MANAGEMENT AND LEAI
EDUCATION

Series Editors: PETER RIBBINS AND JOHN SAYER

The Making of Educational Leaders

TITLES IN THE MANAGEMENT AND LEADERSHIP IN EDUCATION SERIES

The Making of Educational Leaders

PETER GRONN

CASSELL
London and New York

Cassell

Wellington House
125 Strand
London WC2R 0BB

Cassell & Continuum
370 Lexington Avenue
New York
NY 10017-6550

www.cassell.co.uk

First published 1999

British Library Cataloguing-in-Publication Data
A catalogue record for this book is available from the British Library.

ISBN 0-304-70515-2 (hardback)
       0-304-70516-0 (paperback)

Typeset by York House Typographic Ltd, London
Printed and bound in Great Britain by TJ International Ltd, Padstow, Cornwall

Contents

Acknowledgements

A number of special people helped make this book a reality. I am deeply grateful to Professor Peter Ribbins of the University of Birmingham, the series editor, for his unwavering support and perseverance on my behalf. Thanks also to my good friend Ian Ling, who made lots of helpful comments on the draft, to Helen Clements, who chased up numerous references and helped finalize the manuscript, and to Claude Sironi for his excellent work with the diagrams. Many of the ideas in the book gestated during long conversations with three fine teachers and mentors, sadly, all of them deceased. I am grateful to Professor Alan Davies of the University of Melbourne, for his kindness and enthusiastic support of a young scholar, to Professor Thom Greenfield of the Ontario Institute for Studies in Education, for his friendship and deep sense of humanity, and to Sir James Darling, for his patience and openness, and the warmth of his unbounded generosity. My most important debt, of course, is to my wife, Barbara, and daughter, Gabrielle, who have had to endure much but without whose emotional support and help this book would not have been possible.

Introduction

Leadership has been, and continues to be, a source of endless curiosity to academic commentators, journalists, practitioners and the general public. This fascination with the comings and goings of individuals as diverse as celebrities, politicians, sportsmen and women, entrepreneurs, school principals and others, persists despite the typical kind of ho-hum reception now accorded many new works on the topic. 'Not *another* book on leadership!' has become almost the standard refrain. Moreover, the leadership literature increases at a truly staggering rate. In his preface to the third (and most recent) edition of *Bass & Stogdill's Handbook of Leadership* – a publication of genuinely encyclopaedic proportions which comes closest to being the Bible of the field – Bernard Bass (1990, p. xv) notes that the 3,000 original entries in 1974 had more than doubled to 7,500 by 1990. A new student of leadership might well be tempted to ask how much of this vast corpus provides useful, as opposed to merely decorative or ornamental, knowledge. This is a question the eminent scholar Chris Argyris – founder and proponent of organizational learning – asked himself in the late 1970s. The overwhelming bulk of the findings of leadership research, including his own, Argyris (1979, p. 61) claimed, lacked utility and application in specific action contexts. Why? Because 'the theories-in-use that subordinates held were never mapped . . . I never studied the learning system that they created'.

If, two decades later, Argyris's rather disarming observation remains substantially true then little useful purpose would be served by yet one more trek across such apparently well-worn territory. Another contribution to leadership, however, is not hard to justify. For a start, there has been a considerable body of writing since Argyris's confession (a lot of it documented by Bass) which has redirected the field in highly imaginative and innovative ways. Some of this work is discussed below and is the fruit of the labours of scholars, most of whom have managed to avoid getting tangled up in the recent paradigm wars in the social sciences – as Peter Ribbins and I have argued elsewhere (Gronn and Ribbins, 1996, p. 453), leadership studies emerged from the at times paralysing intellectual introspection and turmoil of these battles in remarkably robust form. Indeed, presently there is an extraordinary outburst of creative energy and vitality in the field.

Then, of course, much has happened to dramatically redefine the contexts in which leaders lead and to reshape the expectations of those with whom they work, principally as a result of the impact of two universal phenomena: the globalization of nation-state economies and the resort by governments of all persuasions to market forms of resource allocation and service delivery. And, finally, there has emerged since Argyris's landmark *mea culpa*, to an extent previously unparalleled, a remarkable emphasis on learning. This development is evident in such expressions as the 'learning organization', and even the 'learning society', but it is equally implicit in writings about phenomena like intelligent leadership, knowledge capital and working smarter. In societies whose core business is now more and more the business of learning – as Drucker (1993) thought would be the case – it follows that leaders have to become learners themselves and that they are required to promote the learning of others. Needless to say, such trends have dramatic implications for institutions traditionally devoted to learning, like schools, colleges and universities, and those who lead them.

These developments amount to a new world order both of and for leadership. In such circumstances the key question that arises is: How well-equipped are leaders in this new dispensation to learn and to lead the learning of others? This query prompts a number of subsidiary ones such as: What factors combine to shape the lives of leaders in ways which will ensure that their peculiar mix of personal attributes is acknowledged by others to be leadership? Further, how is it that leaders get to become leaders? Why is the designation 'leader' attributed to some people who are successful and not to others? Which particular barriers – personal, organizational and social – have had to be surmounted in order to attain leadership status? Likewise, what kinds of opportunities have opened up along the way for leaders to exploit and to display their particular brand of leadership? These issues form the central focus of this book.

The Making of Educational Leaders is not intended as a cookbook of recipes or prescriptions on how to lead. Instead, it is directed to those individuals either who aspire to attain formal positions of leadership, or who wish to exercise leadership informally, in a variety of educational settings. It has two aims. First, it is intended to provide a helpful new framework for understanding leadership as a longitudinal and developmental career. Second, it considers in detail the various institutional and role-related tasks which need to be accomplished by aspiring leaders as part of their anticipated career progression, and it offers some helpful clues as to how this might be achieved. While the book is not intended to provide immediately relevant usable knowledge for the solution of particular problems in real-world contexts – i.e. as called for by Argyris and others in the action science tradition – it is, nonetheless, meant to be useful in the attainment of a sense of personal mastery. In summary, the book proposes that, from the point of view of the individual, leadership may be profitably thought of as a progression through four sequential life course stages: formation, accession to office or positions of influence, role incumbency and, finally, divestiture of status, power and role.

This particular conceptualization of leadership has already been dealt with briefly elsewhere (e.g. Gronn, 1993b, 1996, 1997) but *The Making of Educational Leaders* provides the first detailed elaboration of the framework (see Chapter 2). Observers of the careers of public office holders often assert that there is a world of difference between aspiring to and preparing oneself to assume a leadership role, and then being in office and exercising responsibility. This is a distinction, broadly, between becoming a leader and being a leader, and it applies in education and beyond. Because I also recognize the difference in the demands facing leaders and would-be leaders, and differences in the learning experienced in each of these phases (i.e. getting there and being there), I have limited the discussion in this book to what it means to become a leader. The text, therefore, is devoted to the first two of the four stages of the framework.

This book had its origins in two things. First, many of the ideas have been canvassed and sharpened in two subjects taught over a number of years in the Master of Educational Studies and Master of Educational Policy and Administration degrees at Monash University. To those enrolled in Leaders and Leadership, and Leaders and Followers, who were gracious enough to allow me to outline my thoughts and then helped me knock them into respectable shape, I owe a great debt. The second factor, which dictated the precise form taken by the framework, arose out of research into the life of Sir James Darling, the noted Australian headmaster and educationalist. Darling, who died in 1995 aged 96, was an Englishman educated in the English public school tradition. What quickly became apparent when I tried to acquire a more thorough understanding of the English boys' boarding schools during the Victorian and Edwardian eras was that I was witnessing something much more significant than a mere set of forces that had shaped the life of one man. Rather, there was a system of sorts at work – a system with an at times loosely coupled, uneven, ragged or even ramshackle appearance, but a system nonetheless, in which young males were being groomed for leadership roles vital to the running of an empire.

I wondered whether similar preparatory arrangements operated at other times and in other places. Rupert Wilkinson's (1964) early comparative study of the schooling of elites, *The Prefects*, convinced me that I was right. The word which best described these various systems of socialization to elite roles was 'formation'. The remaining key words – accession, incumbency and divestiture – occurred to me when making sense of the phases and overall development of Darling's public life. I next outlined my then rather embarrassingly skeletal and undernourished career framework to two good friends, John Stapleton, of the University of Manitoba, and Peter Ribbins, of the University of Birmingham, who each endured what, at the time, was mere incoherent and innocently expressed thinking aloud. Both men now see considerable merit and utility in the scheme, and either use it themselves or encourage their research students to do so.

It was only when I stumbled upon John Armstrong's (1973) unheralded, long since out of print, but brilliantly insightful book, *The European Administrative Elite*, that the idea of forming leaders really took shape. Armstrong showed how England's nineteenth-century modernizing and industrializing contemporaries (France, Prussia and Russia) adopted a broadly similar system of leader and elite replenishment. He called it maximum ascription and its distinguishing feature was that 'at an early age a very small proportion of the male cohort is selected to occupy the top administrative posts when individuals attain the required age' (Armstrong, 1973, p. 18). In effect, cradles or nursery systems of leader formation were creaming off the well-educated and well-connected male progeny of wealthy and well-to-do, high-status, established families and socializing them, conveyer-belt-like, in selective schools, academies and universities, in preparation for the task of nation-building. What all of these European countries had in common, of course, was that they had been aristocratic and feudal societies and were now imperial powers. In their frontier- or settler-society offspring (e.g. the USA, Canada, Australia and New Zealand), however, the ascription tradition had far less purchase on the collective colonial consciousness, and leadership achievement values (like entrepreneurial self-help and merit) were much more prominent in their paths to nationhood. With a few sectoral exceptions (such as the military) the production of leaders in the new world was, in contrast with 'home', left mostly to chance.

In more recent times totalitarian regimes and command societies aligned with the now defunct Eastern-bloc instituted their own formal methods for producing rank upon rank of stolid, humourless, handclapping *apparatchiki*, and some historians (e.g. Barnett, 1984, p. 24) have been quick to spot the parallel 'prolonged moulding of character, personality or outlook' between young Nazis, Communists and British public-schoolboys. Although ascriptively grounded systems of leader renewal may once have proven culturally viable in rigidly stratified, pre-democratic social orders, their utility in the increasingly diverse societies which now take their political and economic bearings from a globalization compass is questionable if not dysfunctional. Leadership strata drawn from a relatively small number of narrowly selective recruitment sources run the risk of being inbred, brittle, sclerotic and impervious to innovation, and of converging around an extraordinarily narrow range of leader prototypes (typically attributions of greatness and heroism – see Chapter 1). The schools themselves now publicly acknowledge the obsolescence of their traditional approaches to finding so-called natural leaders. Harrow, for example, has introduced leadership training 'to prepare a new generation of gentlemen for the modern world' (*The Times*, 10 January 1998). On the other hand, even where achievement and meritocratic norms have seemingly replaced ascriptive values, there are still significant instances in which elite recruitment remains selective. Thus, in Japan, 'to an extent even greater than the French with their *grandes écoles* and the British with their public schools and Oxbridge', argues Perkin (1996, p. 150), bureaucrats, politicians and businessmen are recruited from a handful of universities 'most of them from Todai, the University of Tokyo, and from one division of it, the Law School'. Notwithstanding such examples, I would argue, societies, sectoral systems and individual organizations intent on efficient learning and adaptation to keep pace with continuously changing economic and technological imperatives are far better positioned by providing access to divergent approaches and routes to leadership.

Finding ways and means of identifying and nurturing potential leadership talent has been a longstanding preoccupation of leadership scholars. Barnard (1956, pp. 82–3, 88), for example, claimed that 'the restriction of the development and supply of general leaders seems to me one of the important problems of our time' and Selznick (1957, p. 15) argued that 'the whole problem of leadership training, and more generally of maintaining and forming elites, should receive a high priority in scientific studies of organization and policy'. More recently McCall (1993, p. 275) has made precisely the same kind of appeal, although Gardner (1995, p. 32) draws attention to the paucity of systematic efforts to detect 'the early markers of leadership'. The identification of competent leadership material is also acknowledged to be a very real and enduring practical problem. *The Guardian* (15 January 1998), for example, reports that of 2,500 advertised vacancies for headships in Britain in 1997 a quarter of the primary schools and about 14 per cent of secondary schools were forced to re-advertise because they 'could not find a suitable candidate'.

There are two broad approaches to the idea of leader formation. First, there is a collective or systemic angle (typically taken by elites and their proponents), which is, broadly, that there exists a need for ongoing supplies or cohorts of requisite replacements to facilitate the maintenance and periodic renewal of institutions. This, in short, is the idea of the reproduction of an elite or leadership stratum. In some cases, as we have seen, leadership groups and elites know precisely what they want and lock in the necessary pathways and arrangements. In other cases they do not and adopt a more *laissez-faire* position. Examples of the former yield recruits conforming to a requisite type – such as the gentleman – whereas in the latter case societies, organizations or occupational groups may be said to 'get the leaders they deserve'. Second, it is possible to monitor the progress of individuals aspiring to leadership roles as they progress down pathways – formally laid out or of their own making – and negotiate the various barriers, constraints, demands or opportunities confronting them. From this point of view Kets de Vries's (1993, p. 3) question: 'What determines who will become a leader and who will not?' makes sense. *The Making of Educational Leaders* acknowledges both of these emphases and provides a detailed elaboration of their interplay in the shaping of prospective educational leaders for their roles.

I anchor the discussion in the text around two core concepts: character and strategy. Character, of course, was (and largely still remains) the essential desired attribute or trait which natural leaders or those supposedly 'born to lead' were meant to embody, as though this particular endowment was somehow there in the blood or taken in at the nipple. Shorn of these kinds of folksy pomposities – and the ridicule to which they were subjected from time to time by the likes of the *Monty Python* crew and facetious witticisms like 'the character-building industry' – the notion of character provides the student of leadership with considerable leverage on the process of formation. Character means nothing more than the totality of the moral, personal and social attributes that comprise the person. The long tradition of scholarly work on character formation in the social sciences – in particular Gerth and Mills's (1964) *Character and Social Structure* – fell into desuetude but has undergone a strong revival in education (see Hodgkinson, 1996; Sergiovanni, 1996). Three main formative agencies, as I argue (in Chapter 3), shape the prospective leader's character: family, school and various peer reference groups. The three main aspects of leadership character are: identity (Chapter 4), values (Chapter 5) and work style (Chapter 6).

Strategy first gained prominence in work on status passage and has been accorded its most recent forthright recognition by Crow (1989). This concept presumes some degree of calculated behaviour as individuals negotiate a career passage through institutionalized pathways and roles. Strategy means the typical patterns or repertoires of behaviour generated in response to ongoing challenges to preferred definitions of the self and one's life goals. A minimalist sense of individual adaptation and adjustment to situational demands is 'coping' strategy. A more active sense of the term – applicable in the case of ambitious, striving, success-driven individuals – would be a designation like 'prudent' strategy. Strategies become evident during accession when, in order to attain formal recognition as a leader, aspirants have to negotiate three important institutionalized processes: succession (Chapter 7), selection (Chapter 8) and induction (Chapter 9).

The various challenges and demands of formation and accession are not just dealt with by individuals at only one point in their lives. Rather, learning, which is central to character formation, occurs throughout the life cycle. Similarly, every time incumbent leaders seek new or different appointments they confront the same accession challenges. The only difference, of course, is that with accrued experience they will have acquired more polish and sophistication in their subsequent candidatures – providing, that is, that they have been successful.

In summary, this book provides a detailed consideration of leadership development and takes a longer time frame perspective on leadership and the acquisition of leadership status than is conventionally the case. As will quickly become evident to the reader, the thrust of the approach that I am arguing for in this book is heavily biographical in its basis, the case for which has been made in more detail elsewhere (see Gronn and Ribbins, 1996). With a few exceptions, this bias goes very much against the grain of orthodox thinking in leadership studies generally, and school and educational leadership particularly, where the preference is still, by and large, for research findings and measures derived from one-off, quantitative, substantially decontextualized, cross-sectionally designed studies. But, as I have quoted Argyris as saying, much of this has long since ceased to be additive, applicable or even helpful. The time is well overdue for the field to take seriously the documented experiences of people as they go about acquiring a sense of themselves as leaders and to pass on the benefits of those insights to those coming up behind them. My hope is that this book will not only show commentators and practitioners how they may best move forward but that it will also advance us a few steps along the path to enlightenment.

DEDICATION

This book is dedicated to the memory of my daughter

LAURA FRANCES GRONN
(26 June 1978–15 May 1996)

At last I have painted my starry sky.

The meaning of leadership

What is leadership? In keeping with the custom normally adhered to by writers on the subject I provide some answers to that question at the outset. Awareness of the typical ways in which leadership is defined is appropriate for practitioners, but especially for aspiring educational leaders, because their expectations of leadership are largely shaped by existing ways of thinking. It is appropriate that the perceptions and expectations which real-world actors do form be the best and most accurate ones available.

This point is especially significant for leaders and would-be leaders in education because schools, universities and colleges have rarely stimulated the production of theories of leadership and administration which are unique to them. The highly influential metaphor of loosely coupled systems, for example, originally propounded by Weick (1976) – not, note, an educationalist but a business and organization theorist – is one of the few genuinely original contributions made by education to the generic fields of organization, leadership and administration. The flow of influential ideas has been overwhelmingly *to* sectors of education *from* elsewhere, rather than the reverse. The pattern of knowledge diffusion between the wider field of leadership and sub-fields such as school leadership and educational leadership tends to take one of three forms: first, commentators in education or schooling frequently ignore or inoculate themselves against work going on in the larger generic field (usually to their cost); second, commentators in the various sub-fields sometimes borrow selectively – and, if Sergiovanni (1996, pp. xiii–xiv) is correct, indiscriminately and usually in unhelpful ways – from findings in the generic field; or, third, commentators in education try to merge findings about leadership regardless of the particular field or source from which they emanate (a recent example is Gardner, 1995).

The approach taken in this book is to synthesize material in broad conformity with the latter course of action. In this chapter, immediately following a brief overview of the state of, and trends in, the field, I distinguish the meaning of leadership and a number of key, related terms; I then say something about leadership and symbolism; I next address the growing popularity of cognitive attributional perspectives on leadership and, finally, I comment on the growing attraction of follower-centrism amongst leadership commentators.

The received wisdom

No one academic domain or professional field of enquiry claims a monopoly over the study of leadership. Bass's (1990) *Handbook* reveals that leadership has been the focus of interest of numerous historians, political scientists, organizational sociologists, various schools of psychologists, business management theorists, educationalists, journalists and social commentators generally. This profusion of stakeholders is simultaneously the field's strength and its weakness. On the one hand, the fragmentation of scholarly endeavour has meant that the study of leadership has tolerated a diversity of traditions and methodologies. Broadly, a spectrum of approaches running from psycho-biographical studies, through run-of-the-mill 'life and times' biographies and narrative accounts of leaders to psychometrically designed measurement studies finds a comfortable place in the sun. The one genuinely serious attempt to integrate or blend the vast output of all this work – as opposed to Bass's (1990) encyclopaedic cataloguing in the *Handbook* – is Burns's (1978) *Leadership*, acknowledged in most quarters to be a *tour de force*.

On the other hand, as I have just suggested, the proliferation of contributors has tended to impede fruitful cross-fertilization in the field and hampered a ready diffusion of findings. Sub-fields and networks of scholars often work in self-contained ways, borrow from one another idiosyncratically, become locked into using well-worn methodologies and, out of apparent ignorance, eschew the kinds of gainful conversations that go on in other scholarly domains. In education, fortunately, this is changing and there is a strong focus of interest on the leadership of organizations to which commentators in the educational and school leadership sub-fields are making an important contribution. The long-term, identifiable historical trend in the generic field of leadership has been away from approaches focusing on leaders and their capacities (great man and trait theories) or actions (situational, style and behavioural theories) – although components of what has become known as the 'new' leadership (see Bryman, 1992) such as transformational and charismatic theories obstinately defy the trend – to a focus on followership, and how and why leadership comes to be ascribed by followers. This aforementioned shift towards follower-centric approaches to leadership includes cognitive psychological, attribution, social construction and psycho-dynamic theories. Two other recent developments are the renewed emphasis placed on values and moral leadership (especially in educational circles), and institutional theories of leadership. Paralleling these trends has been a shift in the level of attention from a venerable tradition in social psychology which focused on the leadership of small primary groups – such as classrooms, clubs, camps, gangs and work crews – to the large organization, especially its upper echelons.

One of the spin-offs of the increased prominence being accorded follower cognition by commentators is the attention given to implicit theories of leadership. And these (as I show shortly) create all sorts of headaches for empirical investigators because, as mechanisms for structuring and filtering perceptions of leadership, implicit theories make it difficult to take the world of leadership at face value. Like their informants, commentators retain their own implicit theories of leadership and they are by no means immune from the processes of attributive reasoning. Despite this isomorphism, it is fair to say that a crude, naïve realism still holds sway within the overall field as expressed in the following set of assumptions which represent the scholarly community's typical attributions or implicit theories about leaders:

- in the pecking order of status, leadership is different from and more important than administration and management;
- there is a division of labour between those who lead (a minority) and those who follow (a majority), and leaders are qualitatively different from followers;
- leader-followership comprises the exercise of uni-directional influence – i.e. leaders do things to, for and on behalf of, followers;
- the appropriate unit of leadership analysis in research is invariably the individual leader;
- organizational leaders are (mostly) formal (and usually top) position-holders or role-incumbents in a hierarchical authority system;
- event outcomes and actions are caused by (i.e. attributable to) the agency of individual leaders; and
- the variability and uniqueness of the contexts in which leadership is exercised are of marginal significance.

The family of terms

Apart from leadership itself, there are four other closely associated words which need to be defined: administration, management, executive and headship. In summary, the position taken here is that leadership is separate and distinct from all four terms. Essentially, administration and management are synonymous: both are alternate ways of denoting the incumbent of an executive role and the incumbent of a headship role is simply another way of designating the most senior person in an executive status system. It is fair to say that while this manner of making the connection between terms would not find universal acceptance there is, nevertheless, broad agreement with it. The essence of the claim made here has recently been well expressed by Lord and Maher (1993, p. 4):

> We can think of leadership as resulting from a social-perceptual process – the
> essence of leadership is being seen as a leader by others. Management, in contrast,
> involves discharging a set of task activities associated with a specific organizational
> position. Leaders may or may not be good managers, and managers may or may not
> be viewed as leaders.

First, the argument that there are different shades of meaning, usage and practice between administration and management needs to be acknowledged as a defensible one but for all practical purposes it can be dispensed with. The most articulate advocate for this distinction in education (and beyond it) is Hodgkinson (1991, pp. 50–3), who insists that the essential ingredient of administration is the manipulation of values and ideas while the essence of management lies in the manipulation of facts and material objects. Recently Hodgkinson (1996, pp. 27–8) has reiterated this broad distinction but then makes allowance for 'semantic convenience' and conventional patterns of usage, and even gently chides Barnard (1982 [1938]) – a father of the field – for circumventing any difficulties of definition by preferring 'executive'. Hodgkinson is trying to sustain a workable distinction between ends (i.e. administration) and means (i.e. management) but if the former subsumes the latter and if, in reality (as he admits), neither operation exists in discrete isolation from the other and the difference is 'one of emphasis', then it is much more sensible to scrap the distinction and substitute one overall functional continuum.

To my way of thinking manager and administrator are optional ways of designating individuals wielding executive authority. The fact that the scholarly field might be known as educational administration in one place, but educational management elsewhere, matters little. And, in the public sector the world over, government agencies, departments, instrumentalities and utilities now reconstruct themselves with such characteristically frequent abandon that they jettison at will any title or label deemed to have outlived its political shelf-life. In Australia, for example, the longstanding Education Department of Victoria has become successively, in less than two decades, the Ministry of Education, the Department of School Education, the Directorate of Education and then the Department of Education, with corresponding titular changes designating the most senior public servant. The point, then, is that cultural and sectoral usages of both terms and their derivatives vary, which makes distinctions between administration and management at best rubbery and at worst almost impossible to sustain. In summary, therefore, administrator and manager are synonymous occupational labels denoting officials or incumbents of offices who are authorized to execute decisions to get others to get work done, and for whose own work and that of others they are held accountable (Jaques, 1970, p. 133).

Leadership, by contrast, is a qualitatively different function from both management and administration – a point readily endorsed by a number of commentators (e.g. Kotter, 1990; Zaleznik, 1977), although not always for the same reasons. Hodgkinson (1983, p. 195, original emphases), on the other hand, collapses leadership back into administration with the emphatic assertion that 'administration *is* leadership. Leadership *is* administration'. Further, he inserts leadership under the manipulation of persons. In his own defence, Hodgkinson (personal communication, 1985) claimed that Burns's (1978) tome *Leadership* could be read (as he had in fact laboriously done) by substituting 'administrator' or 'administration' on every occasion Burns used either 'leader' or 'leadership' without ever once ruining the argument or grossly distorting the text's meaning. Hodgkinson's views on leadership and administration, of course, are influenced by the traditional structure of the British civil service with its higher 'administrative caste drawn from candidates with a background in Oxbridge classicism' (Hodgkinson, 1991, p. 53).

Contrary to Hodgkinson, the position advanced here is that executives (i.e. administrators and managers) need not be leaders, despite the fact that they may be the highest or most senior incumbents in an executive system, and despite the possible (indeed, understandable and probably highly likely) expectations of their subordinates that they should, in fact, lead. Occupancy of a role and possession of the accompanying status that incumbency bestows do not, of themselves, automatically confer leadership status on an office-holder. And the reverse possibility is equally true: leaders, to be leaders, need not hold any formal office at all for, just as a person can manage or administer without leading, 'it is obvious that a person can be a leader without being a manager' (Yukl, 1989, p. 253). Gandhi, for example, one of the most frequently cited examples of a charismatic leader, the spiritual leader of millions of Indians and a driving force for Indian independence during British colonial rule, never exercised any conventionally understood administrative responsibilities in the Congress Party.

Leadership is an ascribed or attributed status, which means that the decision as to whether persons merit being deemed leaders resides in the hands of the other abstracted party in the formulaic dyad within which discussions of leadership are typically cast: followers. In truth, Weber's (1978 [1922], p. 242) observation that 'it is the recognition on the part of those subject to authority which is decisive for the validity of charisma' – i.e. leadership stemming from extraordinary or exceptional personal qualities – applies to all forms of leadership. And when leadership status is accorded by followers two critical ingredients generally come into play: interpersonal influence and identification. Leaders, firstly, are influential persons, whether or not they exercise the kind of formally designated executive responsibilities considered above. Influence means 'significant affecting' (White, 1972, p. 485), whereby a tangible difference in degree or kind is made to an individual or a group's 'well-being, interests, attitudes, beliefs, intentions, desires, hopes, policies or behaviour' (White, 1972, p. 489). Moreover, when followers do ascribe leadership they mentally position themselves, in effect, in a state of readiness as desiring to be influenced. Thus, they deem the leader's influence to be legitimate and they do so willingly and freely. Followers, then, are willing horses, and a leader is an influential person or, as Gouldner (1950, pp. 17–18) once said, 'any individual whose behavior stimulates patterning of the behavior in some group':

> By emitting some stimuli, he [*sic*] facilitates group action toward a goal or goals, whether the stimuli are verbal, written, or gestural. Whether they are rational, nonrational, or irrational in content is also irrelevant in this context. Whether these stimuli pertain to goals or to means, cluster about executive or perceptive operations, is a secondary consideration, so long as they result in the structuring of group behavior.

Another way of expressing the meaning of leadership as influence is to say, as Lantis (1987, p. 197) has, that leadership can be demonstrated only 'when it can be shown that those said to be followers would otherwise have behaved differently'. The legitimate influence accorded a leader may, of course, be grounded in any perceived personal skill, attribute or endowment, and the sum of these attributes may be said to constitute a leader's capital. And because sources of influence do not wholly reside at the apex of organizations like schools, leaders (and leadership) are to be found, potentially, at any level and in any sphere, from the smallest, most transient organization to the largest complex transnational corporation or traditional institution; indeed, 'wherever you are working', comments Lantis (1987, p. 190).

The second distinguishing characteristic of leadership is identification, a Freudian concept denoting an emotional tie or the psychological process of modelling, attachment and bonding between followers and leaders. As the object of followers' identification the leader may simply be the person who, or the image of someone which, followers wish to be like. At a more unconscious level, perhaps, a leader represents the collective followers' inner personal strivings, the one whom they may imitate, or in whom they place their trust, aspirations and longings. In extreme cases the bonding between leaders and followers can become very emotionally charged and, if Freud was right about the unconscious recesses of the mind, then beneath the followers' willingness to be influenced by their leaders there often lurk a host of unarticulated psychological needs which give expression to wish-fulfilment. Leaders, therefore, are potentially very powerful or, depending on the context, even dangerous individuals who can be instruments for either good or ill. Fanatics, to continue with the extreme possibility, are often psychologically unstable and display highly neurotic or borderline psychotic tendencies, and are extraordinarily adept at manipulating primitive mass instincts. On the other hand, a benign inspirational leader is often perceived as saintly and is someone who calls forth mass aspirations in the pursuit of, and allegiance to, highly valuable and socially useful ends.

My claim that leadership is a form of direct or indirect, legitimately expressed, influence finds increasingly broad acceptance among leadership commentators, as Hunt's (1991, p. 57) review indicates – although Heifetz (1994, p. 22) is a recent exception. If influence is paramount, then that prompts the question of why it is that commentators do not simply refer to influence, rather than clinging doggedly to leadership. There is a clue to be found with regard to the last of our four terms to be clarified: headship. As mentioned, headship – as in headmistress, headmaster, principal, CEO and similar 'head of' titles – refers to the highest office in an executive authority system. But headship does not mean the same thing as leadership, for heads of executive role systems are not necessarily and automatically leaders. 'A head', writes Lantis (1987, p. 191, original emphasis), '*may* be a leader but is not one inevitably'. On the other hand, not every commentator accepts the headship–leadership distinction as valid – for Janda (1966, pp. 352–3), for instance, it is 'dubious' – while others draw too hard-and-fast a distinction. Thus, as esteemed a pioneering authority on leadership as Gibb (1968, p. 213) once noted that 'the [reflex] relation between master and slave, teacher and pupil, and frequently that between officer and men is characterized by a type of unidirectional influence which few people would want to call leadership'. Yet, to go on and observe, as Gibb (1968, p. 213, emphasis added) did, that 'leadership is to be distinguished, *by definition*, from domination or headship', is to imply that leadership always lies outside the head role and is precluded, in effect, by virtue of being a head. Clearly, this is absurd. What can be said with certainty, however, is that while headship roles confer formal authority over incumbents, the authority of office does not automatically carry with it the status of leader (Biggart and Hamilton, 1987, p. 432).

A common mistake, then, because of the association often made between a head or figurehead and the influence they might, and are usually expected to, provide is to assume that headship and leadership are synonymous. That is, load senior-level organizational appointees with responsibility and remunerate them sufficiently generously – so the prevailing mindset runs – and organization members have every right to expect of such people that they will provide influence and direction. From that kind of reasoning it is but a short step to depicting what heads do as being leadership, rather than influence, because to be the top or near-to-the-top person means to be the most important or *leading* person. On the logic of this set of assumptions it generally follows that the leading person's influence is meant to be taken as leadership.

The symbolic task of leadership

The activity or task of leadership may be defined as the framing of meaning. The departure point for this idea is the famous summary of sense-making known as Thomas's dictum (cited in Goffman, 1975, p. 1), viz. 'if men [*sic*] define situations as real, they are real in their consequences'. The terms here are relatively uncomplicated: to 'define' means to attribute meaning; the 'situations' referred to are the immediate or long-term circumstances in which individuals find themselves; 'real' means significant and 'consequences' denotes the causal impact of those circumstances on subsequent behaviour. And in this particular phenomenology the sense that is made of an event and the meaning which is attributed to it by an individual is facilitated by pre-existing and culturally shared understandings. Thus, in defining any situation as real or meaningful, therefore, 'those who are in the situation ordinarily do not *create* this definition ... all they do is to assess correctly what the situation ought to be for them and then act accordingly' (Goffman, 1975, pp. 1–2, original emphasis). What makes a particular leader's cognitive act of sense-making significant for followers is her or his capacity to invoke key symbols which reinforce the meanings they choose to frame.

Apart from influence, the other point of agreement amongst commentators is that leadership is an inherently symbolic activity. Because leaders are those persons whom followers are willing to be influenced by and to identify with, followers are well disposed to have them frame meanings on their behalf and to accept the symbols and language in which they cast events. For this reason Smircich and Morgan (1982, p. 258, original emphases) refer to 'an *obligation* or a perceived *right* on the part of certain individuals to define the reality of others'. Entire stocks of cultural definitions and meanings – in the form of ideologies, words, symbols, images and discourse – are available for leaders and can be resorted to as needs be to facilitate the framing of particular episodes and events. Leaders live their careers invoking and manipulating carefully chosen symbols to influence their followers and to defend their interests, and to ensure that their interpretations of events become *the* preferred understandings of reality. Thus, if a leader's symbols are to have semantic force for followers then, Griffin *et al.* (1987, p. 202) argue, leaders are responsible for 'instilling meaning in organization action and events' and they have to 'construct [perceptions of] reality for the followers'. Symbolism is here interpreted in the widest sense, and encompasses messages ranging from carefully crafted and elaborated meta-narrative stories on the one hand to momentary, fleeting 'easily digested sound bites' (Gardner, 1995, p. 298) on the other.

Griffin *et al.* (1987) show *how* it is that a leader's symbols affect followers. Their image of the leader–follower relationship is akin to a cognitively conceived tennis or ping-pong match, in that a zig-zag or stimulus–response relationship of spiralling cycles of behaviour, perceptions of behaviour, perceptions in turn of those perceptions, with further behaviour ensuing, and so on, takes place. For Griffin *et al.* (1987, p. 204) the initial stimulus in this dyadic interchange invariably emanates from the leader, although this need not necessarily be the case. For one thing, the claim that followers respond to leaders presupposes that leaders can be known at the outset of an exchange whereas, as I have argued, if leadership status is largely ascribed then exactly who the leaders are in a particular context has to be ascertained rather than taken for granted. Further, as will become clearer shortly, leadership is more than likely to be a *response* to followership, rather than the reverse. For the moment, however, the virtue of Griffin *et al.*'s micro-cosmology is its emphasis on the reciprocity of leader–followership: neither party, leader nor follower, acts in isolation from, but is instead influenced by, the other in a kind of cognitive two-step.

Acceptance of both these possibilities – i.e. followers as paramount and dyadic reciprocity – results in an amended view of leadership influence. At one level, organizations may be thought of as comprising aggregations of these numerous leader–follower dyads. If so, then an infinite number of hierarchically arranged and authorized task-related, socio-emotional and other dyadic exchanges and interactions comprise the basic reality of every-day organizing. A key defining property of such activity is the idea of 'flow'. Thus, inherent in the work of organizing are various multi-directional flows (in the form of chains, webs and networks) of phenomena like influence, information and symbols which structure the overall pattern and experience of work – hence the common reference to notions like 'workflow'. Such flow imagery is central to recent institutional theories of leadership (e.g. Biggart and Hamilton, 1987; Ogawa and Bossert, 1995), one of the advantages of which is that they provide us with an emergent, rather than a static, view of leadership. That is, particular acts in the overall flow of influence prove more influential than others (i.e. degrees of influence carry greater consequences) for organization members, and these come to be associated with particular individuals and groups so that 'leaders emerge in the course of interactions' (Hosking, 1988, p. 154). Ongoing experience with such people generates expectations about the locus of leadership and the likelihood of its occurrence. As is well known, the tendency in most formal organizations is to embed these expectations in formally defined roles rather than leaving management and leadership to chance. Nonetheless, phenomena like the fluidity, dynamism and potentiality of experience can be thought of as the prior constituent organizing elements, in which case leadership is a structuring activity and might be best considered as an outcome or an effect (more on this in a moment).

The difference made by leaders

Despite these alternatives and possibilities, the widespread and long-standing significance attached to instrumental views of leadership persists. They stem, in large measure, from the assumption (and hope) that leaders ought to be able to, and indeed do, make a difference. For there to be a difference made by leaders means, typically, demonstrating that they act as causal agents who engineer desired effects or outcomes which, but for their actions, would not otherwise have occurred. For the theoretician this entails the satisfaction of relevant counterfactual conditions, whereas in contemporary parlance it means, simply, that leaders can be shown to add value to organizational performance. But this claim about alleged differences does not go without saying. Indeed, from it there follow a number of important implications. One is that if leadership comprises framing meaning and

ensuring that leaders' interpretations win numerical adherence and commitment, then a plausible explanation for followers' identification with
leaders might be that leaders are qualitatively different and better people.
That is, those to whom the status 'leader' is ascribed may well be able to
construct more powerful symbols and exploit them to better effect because
they constitute an inherently better class of individuals than those whom
they lead – perhaps because they are born, rather than made, that way. But
the case for the innate superiority of leaders is a difficult one to sustain. On
this issue, Gouldner (1950, p. 19, original emphasis) dissented, observing
that 'if a *dichotomized* difference is sought between leaders and followers, then
there is none. The difference is most probably a difference of degree,
regardless of which definition of leadership is employed.' Despite the eclipse
of born-to-the-purple assertions of an inherited right to privileged leadership, and the broad triumph of meritocratic leadership norms, arguments
about the alleged specialness of leaders die hard. Thus, in defining leaders as
the transformers of persons and instruments of their moral elevation, Burns
(1978, p. 273) sees a leader as someone who is 'a very special, a very
circumscribed but potentially the most effective type of power-holder,
judged by the degree of "real change" finally achieved'.

One variation on this superiority argument is Zaleznik's (1977, 1990)
comparison of leaders with managers rather than with followers. Previously
Zaleznik (1964, p. 164) had noted that differences in leadership and managerial performance were ultimately 'genetically determined' but that the
neuro-scientific data required to substantiate the claim were then unavail-
able (but see Gronn, 1993b, pp. 353–6). Later Zaleznik (1977, pp. 76–7)
cited psycho-biographical evidence to distinguish the two roles, yet he
provided few examples (although see Rustow, 1970, pp. 4–14). Leaders, he
believed, were predominantly gifted individuals who relied largely upon
personal qualities to lead, whereas managers relied on learned techniques.
Leaders defined goals; managers responded to them and immersed themselves in processes. Leaders took risks; managers preferred to bargain and
play safe. And, finally, Zaleznik claimed that managers were mostly 'once-
born' personality types with a strong need to belong, whereas leaders were
'twice-born' souls displaying a strong sense of personal mission. The corollary of this kind of distinction, however, is that if more prominence is
accorded to leaders rather than managers then management is devalued at
the expense of leadership. Yet, as Fidler (1997, p. 26) has quite rightly noted,
'both leadership and management of organizations are essential for their
successful operation and there is a great deal of overlap [between them]'. If
so, it is small wonder that such distinctions are seen by some commentators
as posing a potentially 'debilitating split' (Krantz and Gilmore, 1990, p. 189)
for organizations, were one function to be privileged ahead of the other,
between being over-led but under-managed, or being under-led and over-
managed.

In direct contrast to Burns and Zaleznik, Jaques has blithely obliterated distinctions between leadership and followership – 'we have found that the notion of "a leader" or "the leader" simply gets in the way' (Jaques and Clement, 1995, p. 6) – and between leadership and management altogether. Instead, in his stratified systems perspective on organizational authority, leadership is subsumed under tightly structured and defined, hierarchically arranged managerial roles, differentiated on the basis of time-span of discretion (i.e. the time taken to conceptualize, oversee and implement decisions) and cognitive complexity (i.e. the levels and types of mental capacity required to conceptualize, oversee and implement those decisions). For Jaques, all managers automatically carry leadership accountability, and to that extent they are managerial leaders. Other observers see the differences made by leadership in still more negative terms. Thus, for Vanderslice (1988), for example, institutionalizing a division of labour between leaders and followers generally results in the disenfranchisement of followers. If, indeed, there is any difference to be made it will not be made by *a* leader, but by leader*ship* – in which leader roles regularly rotate – as her case study of 'Moosewood' (a US restaurant collective) demonstrates, because decision creativity and learning are only facilitated by structures which enable organization members to lead themselves. As Vanderslice (1988, p. 695) argues:

> If we redefined motivation as a willingness to take responsibility, think creatively, and develop processes that benefit both individuals and organizations, we might be less inclined to uncritically accept the need for leader–follower power differentials.

From this perspective, the one overriding and genuine difference that leaders make, then, is a negative one: to de-skill followers and to instil in them a learned helplessness and dependency (Gemmill and Oakley, 1992). Indeed, these are exactly the kinds of alienating effects Spaulding's (1997) sample of 81 US teachers recently reported themselves experiencing as the outcomes of the leadership of their school principals.

Attributions, implicit theories and perceptions of leadership

The idea that leadership is an attributed status was first developed seriously by Calder (1977, pp. 185–7), who suggested that leadership is best understood as a lay term or label – as opposed to an abstract scientific concept for which there exists a universally agreed-upon concrete referent – for a category of (observed or inferred) behaviour intended to express a sense of personal potency. The critical question, perhaps, is less: 'What *is* leadership?' in any abstract sense but rather: 'What *counts* as leadership?' to those according or ascribing the designation 'leader' to a person or persons in the particular circumstances in which the parties are located. Calder then proposed that those lay assumptions with which informants infer leadership and leadership causality from behaviour were the true objects of study for researchers.

This implicit cognitive process of attribution-making (as it has become known) was held to be a cyclical one in which Calder described the steps, typically, as: observation of behaviour; checking of that perceptual evidence against a set of prior assumptions and beliefs about leadership for consistency or disparity; and, in the event of a close fit between the evidence and an existing mental template, conferring or attributing leader status to the persons in question. This line of reasoning – i.e. that leadership is in the eye of the beholder – is broadly consistent with the Weberian view of charisma referred to earlier and, of necessity, draws students of leadership into the analysis of follower cognitions or understanding rather than taking leadership to be a given. Important implications follow for the design of research, particularly questionnaires, because 'implicit leadership theories underpin individuals' descriptions of leaders when answering batteries of questions' (Bryman, 1987, p. 129). What this means is that informants' implicit reasoning about leaders and leadership filters or screens informational cues about the performance of leaders. Thus, implicitly held theories (i.e. unarticulated but intuitively held explanations of the interconnections between informants' assumptions) of what it means to be an effective or an ineffective leader, for example, are likely to prompt informants to attribute greater or lesser degrees of influence to particular individuals through a kind of matching process which determines category assignment. The possibility of this kind of response calls into question the extent to which any actual behaviour is being measured at all by a survey instrument and, therefore, such an instrument's validity (Lord and Maher, 1993, p. 67).

The technical term for the shorthand idea of the template just referred to is 'prototype', by which psychologists mean 'a central tendency of feature values across all valid members of a category' (Sternberg and Horvath, 1995, p. 10). Prototyping is a way of simplifying or reducing the features of an otherwise complex phenomenon down to its barest distinguishing essentials and, in a nutshell, is an economical means by which people deal with cognitive overload and complex problems. Prototypical judgements are made by computing the similarity between an object (an individual and her or his behaviour) and the core, defining attributes or aspects of a category (such as appropriate or inappropriate leader behaviour). In that sense a prototype is like a design model, which is probably close to the popularly understood meaning of the word – as in the idea of constructing a prototype for a new vehicle or piece of equipment, say, prior to drawing up an exact set of specifications for product development purposes. An example in the leadership domain would be Gardner's (1995, pp. 285–90) prototype of the exemplary leader. Apart from shaping perceptions, the other important effect of mental prototypes is that they generate expectations in the minds of followers about appropriate leadership behaviour to be anticipated in future through direct experiences with leaders or when confronted by new information about them. A related form of typecasting to prototyping is stereotyping, another reductionist process. Whereas a prototype is a bundle of attributes clustering around a central tendency, a stereotype is a particularly rigid and inflexible form of categorizing that is narrow, over-simplified, overdrawn and generally impervious to modification. In summary, then, attributional reasoning as regards leaders and leadership entails a recurring cycle of expectations (shaped by experience and knowledge of prior behaviour) which frame perceptions of subsequent behaviour, which in turn either confirms or disconfirms pre-existing expectations through prototypical matching, after which the cycle begins once again.

This cognitive perspective sheds some light on how and why it is that leaders are thought to make a difference. Particularly helpful here is Meindl's (1990) idea of the romance of leadership (RL) – the deep-seated 'faith in the potential if not in the actual efficacy of those individuals who occupy the elite positions of formal organizational authority' (Meindl *et al.* 1985, p. 79). That is, whatever the empirical validity of a leader's actual impact or the difference made by leaders, what counts, Meindl asserts, is the widespread belief that, in the end, it is leadership above all other factors which counts. Needless to say, it is a short step from that point to claiming it to be in the interests of leaders' stability and longevity for them to foster such beliefs. Niccolo Machiavelli (1967 [1640], p. 101), the famous Florentine philosopher, in his masterpiece, *The Prince*, was alert to this possibility when he noted that while princes seemed to be captive of their subjects' perceptions of them they could easily turn the tables to their advantage: 'everyone sees what you [i.e. the sovereign] appear to be, few experience what you really are ... the common people are always impressed by appearances and results'. It is for similar reasons that Hodgkinson (1996, p. 85) refers to leadership as 'an incantation for the bewitchment of the led'. At any event, the RL is Meindl's construct for people's theories or ideas about what makes organizations operate effectively: i.e. the preferred explanation to which people typically turn when they seek to account for events – good and bad, beneficial and detrimental – which affect entire societies or organizations, and the consequences of those events. Most people learn or are socialized to attribute causality to a leader or leaders. The RL, therefore, is a kind of implicit explanation which is drawn on or invoked to explain or account for occurrences and non-occurrences. As such the RL is a causal explanation of performance to which people are psychologically committed and which is drawn on to understand both past events and future possibilities.

Meindl developed his RL idea into an experimental scale – the RLS – in which he provides participants with a series of alternative explanations (e.g. chance, luck, the leadership of a chief executive officer (CEO), market forces) for hypothetical event or vignette outcomes. An example is: 'In comparison to external forces such as the economy [and] government regulations, a company's leaders can have only a small impact on a firm's performance' (Meindl, 1990, p. 169). Under experimental conditions groups of subjects are provided with organizational vignettes in which the contextual details are varied to positively or negatively enhance organizational performance (e.g. rates of

returns on investment, percentages of product market share) and are reques-
ted to account for the hypothesized results from the range of explanatory
options such as the example above illustrates. Invariably, the experimental
subjects nominate individual leaders as the most important causal agency. On
the basis of an accumulated set of experimental findings Meindl concludes that
it matters not which particular source one examines – such as manifestations of
leadership as diverse as the image of leaders in newspaper reports, in students'
theses or dissertation topics, in small business periodicals as well as the
aforementioned undergraduates' responses to organizational stories during
experiments – the same conclusion can be substantiated: leaders, typically, are
accorded potency and given credit for securing positive outcomes and are
blamed for circumstances that go wrong in preference to most other possibilities (Meindl *et al.*, 1985, p. 96).

Meindl's data provide evidence of aggregated individual cognitive attributional reasoning processes and show that leadership prototypes are culturally
constructed. That is, in virtually all societies and organizations the acquisition of leader prototypes is pre-programmed, as it were, by various
attribution formation and attribution diffusion agencies (typically, education systems, reference groups and mass-communication media) which
sanction, validate, legitimate and reinforce key leader attributes. In respect
of visual media, for example, Katz and Dayan's (1986) analysis of televised
images indicates how in most societies the collective public consciousness of
important or 'big' events is shaped, prototypically (or, some media critics
might argue, stereotypically) by their classification into dramatic spectacles
such as contests (clashes between public figures of titan status), conquests
(in which human endurance triumphs against almost impossible odds) and
coronations (recognition of crowning and towering human achievements).
Moreover, Klapp's (1964) early work showed how the actors in these various
social dramas were typecast into the traditional categories of heroes, villains,
victims and fools.

Turning specifically to Klapp's category of hero, along with greatness (the
celebration of superhuman deeds), the quality of heroism (the celebration
of courageous deeds) has been a particularly powerful and persistent leader
prototype. Like greatness, the attribution of heroism has had a historically
close connection to schooling. Of the two, greatness has probably had the
most significant impact on leadership. Indeed, so deeply entrenched did the
belief in great deeds (mostly of males) become that it gave rise to a theory of
leadership change and causation, the so-called great man theory of history.
In one way, this great man view represented the spirit of a particular age – it
served as an apologia for nineteenth-century Victorian triumphalism. The
gospel of greatness was spread by a diverse lineage of scholars, essayists and
promoters. It became institutionalized in a variety of ways, big and small.
Thus, historical epochs became known by the surnames of monarchs and the
chapters of organization histories were typically demarcated according to
the incumbencies of powerful figures. Greatness embedded itself deeply in

the collective social consciousness for a number of reasons to do with schooling. Thus, there was a concentration on the deeds of prominent individuals and their moral precepts in the formal curriculum, and greatness was consciously and deliberately modelled by English headmasters and headmistresses. There even grew up in the nineteenth century English boys' public boarding school, for example, an ethos – sometimes autocratic, sometimes benevolent – known as the headmaster tradition. The particular factors which helped concentrate power in the hands of girls' and boys' school heads included: provision by governing bodies for the payment of heads' emoluments or monetary rewards being made directly dependent on the prosperity of the school; the increased reliance of heads on the moral force of personality in administering their schools to the point where the weight of their public pronouncements gave them some genuine claim (along with the clergy) to be the moral policewomen and policemen of society as a whole; and the extraordinary popularity of school novels (such as *Tom Brown's Schooldays* and *Stalky and Co.*) and magazine stories in diffusing the image of self-styled 'superior' women and men.

Greatness lingers on. As I have pointed out elsewhere (Gronn, 1995), the antecedents of what is arguably the currently most popular type of leadership – even amongst prominent school leadership theorists – Bass's (1985) transformational model, can be shown to link back directly to the great man theory of change. Heroism, likewise, displays extraordinary resilience. As recently as 1995 in the *Guardian* (23 September), for example, the then UK Government's chief curriculum adviser, Dr Nicholas Tate, was quoted as saying that schoolteachers were 'selling Britain short, arguing that Britain's sense of national identity was being eroded because history teachers were ignoring British heroes'. Indeed, the columnist (an Oxford don) noted that:

> If heroes and heroines are myths, a projection of our longings, and if some of their most famous moments turn out to be apocryphal, they are nevertheless a necessary fantasy. We all need, at some stage in life, mentors. We all seek out people to believe in, patterns to follow, examples to take up. We take courage from those who seem stronger or more steadfast than ourselves. We glamorise stars and worship at the feet of gurus.

A sympathetic appreciation of so-called great leaders and heroic leadership would see them to be representing nothing more than simple attempts at different times throughout history to highlight exceptional or extraordinary instances of behaviour in which, for example, the prowess, gifts and achievements of individuals set them apart from their fellows. Gifted and talented people have always been in evidence in virtually every field of human endeavour – literature, sport and music instantly come to mind – and on that score leadership should be no different. But what does make leadership different from these and other spheres, of course, is that in an increasingly complex world societies and organizations can afford less and less to give free reign to untrammelled individual virtuosity. The other problem is that the overall historical report card for greatness and heroism has not been good, so that personages known by appellations such as '[X] the Great' have more often than not turned out to be tyrants, despots and dictators.

Follower-centric leadership

So far in this chapter I have been considering an important body of newly emerging literature on leadership. The review has not been exhaustive and many other recent popular theories of, and approaches to, leadership – e.g. vertical dyadic linkage models, leader–member exchange and path–goal theories, and executive and strategic leadership – have not been discussed because their relevance to education and schooling is far from immediately apparent. The material considered is representative of a broad new trend towards the utilization of constructivist perspectives and has been nominated with an eye to the particular career development needs of aspirant leaders. This trend reflects the growing awareness amongst commentators that leadership is about making connections, 'a cognitive enterprise', as Gardner (1995, p. 296) terms it, between the minds of leaders and followers. Hogan et al.'s (1994, p. 494) observation of the field of leadership, that effectiveness is held to be 'the standard by which leaders should be judged', is probably still substantially valid – and is certainly consistent with the implicit assumptions which Meindl found lying at the heart of people's romanticized views of leaders. On the other hand, if prospective educational leaders undergoing or about to undergo what organizational sociologists often refer to as anticipatory role socialization are to attain a sense of personal mastery then awareness of what is required to become a leader is more appropriate than injunctions about the need to be an effective one. The chanting of mantras like 'effectiveness' tells us nothing about the pre-conditions for being effective and, in any case, ignores the evidence (considered in Chapter 2) that the capacity for effectiveness may well be life-cycle related. So first things first.

The virtue of an approach to leaders and leadership which emphasizes follower-centrism – Meindl's term – is that it is consistent with the sentiments of some of the classic writers in the field. To the alert reader, that might sound suspiciously like an author's attempt to put himself on the side of the angels. If it does then the only reply is to say that it was part of the originality of insight of three of the founding figures whose work has been touched on already – Machiavelli, Barnard and Weber – to point out how, in the end, the stability of personal leadership rested on upward flows of consent, sovereignty and legitimacy. Barnard (1982 [1938], p. 163), for example, was adamant that the authority of any organizational decision did not reside in persons in positions of authority but 'with the persons to whom it is addressed' – which is really another way of saying that popular sovereignty, or the principle of the consent of the governed, also operates within organizations. Moreover, the point is consistent with all that we know about how wider democratic electoral and political processes work, which is that governments invariably lose office when they surrender legitimacy. It should be clear by now, then, that leadership does not automatically go with the managerial and administrative territory, so to speak, in organizations. Rather, leadership can never be taken for granted by the neophyte, because the basis upon which it rests is fickle, capricious and precarious, or as Gardner (1995, p. 288) puts it, 'leadership is never guaranteed, it must always be renewed'. The bestowal of leadership status by followers is no more automatic than is their obedience. This means that leadership has to be worked at, constantly. And it is in this respect, I think, that Valerie Hall's (1996) excellent and highly informative study of six women primary and secondary school heads, *Dancing on the Ceiling*, is germane. Hall demonstrates the extraordinary lengths to which her sample of six went to fashion and project a sense of themselves as leaders in order to make the kind of connections to which I alluded above.

Not a lot is known about the ways in which, amongst themselves as a collectivity, followers go about attributing leadership to others. Much of the work here – which is speculative, but nonetheless instructive – has been undertaken by Meindl. He began by considering charismatic leadership specifically and reasoned (somewhat heretically) that, to better understand the phenomenon, the leader could be left out of the picture altogether thereby permitting research to take place into the experience, recreation and transmission of charismatic effects amongst groups of followers (Meindl, 1990, p. 189). One possible mechanism of the spontaneous diffusion of affective reactions to charisma, he argued, might be something like social contagion. (The epidemiological analogy was and remains deliberate on his part.) A good example of what he had in mind is to be found in Whyte's (1965, pp. 230, 235) classic study of small group leadership in 'Cornerville', *Street Corner Society*, although in this case the contagious reaction to the leader in question was a negative one. During the US presidential campaign of 1940, at a time when 'Roosevelt and democracy did not conflict with Mussolini and fascism in the minds of Cornerville people', President Roosevelt made a speech elsewhere in the country attacking the Italian dictator. All that was necessary to ensure that the speech had a destructive effect on the Italians of Cornerville was that:

> It influenced certain people who in turn influenced others. There was a long process of fermentation in which people interacted to bring about this change of allegiance.

This example highlights the importance of social networks. Comparable structures within organizations would probably include friendship cliques, conversational grapevines and rumour mills – entities bearing a remarkably close resemblance to the features of informal organization on which Barnard (1982 [1938], pp. 114–23) laid so much importance and which he cautioned executives to ignore at their peril. Another example would be the rippling effect of laughter or circumstances of uncertainty or tension in which people look to fellow group members for visual cues and clues regarding appropriate behaviour. Yet one more would be the crowd's responses to their naked sovereign at various points in the dialogue of the well-known fable 'The Emperor's New Clothes'. For Meindl it is the social processes operating in such group arrangements as these which determine whether or not the effects of leadership, charismatic or otherwise, sustain themselves amongst group members.

In a later development of this perspective, Meindl (1993, 1995) has gone as far as suggesting that leadership reduces to a state of mind which emerges amongst followers or a way of thinking about their relationships to one another to which they become attuned. If he is correct then elusive, but nonetheless palpable, phenomena like mindsets, moods, collective arousal states, levels of awareness and temperaments become the focus of research. To market researchers and public opinion pollsters whose life-blood is to take continual soundings and to gauge consumer receptivity for their commercial and political masters, such suggestions regarding the state of the organizational body politick, so to speak, are nothing new. They do, however, have profound implications for the craft and practice of leadership, on the one hand, and for aspiring leaders learning about that same craft and practice, on the other. Anna Neumann's (1995) study of the induction of the newly appointed president of 'Blue Stone College' – in which she unravelled the interplay of the expectations of those who appointed the president, the interpretations they placed on his behaviour as he sought to carve out a new role for himself, his initiatives and their responses to these – provides a good illustration of the former implication. Neumann (1995, p. 271) concludes that:

> leaders who attend carefully to the thinking of those around them and who frame their own thoughts and actions with the beliefs of these people in mind are likely to be better at their work than leaders who articulate visions that have little or no grounding in the realities of those they presume to lead. This does not mean that leaders should simply do what others expect them to do. Rather, they should take, as their point of departure, the thinking and beliefs – the culturally ingrained understandings and values – of those whom they wish to lead. This suggests that a primary task for leaders is forming relationships that will support their own learning about the beliefs and values of those to whom they seek to relate.

As for the second implication – learning about leadership – Calder (1977, p. 203) was emphatic that leadership could in no way be taught as a skill. Instead, the best to be hoped for, he thought, was 'to sensitize people to the perceptions of others – that is, to sensitize them to the everyday common-sense thinking of a group of people'. Would-be-leaders, as he called them, had little choice but to 'respond to the attributions based on the meaning of leadership for each group with which he [or she] interacts'. Likewise, it remains Meindl's (1995, p. 333) considered view that, rather than learning so-called leader behaviours to better control followers, 'the creation and sustenance of interpretive dominance regarding leadership' – i.e. the inter-play of actions with contexts, impressions and reputations – 'would have the highest priority'.

Despite what I take to be the far more realistic overall grip on the situational phenomenology of leader-followership provided by a follower-centric perspective, compared with conventional approaches to leadership, there is a rider. It is that the kinds of suggestions just dealt with above retain a here-and-now, if at times slightly ephemeral, ring to them. They beg the question of what happens over the long term within particular cultures, institutions and generations to shape and predispose prospective cohorts of leaders towards these or the other leadership sensitivities which their propo-nents highlight. That concern brings us back to the key focus of this book, the formation of leaders, and the sorts of arrangements, if any, that different societies and organizations can and do put in place to develop what Gardner (1995, p. 303) refers to as 'an enhanced cadre of future leaders'. But to produce the kind of exemplary, pro-social, leading minds sought by Gardner raises a dilemma which different types of societies, new world and old world, have sought to resolve in one of two broad ways: creaming off talent, followed by intensified, regimented, hothouse prestige cultivation, or happenstance, serendipity and *laissez-faire*. Gardner (1995, p. 304) is alert to this dilemma. His fellow Americans, he says, give every indication that they attach enor-mous significance to leadership, yet:

> By pretending that leadership will happen naturally or that leadership can be inculcated incidentally, we ensure that there will be an unacceptably low number of individuals who can fill the essential desiderata of leadership. And we make it less likely that leaders will emerge from less-dominant groups and less-privileged institu-tions in the society.

Gardner's solution is to invest intellectually in the production of future leaders by trying to familiarize everyone, not just a select few, with the cut and thrust of what being a leader entails, for which he provides a number of helpful suggestions (Gardner, 1995, pp. 305–6).

The argument of this book, however, while broadly in keeping with the spirit of what Gardner is after, is that far more specific guidance should, and can, be provided about the formative obstacles that need to be surmounted preparatory to the assumption of any leadership role and the attainment of a sense of personal leadership mastery. As I have already indicated, these boil down to three major personal challenges to be confronted in respect of identity, values and work style, and three important organizational hurdles to be prepared for and to negotiate: succession, selection and induction. In endeavouring to make the case that what it means to be a leader is best understood through followership, and then from within an overall longitudi-nal time frame, no particular presumption has been made about whether the prospective leader is to become, necessarily, a principal, a classroom or leading teacher, a curriculum co-ordinator, a college director or whatever. One consequence of this openness, of course, is that the subject matter of the book, 'the leader' and her or his leadership, becomes something of a moving target – but that is unavoidable. There should be no presumption on the reader's part that I have any particular role in mind. That said, if there is any evident bias towards role incumbency of one sort or another in the research which I have discussed throughout the text then the reason for that is a simple one: it reflects the traditional predisposition of commentators to think of leadership solely, or mainly, in formal, role-related ways. Where possible, therefore, in such cases I have drawn whatever relevant inferences I could for other roles or for leadership viewed informally. Moreover, in keeping with the spirit of openness I have adopted, I allow for the possibility of leadership manifesting itself at any level of any educational organization. Finally, my remarks apply with equal force to prospective leaders of both sexes.

Hodgkinson has remarked on a number of occasions that we are, all of us, either administrators or administered. He is right. Equally, we all lead, for at least some of the time, or are led, for pretty well all of the time. Some of us want to be leaders. Others are content to be followers. We make choices, or at least we like to think we do. How and why it is that particular choices in respect of leading and following come to be made throughout our lives, and what the parameters and confines are within which those choices are made, are part and parcel of leadership careers, the subject of the next chapter.

CHAPTER 2

Leadership as a career

Before examining the ways in which the formative years of educational leaders and would-be educational leaders are moulded and shaped by key agencies, I outline a longitudinal framework with which to synthesize those leaders' experiences. This framework is the outcome of a search for the most economical way of utilizing the vivid insights available in biographies of leaders. An economical means was necessary to encompass the diverse sets of experiences undergone by leaders during vastly different eras and in dramatically different cultural milieux in order to make meaningful comparisons. The initial impetus for this was pedagogical for I wanted a way of enabling students of leadership to be able to compare leaders' lives at any one point in time across space, place, circumstances and time, in order to provide them with a vantage point from which to get their own lives as possible future leaders into perspective. The essence of what I wanted was some means of doing justice to the uniqueness of individual experience while at the same time bringing together shared features and anchoring them around core themes.

Eventually, I decided on the concept of a leadership career. But before I outline the particular advantages of a career perspective some prior questions require an answer. First, why should knowledge of both the broad sweep and detail of leaders' lives be of more than passing concern and interest? Avolio and Bass (1988, p. 46) have drawn attention to the paucity of systematic psycho-historical studies of leaders, for example, despite 'the wealth of information in biographies of world-class leaders'. The most powerful reason why biographies of leaders are worthy of consideration is that they take students of leadership right to the very heart of an argument at the centre of social theory which has undergone a resurgence of interest over the last 15 years or so. This argument concerns the nature and constitution of what used to be known as free will or voluntarism (as opposed to determinism) but which now mostly goes by the label of human agency. Simplifying matters, the focus of what is at times a very complicated and attenuated scholarly debate concerns the proper relationship between agency and structure. This deals with the uptake of human actions (i.e. their outcomes and effects), and the causal connection between those actions and the social structures in which they take place, particularly in respect of the perpetuation of, or alteration to, those social structures (wholly or in part) through time – processes known technically as morphostatis and morphogenesis respectively (Archer, 1995).

In this chapter I show how leadership may be profitably conceived of in career terms, and how the four-stage career framework I outline in detail provides a useful comparative approach for ordering the experiences of leaders while retaining the analytical dualism between, rather than conflating or eliding, agency and structure. I begin with a brief explanation of how the framework emerged, I next consider a number of important writings on career and then, finally, I provide a detailed elaboration and illustration of each of the four stages or phases.

Antecedents of the framework

Two scholars, in particular, were influential in their own spheres in initially focusing my attention on the importance of human agency. The first of these was the late T.B. Greenfield. For reasons which are not entirely clear the social sciences took what might be called a subjectivist turn from about the mid- to late-1960s. In educational administration that shift can be dated precisely, 1974, when Greenfield delivered the first of a series of spirited criticisms of the epistemological and ontological assumptions on which he believed the field rested (for a selection see Greenfield and Ribbins, 1993). For about the next two decades Greenfield had both his supporters and his detractors. Whatever the merit of his intellectual position during that period – over which the argument still rages (see Park, 1996) – one of Greenfield's most important and enduring contributions to educational leadership and administration was to focus his peers' attention fairly and squarely on the individual administrator and leader. One of the consequences of the vehemence of his attack on the field and the warrant of its claim to a scientific knowledge base, and of his passionate endorsement of what might be termed the *verstehen* side of Weber's sociology, was, as I have argued elsewhere (Gronn, 1994, p. 226):

> To heighten everyone's awareness of what administrators brought with them to their roles by way of personal resources and their understanding of the intentions informing their actions.

Thus, phenomena like administrators' and leaders' temperaments, values, interests, personalities, feelings and emotions, and the connection between these and their actions, were overriding concerns for Greenfield.

During this turbulent period, another keen observer of leadership and administration, sharing concerns not dissimilar from those of Greenfield, only in his case working in the domain of political psychology and from the perspective of psychoanalysis, wrote an important and widely acclaimed book entitled *Skills, Outlooks and Passions: A Psychoanalytic Contribution to the Study of Politics* (Davies, 1980). In addition to displaying the wealth of his original insights and his distinctively crisp, sprightly style, the particular virtue of A.F. Davies's voluminous study was that in it he had subsumed a vast range of clinical and biographical information beneath an inventive array of classifications, much of it concerned with administrators (albeit civil servants rather than school and educational managers) and political leaders. Like Greenfield, Davies too, in his own way, had shown how in the study of society and organizations it was possible, so to speak, 'to bring the people back in' to the analysis. Neither man's writings, however, had had sufficient to say about the constraints on human action and the ways in which human beings assume the identities and roles they do due to processes such as socialization. Indeed, in Greenfield's case I suggested (Gronn, 1994) that there was another side to Weber which dealt with this relationship between social structure and social action, but which Greenfield had ignored.

What eventually gave me the departure point for what I was after were two other sets of important writings which paid careful attention to the contexts for action. The first included some of the early chapters in Gerth and Mills's (1964) classic, *Character and Social Structure*, which discussed in detail the ways in which institutions shape people for the performance of diverse social roles. Two passages in particular, while by no stretch of the imagination the final word on the matter, leapt out at me (Gerth and Mills, 1964, pp. 173, 161–2):

> Institutions not only select persons and eject them; institutions also form them.

and especially:

> Were we fully to trace out the biographies typical of a society's members, from before birth until after death, we would also have to study a great deal about the roles and institutions of the society. For the biography of a person consists of the transformations in character which result from abandoning roles and taking on new ones.

The other piece was a short, but highly stimulating and evocative article by the management theorist, Rosemary Stewart (1989), in which she reviewed a growing body of first-hand observational fieldwork investigations of the day-to-day work of managers in a variety of settings (including education), following the important leads given by Mintzberg (1973) and Kotter (1982). Stewart (1989, p. 4) provided a comprehensive 'map of the field of study' and outlined numerous possible avenues for future research into the work of managers, the pertinent one of which was the link between influences such as biographical data, education, career and personality, and the ways in which managers from different cultural and organizational backgrounds construed and performed their jobs.

Although in some ways career might seem to be a fairly well-worn concept in organizational sociology and occupational psychology, I saw it as capable of being sufficiently reworked to encompass individual and collective aspects of leadership pathways and trajectories. Gerth and Mills (1964, p. 94), it seemed to me, were right: career is one of those general terms with which we can 'knit interpersonal situations into social structures' and which enable us 'to locate types of persons within social structures'. At the same time, however, career is a notion which, like the concepts of character and strategy to which reference was made at the beginning of this book, requires careful use. There is no doubt that there are numerous people in all walks of life, but especially in the professions, who are ambitious, and who quite consciously and unashamedly define occupational goals for themselves early on in, or even beforehand in the period leading up to, their working lives. Equally there are those for whom the overall pattern of their paid employment evolves or just happens, for whom there is no particular blueprint and who may be said, literally, to fall into pursuits like teaching and administration. Needless to say, any preferred framework for ordering leadership experience has to be able to accommodate both of these contrasting polarized ways – calculation and serendipity – in which roles come to be occupied.

A closely related point is that leadership careers can be viewed either prospectively or retrospectively. On the one hand, if evidence is available of people monitoring and reflecting on their leadership experiences while they are actually undergoing them, and if that evidence suggests these same people do in fact see themselves as consciously constructing careers, either in conformity with some originally conceived plan of their own or deviating from it to some degree, then that is one thing. In such instances it would be perfectly legitimate for an interested onlooker or student of leadership to impute some degree of conscious intention and coherence to the experiences of those concerned. Similarly, those individuals in question may well see or describe themselves as somehow being 'in formation', or as being prepared or preparing themselves for leadership. Equally, however, they may well not. And because leadership cannot be fore-ordained – i.e. there is no foolproof way of predicting who will become a leader and who will not (because knowledge of who gets to be attributed with leader status is only knowable *after* the attributions have been made) – most leadership careers have to be reconstructed by looking backwards. Leaders themselves can look back and undertake that reconstruction, either as collaborative life history informants, as autobiographers or as the compilers of memoirs, or it can be done on their behalf, with their knowledge and agreement, or without these (if they are deceased), by biographers. Either way, only with the luxury of hindsight is it possible to say, for example, that particular segments of experiences slot into categories or sub-categories of a nominated career phase or stage.

Thus, in the various parts of this book in which I put forward an idea like strategy I can easily run the risk of being accused of imposing an order and logic on an individual's experiences for which there simply is no evidence and which, therefore, is not warranted. In short, I would stand guilty of failing to adequately take account of accident and chance. My answer to that anticipated objection is threefold. First, in some cases of leaders, the evidence is simply overwhelming: they will and do consciously devise strategies for getting on and upwards as leaders, and as fast as is humanly possible. Second, where they do not choose to do so by deliberate intention they can, nonetheless, be seen as having done so by default. That is, in a retrospective reading of their actions it is sometimes possible to detect a pattern which, while not adding up to an avowedly calculated response from the outset, still bears all the hallmarks of a considered response to the vagaries of circumstance. Third, on the basis of an accumulated body of research evidence, I am advancing in the pages of this book the utility of the idea of prospective leaders learning to think strategically as regards themselves and their future careers. In that respect I have slipped across a line that is often drawn between a study which reports an empirical set of findings and one which adopts a normative posture in relation to those data. My defence, for what is in some quarters seen as unpardonable, is that if the record of experience is to be learnt from in the pursuit of role mastery, then there simply is no other option.

Organizational and occupational careers

The popular understanding of career has traditionally been associated with occupations and paid employment. When used in this connection career necessarily entails the particular physical or mental labour required to be performed, but it has generally carried a wider meaning than the actual labour, tasks or duties that together make up an occupation. Thus, when considering their future employment, and provided they were fortunate enough to be part of a generation faced with relatively rosy or buoyant labour market prospects consequent on full employment, potential school-leavers generally used to be counselled to prepare and position themselves for career openings in one of the professions or the skilled trades, rather than merely seeking out random job vacancies. Perhaps they still are. Likewise, when applied to leadership, the notion of career communicates more than the straightforward idea of task performance. In both spheres – paid employment and leadership – career has usually signalled the idea of a field of human endeavour in which there is ample scope for, and the possibility of, sequenced and planned movement and, therefore, some sense of anticipated trajectory. Pursuit of a career does, of course, bring with it financial reimbursement, but there is also a number of other equally important compensations and rewards such as status, scope to express one's individuality and identity (i.e. to perform in a way in keeping with one's personal needs) and the capacity to foreshadow and realize one's potential. There is also an implied notion of commitment to a course of life and perhaps even a sense of craftsmanship as well.

It is important at the outset to consider the idea of leadership careers alongside those to do with employment because commentators' assumptions about the latter have frequently informed discussions of leadership. As will be seen in a moment, however, some of the recent thinking of occupational sociologists has shattered the kinds of cosy assumptions traditionally associated with career theory. Moreover, these new perspectives also have dramatic implications for the styles of leadership now thought to be appropriate for changed workplaces and organizations in a globalized, post-modern world. They may even be such as to render any claim which purports to view leadership as a career highly suspect. But before showing how such a view of leadership can be sustained in the face of these trends, I begin by considering some of the typical ways in which commentators have conceived of careers.

Sociologists have tended to think of career in the sense of an individual's life course, i.e. as a way in which 'to refer to *any* social strand of any person's course through life', as Goffman (1976a, p. 119, emphasis added) once expressed it in a celebrated essay on the moral career of mental patients. An expression like 'course through life' has no necessary connection with work or employment. Rather, it captures the biographical experience of time and signals a sense of journey or passage, which is what Goffman (1976a, p. 119) particularly seems to be driving at when he refers to:

> the regular sequence of changes that career entails in the person's self and in his [*sic*] framework of imagery for judging himself and others.

In Goffman's essay the adjective moral is juxtaposed with career to form 'moral career', by which he means the well-being and welfare of individuals in respect of the particular characteristics of personhood that constitute them as human beings. In the case of mental patients these defining attributes come to be shaped by prolonged incarceration in a particularly demanding institution – small wonder, then, that Goffman (1976a, p. 154) refers to a patient's moral career as 'a given social category' and to 'a standard sequence of changes' in one's conception of self and others. Such remarks, as Goffman intended, apply beyond the sphere of mental health and communicate a strong sense of careers in general as being patterned or socially constructed life experiences.

What Goffman demonstrates is that there is a symbiotic relationship between individuals and the institutional contexts from which their identities emerge, with a bias in the connection towards institutional determination – an instance of what Archer (1995, p. 100) refers to as over-socialization. Individuals' careers, as I shall demonstrate in the case of leaders, are indeed structured for them, but those same individuals are still able to negotiate particular identities and pathways of their own choosing from within those structured options available to them, and to some extent determine the pace with which they move along them. Given this idea of a career broadly conceived of as a life course, what are the principal perspectives which commentators have adopted on careers?

The first point is that career can be understood in two broad senses:

objectively and subjectively (Stebbins, 1970, p. 34). A career thought of objectively means an overall view of socially defined or institutionally patterned career lines (as in Goffman's example of incarcerated mental patients), whereas a subjective perspective on career refers to an individual's understanding and feelings about her or his career experiences. A slightly different way of making this distinction is Gunz's (1989, pp. 226–8) differentiation between a macro (or societal and organizational) perspective and a micro (or individual) view of career. Second, the location of career roles is important, for, while individuals work in a chosen occupation or vocation, it is particular organizations which demand their immediate loyalty. Thus, a newly appointed principal, for example, is influenced by the cultural dictates of a particular organizational setting. These two dualistic commitments open up numerous possibilities for tracking careers. At any time during an individual's career, for example, movement between organizations (e.g. from schools to colleges) is possible but without her or him necessarily having to switch occupations (e.g. they may transfer as principals or leading teachers). Alternatively, individuals can change roles and jobs within the one location (e.g. through internal promotion from teacher to administrator). Whichever path is taken, different combinations of role learning and cultural adjustment will vary in the severity of the demands they impose. When there is a twofold change – a career switch and organizational relocation – the tension and dislocation for one's sense of self and domestic lifestyle can be profound, as Mealyea (1988) found in his study of self-employed tradesmen and women who, in mid-career, decided to become schoolteachers.

Career progression is understood generally as a desired, vertical, ladder-like movement through age-related and time-phased stages. The various locations occupied by individuals at any one time generate corresponding expectations and perspectives of career trajectories. Thus, early career restlessness contrasts with the transitional rethinking typifying the mid-career years, as one's early dreams are re-evaluated (Levinson *et al.*, 1978), and the more reflective and winding-down sensations experienced in one's twilight years. Career movement also usually entails the achievement of higher rank – a phenomenon known as status passage – and Schein (1991) has shown how an individual's organizational function (e.g. responsibility for particular tasks) and centrality (as an insider or an outsider in respect of overall power and influence) change sharply with acquired status. Factors like these combine to create 'chains of opportunity' (Gunz, 1989, pp. 233–4) which, depending on whether they facilitate or impede the speed of desired or timetabled movement through career, represent subjectively understood feelings of progress, betterment, improvement, wasted chances, consolation or resignation, as the case may be, to the individuals concerned.

Mid-career is one transition point that has come under increased scrutiny (Kearl and Hoag, 1984). If career advancement is experienced as akin to ladder climbing or like moving up an escalator, then opportunities for, and the pace of, advancement appear to slacken with the onset of middle-age and the assumption of middle-management responsibilities. Martin and Strauss (1956, p. 104) noted how it was at this career point that the possibility of being sidelined first became likely for managers. The pioneering work in this area, particularly as regards men, was completed by Levinson *et al.* (1978) in the popular book, *The Seasons of a Man's Life*, in which it was argued that adulthood comprises a series of alternating stable periods and transitions during which former conceptions of identity are discarded and new ones initiated. It is in the 30s age-range that career-oriented individuals have a sense of climbing and of achieving their aspirations. During the early 40s, however, one starts to look over one's shoulder, and sense of meaning and direction are called into question. This searching and questioning is experienced as particularly difficult, especially by men, because residues of earlier unfinished psychological business begin to surface. Women freed of responsibilities for family formation, by contrast, may experience a comparably different rhythm and find the mid-life years provide them with a second wind.

Smoothness of career passage, then, is rarely the norm. Critical turning-points and transitions (e.g. being passed over for promotion, lateral appointments, demotion) entail temporary or lasting setbacks which may be experienced as loss or even grief. Moreover, career disincentives such as reduced pension or superannuation entitlements for working beyond certain age limits are often encountered. Two critical factors in determining both the mode and speed of career advancement are timing and strategically located personnel. Speed of movement is often dictated by ingredients such as age, level of experience, skill, seniority and formal system requirements. In this last respect some career moves may be regularized (e.g. automatic annual re-grading through salary increments) and some may even be mandatory (e.g. in Australia, for teachers, initial appointment to a rural school before a metropolitan position). Strategic personnel are those well-positioned senior individuals who count or exercise clout in respect of organizational power and influence. They include various patrons and sponsors who provide leverage and important advice on career openings, promotion and shortcuts to success, as Marshall (1985) found in her field study of US male and female assistant principals, although this was less so in Hall's (1996, pp. 54–8) study of six UK women heads. In both studies, however, aspiring school administrators learned the value of watching their peers and superiors to try to acquire models of appropriate future role behaviour and ways of presenting themselves as educational leaders.

Individuals are often required to possess set prerequisites, both for career entry to guarantee their licensing and registration following pre-service training, and for further career movement. These may include formal academic credentials, references or testimonials of character and, particularly for accelerated movement, some evidence of reputation and track record. Such details reflect the fact that career movement in organizations is usually formally structured along particular tracks or pathways, determined by qualifications, graded into levels of responsibility and competence and, in many instances, determined by formal industrial relations agreements and awards. The demands and personal costs of status passage and movement along such pathways vary for the individual, particularly in respect of decisions to enter professions like medicine, teaching and social work. If the circumstances of occupational preparation and training are tightly structured, and if the demands imposed on the individual are particularly intense (as with the induction of defence service personnel), then the effects can be stressful. Old identities may well have to be discarded in order to reconstruct oneself into a new person (Khleif, 1980, p. 208, original emphasis):

> It is as if the trainee must consciously deny the moral worth of his [*sic*] old self, must consider it a form of deviance or relevance, as a *pre-condition* for acquisition of his new identity.

In the case of prospective North American school superintendents, for example, Khleif (1975, p. 303) found that a technique of batch processing was utilized to ensure that the trainee men enrolled acquired the necessary sense of dress, vocabulary and self-assertiveness demanded by the trainers. Thus, 'rookie superintendents are not asked to repudiate their old occupational identity, only to transcend it!' New administrative identities are acquired by means of status reduction.

At the summits of a variety of conventionally understood organizational careers await the glittering prizes – numerous privileges and rewards yearned for and esteemed because of the tangible monetary gain, security, comfort, status and power they bestow. Their attainment is usually legitimated by various organizational norms and cultural values, and by various occupational ideologies (e.g. professional ethics of service to society). Their pursuit is also justified by each individual's personal search for meaning, fulfilment, utility and self-actualization, and is further warranted by the social significance attached to those values forming part of the work ethic such as hard work, the pursuit of success and delayed gratification.

This summary overview has sketched in a few of the major features of organizational careers as they have been broadly understood in education and elsewhere up until recently. There is, however, a quite dramatically different view of careers emerging which challenges virtually every assumption on which the picture just painted has been based. The essence of the argument is that the vertically integrated and co-ordinated, stable, hierarchical, complex and interdependent conglomerates which have characterized the world of organizations for so long, and in which careers have played themselves out, are now being replaced by drastically trimmed-down units predicated on the need for rapid adaptation and flexibility, or even by networked and cellular organizational forms. And just as these huge corporate and human service juggernauts are having to redefine themselves, then so, likewise, must careers and our conceptions of them. Increasingly, independent or quasi-independent individuals trading on the name and goodwill provided by formal organizational membership or affiliation are to be seen working in consultative, networked and consortia arrangements *across* organizational boundaries rather than *within* bounded organizational forms. Careers can no longer be thought of, therefore, as lifelong but are instead being described as boundaryless (Arthur and Rousseau, 1996) and protean (Hall, 1996).

Protean signals the ability to adapt and change one's identity quickly, and to re-position oneself at will as quickly moving circumstances require. Career theorists now refer to the idea of a new career contract – less in respect of commitment to a particular organization or vocation but as regards a new understanding or agreement with oneself to construct a self-determined, do-it-yourself career of choice (Hall and Mirvis, 1996, pp. 20–2). Such claims rest on the assumption that in a knowledge-dependent economy power resides increasingly with persons rather than with formal positions, and that organizational minimalism (as embodied in the paradigm of the small, flexible, Silicon-Valley-style, high-technology company battling not just to define the game, so to speak, but to define it and then stay out in front of it) is the shape of things to come (Arthur and Rousseau, 1996, pp. 5, 10). The limited available evidence about how firms adapt to these extreme pressures is that they do not wholly jettison their existing managerial arrangements but instead develop hybrid 'semi-structures' (Brown and Eisenhart, 1997, p. 28) on which they rely to position themselves at a tolerable point somewhere between complete order and total chaos. Perrow (1996, p. 310) questions the desirability of these developments and suggests that this alleged career boundarylessness is only likely to be an option for a privileged minority of mainly professional employees, and that despite popular rhetoric about downsizing, the evidence in the USA is that 'slightly smaller big firms [are] still in command of the field'.

The extent to which these imperatives are likely to spill over and take hold in the education sector is not yet clear, although substantial evidence is available of systems adopting various forms of contracting out of educational services, and the numbers of international networks of educational policy entrepreneurs pursuing their own boutique and niche careers are increasing. The other interesting development in the field of leadership which parallels the image of protean careers is Lipman-Blumen's (1996) idea of connective leadership. Globalization, she believes, is simultaneously creating a far more diverse and interdependent world. The template of the new dawn is still taking shape, but life in organizations will be characterized by discontinuity, the fragmentation of experience, plural values, very condensed time frames and a truncated sense of space and place. Moreover, the world of organizations is likely to become a kind of vast sprawling Lego-land in which the leader's job 'is to connect pieces of one organization with parts of another and then take them apart when the task is done, reusing some components and adding new ones to build an ongoing series of structures' (Lipman-Blumen, 1996, p. 207). Her metaphor for the range of leadership dispositions and instantaneous style shifts required to deal with rapid change is not proteanism or the visual image of the collage, but the artist's palette. Here, like the three primary colours, a trio of core style attributes (direct, relational and instrumental behaviour strategies) give rise to nine combinations, shadings and gradations of leadership initiatives. One of Lipman-Blumen's prototypes of the emerging connective leader is Anita Roddick, founder of The Body Shop.

Far from heralding the redundancy of a career-derived framework for understanding leaders, these new parallel developments and possibilities in career theory and in leadership suggest that it is as pertinent as ever. The biographical, life-course career approach to understanding leaders' lives towards which discussion in this chapter has been directed certainly feeds off a number of the traditional, orthodox assumptions made by career theorists (linear sequential progress, pathways, passage, etc.), but it is still able to accommodate readily the idea of emerging career autonomy. It matters not whether leaders' careers are pursued wholly or only partially within formal organizational boundaries, or even across them; potential leaders will continue to pass through a period of intense preparatory learning, or formation as I term it, and they will still take the bearings for their leadership in relation to, and build their follower constituencies from, the membership of organizations of one sort or another. In short, leaders can be expected to continue to define roles for themselves, for which followers will be required, a long way into the foreseeable future. And the fact that the locations in which they will do so are likely to shift dramatically by no means spells the end for leadership careers.

A career model of leadership

There are two important advantages to be gained by approaching leadership from the perspective of career. First, the student of leadership obtains a more informed understanding of the various contexts in which leaders lead. Leadership, as has been argued elsewhere (Gronn and Ribbins, 1996), by virtue of its attributional basis, is heavily context-bound. A career focus explains how contextual factors structure a leader's actions as part of their zone of discretion (see Chapter 6), and how they shape a leader's agency. Second, the field of leadership studies lacks a sound comparative point of reference against which to map leaders' biographical experiences and activities. It is one thing to scrutinize leaders as individuals in isolation, but the field has remarkably few useful benchmarks or parameters for examining the circumstances of leaders' lives in relation to one another, and also in respect of the cultures and societies from which they emerge. Yet, from the perspective of globalization and the better appreciation of different, deeply entrenched cultural approaches to problem-solving the provision of such a scheme is timely.

The following analytical framework distinguishes three macro contexts which structure the trajectories followed by leaders' careers: historical, cultural and societal (see Figure 2.1). What these contexts mean is that all leaders are born at a time which is not of their own choosing, and that they live for the bulk of their early formative years and beyond in civil societies within nation-state boundaries in which they are socialized according to cultural assumptions and values which, once again, are overwhelmingly not of their choosing. Historical contexts position individuals as members of age-group cohorts or generations that are reared in the different eras into which world history divides itself (the Victorian Age, the Cold War, the Swinging Sixties, etc.). The designation 'cultural' is an acknowledgement of differences of relative status and dependency between nation-states – such as imperial subordinacy and hegemony – the spread of huge ethnic, linguistic and religious diasporas across the globe (regardless of nation-state boundaries and frontiers) and differences in rates of influence and the diffusion of cultural values – seen in such common distinctions as old and new world, metropolitan and frontier, and imperial and colonial societies. A leader born into a particular civil society, therefore, is the product of a specific era and is moulded according to the mix of cultural assumptions chosen by her or his primary carers, and in turn embodies or becomes the bearer of those values which have left their mark. An illustration of the way these categories shape a leader's early identity is Sir James Darling. Born in 1899 into a middle-class English family, and reared in Edwardian times, Darling departed what was, for the most part, a paternalistic, class-ridden, and imperialistic nation to begin a new life as a first-time headmaster in 1930. He arrived in Australia, then a far-flung, underpopulated, culturally dependent, capitalist, predominantly white dominion but a country, nonetheless, fiercely proud of its democratic egalitarianism (Gronn, 1986b). Within the broad parameters of history, society and culture, then, can be located the microcosmic details of each individual leader's life. These can be thought of as comprising four sequential phases listed in the inner vertical rectangle within Figure 2.1: formation, accession, incumbency and divestiture.

Formation

Leader formation, as has been suggested, is to be understood in two main ways. From the perspective of the overall society or key sectors within it formation refers to the totality of the institutionalized arrangements which, either by intention or effect, serve to replenish or reproduce cohorts of leaders. Looking back from the point of view of those individuals who can be said to have arrived, so to speak, and who at any one time comprise the aggregate of available leaders, formation means those preparatory socialization processes and experiences which served to later position them in their previous incarnation as leadership aspirants in a state of social and psychological readiness to assume responsibility and authority. It is in this formative period, from infancy to early adulthood, that the scaffolding of a

HISTORICAL ERA

c.1850

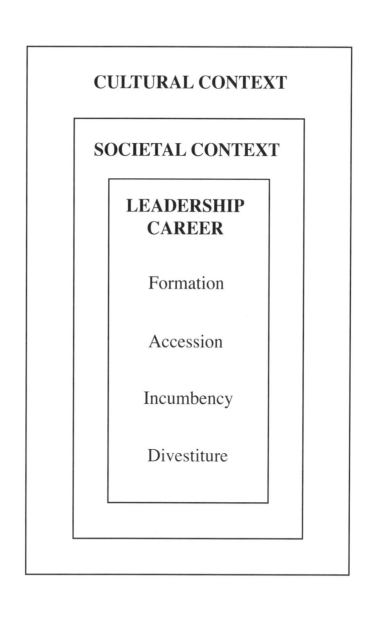

Figure 2.1   A career model of leadership

character structure – 'the essential [moral, social and psycho-physiological] properties of people who hold and want institutional responsibility' (Kaplan, 1990a, p. 419) – is erected. The three principal institutions which shape individual character are families and their modes of upbringing, schooling and educational agencies, and a variety of peer and reference groups.

Briefly, every family type, no matter what its particular social class location, its ethnic basis, its religious or secular affiliations, its gender composition and the division of parental labour on which it relies, transmits key assumptions about appropriate adult behaviour to its offspring. Typically, this includes things like standards in regard to matters of taste, religious and moral values, and attitudes to authority which are either deliberately inculcated by parents or parental surrogates or, if they are not, are resources which children are left to acquire through their own devices. The formal cognitive and affective cultures of school classrooms or related learning environments, along with the informal culture of student life, ensure that forms of schooling either reinforce or subvert the family unit's influence. And just as family and community life is lived within prevailing ideologies of child-rearing in any one historical era, so too is schooling and education predicated on dominant pedagogical ideologies about desired educational outcomes and the appropriate institutional arrangements for their delivery and attainment. The extent to which the core activities undertaken by these three sets of agencies cohere, and the extent to which the intended and unintended messages they transmit are consistently communicated will determine whether or not the formation of a society's young people occurs within a tightly or loosely coupled culture of values. Whenever the connections between them are tight, for example, the requisite pre-conditions for what some sociologists refer to as strong inter-generational closure and the acquisition of social and cultural capital are ensured. Yet, various sub-cultural reference groups (adolescent peers, friends, mentors and consciousness-shaping popular media) provide additional sources of personal and social identification, and hedonistic gratification to the young. Again, the values these groups communicate and the effects of the messages they transmit either reinforce the consistency and direction of socialization experiences sought by families or they lay the basis for potentially adversarial and counter-cultural styles.

It is further suggested that the core aspects of leadership character which these three socialization agencies fashion comprise a conception or definition of self and identity, a preferred working style and an outlook or set of values (see Chapters 4–6). The suggested causal relationship between these elements of the formation process is summarized in Figure 2.2.

Accession

Accession refers to a stage of grooming or anticipation in which candidates for leadership roles rehearse or test their potential capacity to lead by direct

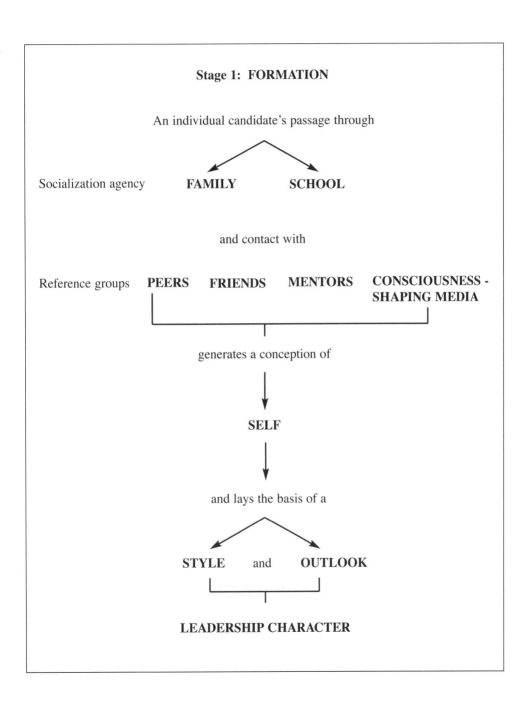

Stage 1: FORMATION

An individual candidate's passage through

Socialization agency   **FAMILY**   **SCHOOL**

and contact with

Reference groups   **PEERS   FRIENDS   MENTORS   CONSCIOUSNESS -
SHAPING MEDIA**

generates a conception of

SELF

and lays the basis of a

STYLE   and   **OUTLOOK**

LEADERSHIP CHARACTER

Figure 2.2   The process of leader formation

comparison with existing leaders and the field of their prospective rivals for advancement. As is shown in Figure 2.3, accession is also to be understood from two perspectives. To the onlooker or observer, it is a period marked by various forms of public display by leadership rookies – analogous in human terms, perhaps, to behaviour such as wing-stretching and preening in the animal world – which is intended to alert potential role sponsors, gate-keepers and talent-spotters that one is worthy to be acknowledged and taken into account, and to impress those sitting in judgement by reliance on various forms of publicity and impression management that one is ready, willing and able to lead. Prospective leaders have to satisfy their potential critics on two counts. First, their assessors need guarantees that anyone marked out from the pool of aspirants or potential candidates is sound. Soundness signifies that the individual in question is reputable; i.e. that their career reputation to this point in time is unsullied and unblemished. Second, they need to be assured that any candidates for leadership responsi-bility are highly credible; i.e. that they have fashioned, road-tested and have at their disposal a workable performance routine.

From the point of view of the aspirant, if she or he is to conform to anticipated institutional demands then they have to measure up in these two important tasks to be accomplished and the expectations which go with them. To do so may require the repression, subordination or re-channelling of individual needs, for to meet the first challenge means to undertake the necessary internal psychological construction (and, if necessary, continual reconstruction if success is not to prove elusive) of oneself as reputable and sound. And to meet the second is to begin assembling and rehearsing a role repertoire or the rudiments of what may eventually become a preferred working style. Both of these mandatory inner, subjective work tasks are geared towards what Karen Horney (1950, p. 308) once referred to as self-realization or the development of one's special gifts or potential. Apart from access to a supportive or 'good enough' (Winnicott, 1965) external facilitat-ing environment conducive to growth, an important internal pre-condition for self-realization is individual self-belief. There are two sides to the coin of self-belief: a sense of efficacy, or the acceptance of one's potency, compe-tence and capacity to make a difference to organizational outcomes; and self-esteem, or positive feelings of one's worth and value. Horney's *Neurosis and Human Growth* suggests that the path to self-realization, self-assertiveness and the achievement of mastery is invariably fraught with self-conflict. Furthermore, it is well documented (e.g. Zaleznik, 1967; Kaplan, 1990b) that the strong motivation to achieve and be successful displayed by many leaders and would-be leaders often masks a profound sense of inadequacy and failure. The fact that the manifold ways in which inner psychological turmoil expresses itself can be masked so successfully at times by candidates for leadership, therefore, makes the institutional hurdles of succession, selec-tion and induction both precarious for leadership aspirants to overcome and

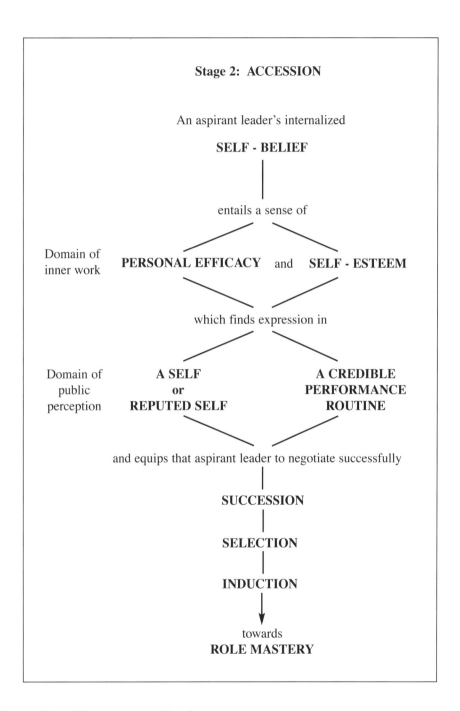

Figure 2.3 The process of leader accession

difficult for organizational gatekeepers to manage (as will be made evident in Part III).

It is during this accession phase that aspiring leaders become alert to vacancies and openings as these arise. If the prospect of being a leader becomes particularly enticing at this time they may even begin searching systematically for positions by scanning advertisements, putting out feelers, taking soundings or by networking. Candidates for leadership learn quickly in this period that the knack is to position themselves or to jockey with one another for preferment. It is for these kinds of reasons that alignments and working agreements are struck with patrons, sponsors and strategically positioned organizational tribal elders while the hopefuls and young men and women in a hurry await a call to office. Finally, while it is difficult to be precise about the duration of accession, this stage is more likely to be an attenuated and interrupted one for women than for men, especially if decisions about career possibilities are delayed or have to be balanced against competing demands such as child-bearing and family formation.

Incumbency

The two remaining stages in the framework, which are not the prime focus or purpose of this book, can be dealt with reasonably quickly. The third stage is incumbency or leadership proper. By this stage leaders have developed and honed their public personas, they have learned to project their authoritativeness, and they now seek to give further expression to their quest for mastery and self-realization by gaining experience through circulating amongst various elite postings and leadership roles. If they happen to be leaders who hold down formal appointments then, as successful candidates, they will likely have undergone and survived both formal and informal induction into their new responsibilities. Thereafter, every subsequent role switch will require further induction into organizational and workplace norms. Provided the match between their personal needs and the requirements imposed by their roles is congruent, so that what might be termed a requisite fit is achieved (i.e. they are not like square pegs in round holes), then incumbent leaders will be able to go some way to meet their need to self-actualize. The attainment of this kind of psychological fulfilment, satisfaction and equilibrium is, of course, dependent on their successful reconciliation of the three core elements which determine the extent of the degrees of freedom available in any institutional role: external constraints, situational task demands and opportunities (Stewart, 1989). The precise mix of these elements and exact nature of the role, and the expectations accompanying it will shape the fine detail of the expression of a leader's hitherto emergent image of self, style and outlook – as I suggested at the outset. In summary, being a leader, either formal or informal, facilitates expression of that person's sense of potency, ambition and vision.

As an addendum to these points, in a recent discussion of headteachers' careers Day and Bakioglu (1996) have identified a series of developmental phases and sub-phases undergone by heads which are compatible with the framework being outlined. They break down what I label the period of incumbency into four sequences: initiation (which overlaps with much of what in Chapter 9 I refer to as induction), development, autonomy and disenchantment. Day and Bakioglu's data (derived from questionnaires, documents and interviews with more than 30 school heads), like those of Hall (1996, pp. 88–113), provide numerous instances of the kind of inner psychological tug of war – which I suggest typifies leadership accession – recurring in the early years as the new incumbents wrestle with their fears and uncertainties. Headteacher P's confession about the kinds of internal conversations still swirling around in her or his mind after six and a half years in the job as a school head is a good illustration (Day and Bakioglu, 1996, p. 213):

> I've always got inside me a question which says 'Am I doing the job as well as I could?' 'What am I doing wrong?' And you sometimes think, when you get something right, you know, it goes down well but you've always got a question about this because you don't have anyone coming and saying 'We've seen quite a lot of practice around the Authority (School District) and what we see you doing is great'. You don't get that very often. You don't actually know, so you are uncertain. I am uncertain all the time about how competent I am. Am I doing a good job? And you have these crises that occur when you do feel inadequate from time to time and you think, I am not keeping on top of it, it is too much, I am not coping. I need somebody who's got more capacity than I have, I am burned out. You get these sorts of feelings from time to time, but somehow you get over those and you come back again.

It was only during Day and Bakioglu's suggested period of autonomy that these school heads felt themselves to be genuinely effective and productive leaders or, in my terms, had attained role mastery. Ironically, however, this achievement meant that a significant proportion of Day and Bakioglu's (1996, p. 219) informants had plateaued and given up learning: instead they were found to be engaging in actions which 'were designed to maintain what is rather than develop what might be'. They had become sluggish. They lacked motivation and resisted change. In effect they were behaving as though on automatic pilot. Effective leadership in their case, then, seemed to be something experienced for a limited period of about four years at most, as well as within the first eight years of a headship, for reasons 'connected with life-phase and social-psychological factors' (Day and Bakioglu, 1996, p. 224).

Divestiture

The fourth stage in a leadership career is divestiture. At some point in their lives, due to factors associated with ageing, illness, lack of fulfilment or incapacity, leaders have to divest themselves of leadership by releasing their psychological grip. That process of letting go may come about voluntarily or involuntarily. It may be planned or unplanned. It may be experienced by the leader, organization or the sector in which she or he has been working as either smooth or traumatic. In cases of voluntary departure, for example, in which leaving office or letting go has been carefully planned for, leaders deliberately make up their minds (usually by retirement or resignation) to relinquish appointments. In cases of involuntary departure, on the other hand – due, perhaps, to the abolition or elimination of one's role or, in extreme political circumstances, because of a coup or even death – someone else usually makes the decision on the leader's behalf. Whichever of these two routes are taken, loss of status and office (and its much-sought-after trappings) means experiencing an almost certain feeling (akin to grief) of lost potency and influence, and of having to witness the possible modification or even destruction of one's leadership heritage or legacy at the hands of a successor. To let go amounts to a King Lear-like gesture which acknowledges that leaders have a shelf life, so to speak, and means a denial (to them) of their immortality and indispensability.

Ribbins, in two recent studies of a sample of headteachers in UK special and primary schools (Pascale and Ribbins, 1998; Ribbins and Rayner, 1998), has confirmed the broad pattern of career progression encompassed in the four-stage framework proposed in this book, but with one minor modification to this last divestiture stage. Instead, Ribbins suggests 'moving on' (Pascale and Ribbins, 1998, p. 12):

> This alternative route is seen to involve a phase of reinvention or rebirth, in which the incumbent moves on towards a newly created professional life, within a significantly different context and with newly created peers.

Ribbins and his co-authors also incorporated Day and Bakioglu's (1996) four phases of incumbency but their data did not confirm the latter's posited disenchantment. As an alternative Ribbins proposes 'advancement'. His suggested modifications yield two alternative potential career routes (Pascale and Ribbins, 1998, p.13; Ribbins and Rayner, 1998, p. 7):

Route 1: Career progression as potentially negative and destructive
1. Formation
2. Accession
3. Incumbency: initiation, development, autonomy, advancement as disenchantment
4. Moving on: divestiture

Route 2: Career progression as potentially progressive and creative
1. Formation
2. Accession
3. Incumbency: initiation, development, autonomy, advancement as enchantment
4. Moving on: reinvention

There are two points here, neither of which requires modification to the framework because the possibilities Ribbins's data open up are readily accommodated by it. First, while Day and Bakioglu (1996, pp. 220–1) do report compelling evidence of their principals' disillusionment, fatigue and psychological retreatism, all of which signals a loss of professional generativity, this phenomenon is not to be confused with divestiture. Like every boundary-marking ritual or rite of passage in life, divestiture implies a changed status and identity. This dual switch may well be accompanied by the kinds of feelings expressed by Day and Bakioglu's sample, but equally it need not be, for leaders are just as able to divest themselves when they are at the height of their powers. This is the kind of thinking frequently being alluded to by politicians and other public figures if they express the wish to leave office when they are 'on top', 'as a winner' or 'at a time of their own choosing'. If indeed Day and Bakioglu's notion of disenchantment does imply 'a pattern of creeping negativism' (Ribbins and Rayner, 1998, p. 7) then the same cannot be read into divestiture. Second, 'moving on' raises the question of when finality means finality. Let me be clear: I mean by divestiture that erstwhile leaders have abandoned any future ambition to lead. I make no assumption about the age at which this occurs. After he retired as headmaster of Geelong Grammar School in 1961 at age 62, for example, Sir James Darling became Chairman of the Australian Broadcasting Commission (until 1967) and continued to exercise leadership in a variety of other spheres, including the writing of influential fortnightly editorial reflections for the Melbourne *Age* newspaper until a couple of years before his death. Of course, leaders may also move on to interests and spheres other than leadership, and this may entail Ribbins's notion of reinvention. Yet they can also reinvent themselves from time to time while still being incumbents. But neither of these possibilities, as I say, rules out divesting or letting go at some point in time.

I now turn to the question of the extent to which aspirants moving through these early career phases deliberately choose their passages and pathways in order to maximize their personal advantages and gains as part of a calculated career plan or strategy.

Career strategies

Reference was made earlier to some important distinctions between the various levels at which career could be understood. Briefly these were a macro or institutional perspective on career systems, on the one hand, and the subjectively understood micro level of individual experience of careers, on the other. The idea of a strategy is seen by a number of analysts to be the point of intersection between these two levels and as according significant scope for individual agency and creativity. But the key questions are: How much agency? And what makes this possible? Morgan (1989, p. 29), for example, has pointed out how an indiscriminate application of the idea of strategy to a range of human activities 'may seem to surrender too much to the forward march of rational calculation'. This is an allegation to which some of the more recent developments on boundaryless careers – which seem to be signalling the possibility of an even greater emphasis on agency and freedom from over-determining career systems in the near future – may be susceptible.

A career strategy has been defined by Evetts (1992, p. 11) as denoting 'how individuals negotiate and manage external constraints both formal and informal'. Evetts (1987, p. 27) found not only that English women primary school heads, for example, usually prepared themselves for failure and rejection in respect of their possible attainment of senior leadership roles and appointments in education, but that as far as the shouldering of family responsibilities was concerned, these were 'not minimised or even shared by these women heads'. Rather, 'they had to continue to meet their family and work commitments, balancing one against the other, for the whole of their working lives'. Such experiences made their career progress intermittent and haphazard. In the case of male and female secondary heads Evetts (1993) explored the kinds of accommodations made by heads and their partners or spouses, and the tensions these generated, in their efforts to ensure that one or both parties could pursue full-time career employment. The following patterns were discovered: single careers (with a division of labour between homemaker and careerist – traditionally female and male respectively, but seen to be changing and becoming increasingly a temporary life-phase arrangement); dual careers (both partners pursue careers but incorporate a postponement strategy for child-rearing, a modify-and-adapt strategy to support one of the partners and a balancing strategy in which each supports the other); irretrievable breakdown (the partners try but, unable to accommodate one another, go their separate ways).

Apart from Evetts's important pioneering work on these ways in which aspirants for school leadership roles balance and trade off their various domestic and work-related demands, there are as yet no comprehensive studies of educational leadership attainment strategies. There are some pointers to hand, however, in related areas of education. In an early and comprehensive analysis of pupils' responses to schooling, for example, Woods (1979, pp. 63–83) classified eight strategies or typical modes of adaptation: ingratiation, colonization, intransigence, retreatism, ritualism, rebellion, opportunistic compliance and instrumental compliance. Were one to follow the lead provided by Woods it would be possible to distinguish the career ends towards which individuals might direct their energies from the means available to pursue them. On the one hand, then, there would be the options and possibilities for leadership which individuals perceive as open to them within the broad parameters defined by factors like industrial awards and the particular external constraints to which their educational organizations are subject (e.g. state-mandated policies for staff deployment, promotions and transfers). On the other hand there would be the resources, both personal (e.g. particular skills) and organizational (e.g. professional development programmes, subsidized further education), which make their attainment possible. Arranged together in a diagram these two broad dimensions might form a useful matrix of hypothesized possibilities.

Because it is not my intention in this book to commend the desirability of devising accession strategies, let alone to endorse particular examples for adoption, I have deliberately drawn back from trying to define any such set of career strategy types. Moreover, there would be little point in recommending an abstract universal typology bearing only minimal connection with any context. After all, one of the sources of the appeal of Woods's category labels is that, while they do have general utility, in his discussion they emerge inductively from, and therefore they are anchored securely in, his particular context-bound data. Accordingly, to connect with a point made earlier in this chapter, the most that I am prepared to suggest is that those who happen to aspire to leadership roles might be counselled to begin thinking strategically. That is, they would be well advised to make themselves aware of the particular attributes of character which are likely to best equip them to perform their prospective roles (those factors I discuss in Part II), and which are calculated to impress selectors, along with the intricacies of the major organizational processes to be negotiated if they are to be seen by their peers as leaders (see Part III). I am emboldened in the modesty of this recommendation by some recent findings of research on headships in special education in which Ribbins and Rayner (1998, pp. 14, 16) note the importance of a 'significant element of chance' and the 'strong element of serendipity' in the choice of special, as opposed to mainstream, education as a career sphere for young teachers. To do more than I have done would be to yield to the forward march about which Morgan warned and that, indeed, would be a retrograde step.

CHAPTER 3

Formative agencies

At this point in the discussion it should be clear that leader formation means, in effect, the process by which leaders are made or constructed, but without these two latter words necessarily being taken as implying any kind of crude or over-drawn notion of a mechanical production-line system. And the idea of formation is not as remote from the general public's consciousness as might be thought at first. Indeed, journalists the world over are forever compiling biographical profiles of major public figures in the weekend colour supplements of major metropolitan daily newspapers. The only differences between these kinds of popular accounts of leaders and what I am proposing in this book are that reporters tend not to use words like formation – although from time to time they will use an expression such as 'the making of a prime minister' or something similar. They tend, also, to highlight dramatic features in the past lives of their subjects to give a story-feel to the readership and generally they are not concerned about drawing the explicit kinds of comparisons which the framework proposed here will permit. On the other hand, one of the important factors which unites both approaches is the urge to try to discover what factors drive leaders in all walks of life to behave as they do, and with what effect, and to ascertain how it is that they have managed to attain the particular positions of influence which they currently occupy.

This chapter provides a detailed consideration of the ways in which the various agencies and reference groups itemized earlier in Figure 2.2 shape a prospective leader's formative years. It is written from an institutional point of view, the first of the two angles which I have suggested are the appropriate perspectives to take on leader formation. With this objective in mind one particularly useful point of departure is Armstrong's (1973) discussion of the recruitment of higher civil service administrators in four European nations (Britain, France, Prussia–Germany and Russia–USSR) during the processes of industrialization and modernization. Armstrong described a broadly ascriptive system of administrative preparation in which completion of a secondary education dominated by a classical curriculum was sufficient to secure elite entry. Apart from a few instances of the specialist preparation of these four elites (e.g. engineering training in Prussia) achievement norms intruded only minimally, so that Armstrong's consideration of higher education was essentially confined to its role in topping up and extending generalist secondary schooling. But with the growth of knowledge, the expansion of higher education provision and the broadening of social access to the university sector during the twentieth century values associated with achievement and merit, rather than ascription, have increasingly come to legitimate the formation of most contemporary leadership strata. Crucial here has been the role played by the higher education sector in Europe and North America, particularly, in dispensing specific management education knowledge to prospective leaders and managers.

In the discussion which follows ascription and achievement are considered as alternative institutional modes of leader formation, and illustrative examples of each approach are provided. I also suggest, however, that because a fundamental reappraisal of the role of higher learning in the preparation of leaders and managers is currently under way, to these two historically significant models there needs to be added a third: customization.

Three formative approaches

Armstrong's ascriptive model was a form of anticipatory socialization in which the offspring of a socially exclusive stratum was selected and segregated at a young age for later elite roles. Its preparation was marked by 'the potential for an uninterrupted line of *reinforcing* socializing experiences from infancy to the attainment of top positions' (Armstrong, 1973, p. 20, original emphasis) in which the bases of selection were criteria such as heredity, family status and an aristocratic outlook. By contrast his maximum deferred achievement model was one in which 'no selection is made among the male cohort until its members reach the appropriate age level for high administrative posts. At that point, the required number of men are selected by some process which gives all – as far as discernible social characteristics go – equal access' (Armstrong, 1973, p. 17). Clearly, ascription would be more likely to produce a closed, unified, exclusive elite recruited from a narrowly defined social base while reliance on forms of achievement, particularly educational criteria, would guarantee a more open and socially variegated elite cohort.[1]

As an example of ascription I consider in detail the instance mentioned earlier in the Introduction to which Hodgkinson (1991, p. 77) refers from time to time as one of the few traditions of preparing leaders in the humanities (an approach with which he is completely in sympathy), viz. 'the generalist tradition whereby leaders are schooled in the classics'. This is the case of the English public schools. The advantage of this choice is that it permits consideration of the interplay of all of the components in the career framework outlined earlier, rather than requiring a separate review of each element in disembodied isolation. I illustrate achievement by considering the deliberate and planned use of higher education and equivalent forms of training to prepare managers and leaders. Formal preparation in management education programmes commenced in the USA around 1900 at a time when general theories of management were first beginning to be articulated, and was later adopted in Europe, Australasia and elsewhere. The historical emergence of achievement as a basis on which to make judgements about leadership capacity paralleled an increasingly wider social dependence on meritocratic criteria and the rise of professional occupational groups in modernizing societies throughout most of the twentieth century. For Gouldner (1950, p. 4) this trend represented the triumph of the bourgeois liberal idea that leadership was something which could be learnt. In that respect achievement signalled the eclipse of the ancient ideal of being 'born to the purple' – i.e. the assumption that leadership was the rightful monopoly of a particular privileged class or stratum claiming to possess an inborn instinct to rule.

On the other hand, it would be a misreading of history to claim that preparation based on universalistic achievement norms embodied in formal credentials has ever completely superseded a dependence on particularistic ascription in the making of judgements about leadership capacity. But just as the latter was eventually forced to provide space for the former in the evolution of preparatory systems, so now, I shall argue, achievement is currently being re-conceptualized to align it with an increasing demand for workplace-related (as opposed to esoteric) knowledge. To Armstrong's ascription and achievement, then, there needs to be added a third evolutionary phase: customization. This rather ugly word is, for the moment, the best available term with which to describe this recent vocational development. Essentially the trend towards customization signals the provision and delivery of knowledge capital in a form calculated to best meet the workplace demands and needs of those who will be served by it as opposed to the dispensing of knowledge in ways consistent with the traditional interests of higher education providers. The illustration I give of customization in leadership is the Frontline Management Initiative (FMI) in Australia. These three overall trends – ascription, achievement and customization – are outlined in detail in the next three sections.

Ascription: The triumph of the gentleman

There are a number of sound reasons for the choice of the public school gentleman as the case illustrating ascription. The first is that, although most historians would probably agree that the generalist tradition of the gifted amateur, as it is sometimes known, reached its apotheosis during the Victorian and Edwardian eras, it still exists within the living memory of many of the current generation of leaders in education and beyond – numerous examples of whom were themselves schooled in this tradition or its more recent versions. Second, the amateur tradition was far-reaching in its influence and derivatives of it were diffused widely around the world. Third, and most importantly, its effects as a system of leader and elite formation are still being felt, and assessed by historians. The significance of this point cannot be over-emphasized for, as I shall point out, one of the important litmus tests of any mechanism warranting the designation 'system' – either as something deliberately intended or as the unintended outcome of a confluence of activities – for shaping a caste or stratum of leaders is what that system yields by way of quality of policies and decisions from the scores of cohorts who pass through it. These effects, needless to say, are longitudinal ones and are qualitatively different from the immediate outcomes usually anticipated from short-lived leadership workshops and training programmes. Because the kind of custodial grip of the institutions I have in mind endured over the period of the highly impressionable years at the beginning of the life cycle, the effects in question are best understood as analogous to the greenish watermark left on a porcelain bath – imperceptible while the tap is dripping but clearly evident over time. Finally, it is the impact of a recent highly critical assessment of these effects of the amateur tradition on a leading member of Baroness Thatcher's first Conservative Cabinet, Sir Keith Joseph – who seized on one historian's explanation for the alleged 'British disease' and used it to justify the Government's vision for an entrepreneurial Britain (Annan, 1988) – that makes it such a timely case.

While the English public schools example illustrates exceptionally well the role which education has played in moulding an elite corps of leaders, some historians dispute just how deliberate the public schools' influence was. On the one hand, Wilkinson (1964, p. vii), for example, notes the schools' 'self-declared responsibility for producing national leaders' and Gathorne-Hardy (1979, p. 210) writes that 'public schools did see themselves as producing leaders' yet, on the other hand, Percival (1969, p. 13) disputes these claims and believes the idea of schools acting as breeding-grounds for empire-builders to be a 'questionable' one. The point is that the combination of a childhood spent in what were often large extended families, followed by preparatory schooling, boarding school, and then a degree from either Oxford or Cambridge university functioned, by default or design, as an apparatus for producing leaders. And the archetype of that leadership was known as gentlemanly power or the leadership of the gifted amateur.

In late nineteenth-century England there were various understandings of 'public school'. Narrowly defined it meant the nine great schools investigated by the Clarendon Commission in 1861: Winchester, Harrow, Eton, Westminster, Charterhouse, St Pauls, Merchant Taylor's, Rugby and Shrewsbury – a mix of ancient, grammar, charitable and other foundation schools. They were all Anglican, fee-paying, boarding, national rather than parochial in the markets they served, and shared an important community of interest through competitive games. These nine sat at the apex of a system comprising other newer, purpose-built proprietary schools modelled on them (e.g. Wellington, Clifton, Cheltenham, Marlborough) which had been founded recently to cater to a burgeoning middle- and upper-middle-class demand for school-ing, and sundry other religious foundations. Honey (1977, p. 284) puts the total number of them at anywhere between 22 and 64 – depending on the degree of their self-consciousness as 'public' schools – for the period *c.* 1880–1920. The five ideals for which this group stood were set out clearly in *The English Tradition of Education* by Cyril Norwood (1929), Headmaster of Harrow, and a leading member of the Headmasters' Conference: religion (i.e. Christianity), discipline or character, the intellectual ideal of culture, team games and service. The gentlemanly disposition, which was the product or outcome of the translation of these ideals into practice, comprised a combination of godliness and good learning (Newsome, 1961), a code of behaviour embodying such virtues as civility and piety or, as Wilkinson (1964, p. 10) terms it, a leavening of moral earnestness with gentility. Perhaps the pithiest insight into this remarkable human species comes from Laski (1940, p. 13), who described the gentleman as someone who 'is rather than does; he maintains towards life an attitude of indifferent receptivity'. As to the gentleman's mode of leadership, Laski (1940, p. 22) observed (with a heavy dose of irony) that the gentleman 'can administer with less bureaucratic irritation than any other type I have known. He can arbitrate commercial or international differences with the same fine equity that he umpires a cricket match.'

The first element in the infrastructure which produced this imperial prototype of the gentleman was a curious *ménage à trois* comprising parents, children and nannies. Generalizations about family life during the Victorian and Edwardian eras are notoriously difficult to sustain. Broadly speaking, however, this was a period during which patterns of dominance and submis-sion between parents and their offspring, and between husbands and their wives, came to be quite sharply defined, and in which nannies played a crucially important role in the socialization of young men. Reliance on nannies became widespread amongst the English middle classes. As regards his children, the Victorian and Edwardian paterfamilias was, for the most part, psychologically absent or remote. By sheer weight of numbers men controlled all the key sectors and institutions of English imperial power: politics and public administration, the church, the army, the universities, the professions and business, so that virtually all the public role models available to young boys were male. With a few exceptions it was only in nursing, social work, the religious orders, temperance and girls' schooling that significant numbers of women in leadership roles were to be found. The lot of the reasonably well-off woman, as Virginia Woolf (1938, p. 12) remarked later, was that 'all the weapons with which an educated man can enforce his opinions are either beyond our grasp or so nearly beyond it that even if we used them we could scarcely inflict one scratch'.

In the rearing of middle-class children, nannies occupied a kind of half-life suspended between the parents and the servants of the household. Children ate meals with nanny in the nursery, played with her there, walked and played with her in the garden, and very often slept in the same room as her. Access to one's mother in the early formative years was frequently restricted to set-piece occasions – late afternoons in the drawing room, on Sundays or for family events. Nanny, then, was in a potentially very powerful position *vis-à-vis* 'boy'. Some nannies were held in very deep affection by their young male charges, particularly if parents proved to be neglectful of their progeny. Sir Winston Churchill, for example, was especially close to his nanny (Gathorne-Hardy, 1985, p. 30):

> He never forgot Mrs. Everest. Even in extreme old age, in lucid moments, he would suddenly refer to his love for her; and for many years after she died he paid an annual sum to the local florist for the upkeep of her grave.

The uniqueness of nanny's succouring position and potential for influence invites speculation about her effects on successive generations of English boys who became leaders in public life. (Recent vocal supporters of public-sector entrepreneurialism, armed with such epithets as 'nanny state', of course, deem nannydom's effects to have been baleful.) The most that can be said with assurance is that in many big households nanny (invariably a working-class woman) was formally the surrogate parental figure and psycho-logical rock, so to speak (although not always beneficent), and that her kingdom was the nursery (Gathorne-Hardy, 1985, p. 77). It was this security of nursery and nanny from which little boys at about age eight were ejected when they were sent away to prep school, the next step on their journey to becoming gentlemen. At this point, then, the mechanism at the heart of maximum ascriptive selection – 'random infants could be removed from their natural families for complete socialization by societal agencies' (Armstrong, 1973, p. 20) – really began in earnest.

In the nineteenth century, English preparatory schools prepared boys up until about 13 years of age before they went on to a public school (Leinster-Mackay, 1984, p. 2). Prep schools, as they were known, were an essential component in the English educational infrastructure because as feeder institutions gravitating like satellites around the bigger prestigious boarding schools their job was to produce candidates for scholarships. Prep schools were established as mostly private ventures by entrepreneurial clergymen or former public school masters. Their numbers mushroomed in the last quarter of the century as the rising middle classes sought the desired social spit-and-polish or cachet conferred by public schooling. For reasons of more congenial climate, most of these institutions were located in the south-east corner of England in spa towns and seaside resorts. Living conditions in prep schools were invariably spartan and occasionally even ghastly. Temple Grove, for example, one of the so-called 'Famous Five' – an elite group of five prep schools 'to which dukes would be pleased to send their sons' (Leinster-Mackay, 1984, p. 40) – was primitive:

> In the dormitories snow piled frequently upon the blankets and ice formed on the water jugs: the lavatories … would have been condemned in a slum tenement.

The experience of prep school could be awful and many boys were emotionally scarred by it for life. The very young and orphaned future Lord Somers (later Governor of Victoria), for example, was utterly miserable for much of his time at Mulgrave Castle, Whitby, Yorkshire, as he described in a letter to his sister Verena (cited in Gregory, 1987, p. 14):

> I have got into an awful row because I ran away again. I nearly got expelled. I have been birched by His Lordship [the proprietor, the 3rd Marquis of Normanby and a Canon of Windsor] but not publicly. I want His Lordship to forgive me but I don't know how to do it. The boys are all horrid what shall I do?
>
> I do feel so unhappy because I wish I had not tried to run a way a second time it is awful. The confirmation is being held today. I do wish I could come away but I can't. Oh it is horrid.

Small wonder, then, that Gathorne-Hardy (1979, p. 198) describes a lad's prep school years as 'that terrible piercing loneliness of small children cast out from their homes. It is without question the most important single aspect of public school education.'

The public schools themselves represented a form of institutionalized paternalism. Unlike Barnard, who saw organizational authority as being sanctioned from below, Norwood (1929, p. 75) took the opposite view about the public schools: 'authority comes from above, but all share in delegated powers for the purpose of living a common life'. Moreover, in a pithy disavowal of 'the pseudo-freedom of many-headed uneducated democracy' Norwood (1929, p. 79) justified public schooling as a system of training 'in which the boy is taught to choose what he ought to choose, and that is the real freedom' – a sentiment which even the most hard-headed totalitarian would find difficult to match. Paternalism was particularly evident in the boarding houses to which the boys were assigned upon their enrolment. Here, where authority and control lay with the house prefects, they were expected to eat, live, study, sleep and make friends for the next five years or so. Fagging was an essential (but unwritten or informal) component of their boarding house socialization and had long passed into public school folklore. It was a feudal custom in which junior boys were meant to run errands and perform chores for senior study-holders, in return for which loyalty they were afforded the protection of the older boys. Sometimes this relationship worked to the mutual interests of both parties; at other times it was abused (often sexually) – usually to the detriment of the younger boys. The fascination of commentators with boarding house life has brought forth a torrent of words – novels, essays, memoirs and stories – both positive and negative. Harold Nicolson (1984, p. 99), the diplomat, recalled how at Wellington the rule which restricted his friends to those in his house meant that his immediate circle of acquaintances was effectively reduced to about 10 lads – a policy calculated, he believed, to foster the very sexual 'vice' (as it was known in public school argot) that it was intended to contain. Nicolson was made to feel an emotional cripple as a result. Apart from some rather frustrating experiences as a newcomer in his house at Repton, Darling, on the other hand, recalled his time there as basically a happy one (Gronn, 1986b, p. 35).

Classes in the public schools were organized into sequentially ordered forms (4th, 5th, 6th, etc.), subdivided into upper and lower divisions, and with the curriculum subjects grouped according to sides (classics, modern and army). The quality of the teaching varied immensely, both within and between schools. Some masters were genuinely fearsome and intimidating. If, however, a boy was lucky enough, and was able to endure the occasional pedagogical mediocrity until he reached the Upper 6th, he might then encounter some genuinely inspiring and truly intellectually towering masters. At Repton, after some experiences in the 5th form with a much-loathed master nicknamed 'the Cossack', Darling, for example, was taught in the 6th by two spell-binding and brilliant men, D.C. Somervell and Victor Gollancz (see Gronn, 1990). Some of the particularly important formative agencies which brought these influential masters and senior boys together were school societies and clubs. Debating societies, for example, provided a priceless preparation in the art of public speaking on questions of the day and proved a useful apprenticeship for later public office.

For all of the high-blown rhetoric of their apologists like Norwood about character, nobility, honour and the importance of team-spirit, however, many of these muscular Christian public schools fostered a kind of gung-ho, macho culture of philistinism, athleticism and bullying. This was graphically captured in novels like Thomas Hughes's *Tom Brown's Schooldays* – in the image of the dreaded Flashman and his acolytes torturing young Tom before an open fire – and H.A. Vachell's *The Hill.* One particularly intimidating individual for younger and more tender boys was the 'blood'. Vachell referred to these sporting heroes as 'tremendous swells, grown men with a titillating flavour of the world about their persons', and Alec Waugh in *The Loom of Youth* (the first school novel to be genuinely critical of the public schools and the publication of which in 1917 provoked an outcry) provided this vignette:

> He strolls in as if he had taken a mortgage on the place, swaggers into the inner room, puts down his books on the top of the table in the right-hand corner – only the bloods sit there – and demands a cup of tea and a macaroon.

So pervasive was the stranglehold of these schoolboy idols on Charterhouse just prior to the Great War, for example, that Frank Fletcher, the newly arrived headmaster from Marlborough, was forced to connive with sympathetic senior boys to quell their dominance (Gathorne-Hardy, 1979, pp. 338–9).

It was the hegemony of the classics which was the hallmark of the English public schools. This situation reflected the perpetuation of an aristocratic style in the moulding of human character and was made possible by the dominance of the education system by the universities of Oxford and Cambridge. Critical determinants of the influence exercised by these two ancient institutions were their control of the secondary school examination system and the awarding of much-sought-after scholarships and fellowships, particularly to classicists. Another factor in fostering the Oxbridge–schools link was the high proportion of Oxbridge classics graduates amongst the headmasters – 92 out of 114 of them as late as 1914, according to one source (Parker, 1987, p. 86). The classics were believed to discipline the mind and to develop a general reasoning facility capable of being applied in any sphere, a pedagogical justification which persisted right up until World War II. 'It is possible to be very learned without being educated', claimed Norwood (1929, p. 93), 'but true knowledge, even though limited, if rightly applied, fits men for life.' Or, as Burgess, one of Waugh's characters in *The Loom*, said at the Fernhurst School Debating Society, in response to the charge that Greek was useless in business, 'the Public School man should be too much of a gentleman to succeed in business ... he should follow the ideals set before him by the classics. Nearly all the poets and politicians of to-day are Public School men.' There were also various moral and aesthetic arguments advanced for the study of classics, most of which turned on the assumption of Roman and Athenian cultural superiority. Yet the study of these early societies was not always straightforward and uncomplicated because the eroticism and military glory in the writings of many of the Ancients proved difficult to square with a Christian cosmology. Considerable lengths were gone to, therefore, in order to neutralize this classical mythology by the liberal application of dollops of Christianity – 'rather like spraying roses for greenfly' (Parker, 1987, p. 90).

The influence of mentors was probably felt for the first time in the 6th form, or slightly later at university. In addition to mentoring, in other epochs and in other societies and cultures, the media shaping the consciousness of the young would have included elements as diverse as town meetings, public trials and proclamations, and Sunday-school attendance. In the present day, of course, they encompass the entire gamut from comics, magazines and newspapers to television and computer games. The electrifying experiment in political education unleashed by Gollancz and Somervell at Repton in 1916–17, for example, left its mark, not just on the 6th and Darling, but on the entire school and at some personal cost to both men. In the eyes of conservative educational die-hards at Repton, the Civics Class and the ill-fated magazine – *A Public School Looks at the World* – founded due to the influence of the two masters, were viewed as subversive, even treacherous, and (in today's terms) as politicizing the boys. Yet the experience generated a strong sense of idealism and an extraordinarily close bonding amongst Darling's peers, heightened by the knowledge that army service and the very real possibility of death awaited them not far away in France. Gollancz, as Darling (1978, pp. 29–35) later attested, was a mentor for him, and his experiences at Repton helped subsequently to temper his own response as a wartime headmaster in 1940 at Geelong Grammar School to the charismatic influence of a young, vibrant and equally inspirational teacher of history, Manning Clark, later a famous Australian historian. Another important mentor during Darling's early career as a schoolmaster in the 1920s was his former Repton headmaster, William Temple (then the Anglican Bishop of Manchester and later Archbishop of Canterbury). While he was teaching in Crosby, Liverpool, Darling would come and stay with Temple and his wife at weekends. The two men would talk about all manner of things, including religion, and they both corresponded fairly regularly. Darling's letters to Temple, particularly when he taught at Charterhouse (1924–9), disclosed the kinds of doubts typically experienced by an idealistic young man teaching toffs at an English public school (Gronn, 1986b, p. 39).

It is probably worth diverging at this point in the articulation of this English historical example to observe that mentoring is one aspect of leader formation which, in a number of organizational sectors and spheres throughout the 1980s and 1990s, has been taken so seriously in the professional development of organizational personnel that it has become mandatory in a number of workplaces. Even though as a young protégé of Temple Darling gave voice to some of his immediate concerns about schoolmastering their discussions were mostly life-related. Clearly there would seem to be a place for both intrinsic and instrumental purposes in mentoring, but the problem with the contemporary urge to mandate mentoring in the workplace is that it often backfires or is undertaken in a half-baked manner. Geoffrey Serle (1982, pp. 480–1), the biographer of Sir John Monash, the famous Australian corps commander in World War I, cites some remarks made by his subject in 1923 which he directed specifically to the education and advancement of young men, but which encapsulate very succinctly the contemporary pragmatic impulse to institutionalize mentoring:

> When you come into contact with successful men [*sic*], study them and their methods; try to discover the factors which have led to their success, and model your own methods upon them.

Part of the recent surge of interest in role-modelling and mentoring in organizations is motivated by a genuine desire to facilitate the career advancement of young professionals and, in the case of women, for example, to remove barriers to progression such as glass ceilings (see Ragins, 1989, 1995). Some early critics (Shapiro *et al.*, 1978, p. 56), however, predicted that the idea of assigning mentors to women 'would probably be an exercise in futility'.

Misgivings with mentoring stem partly from the belief that to try and legislate, as it were, for regular pairings between senior and junior organizational members ignores a considerable body of evidence which suggests that fruitful mentoring relationships occur naturally and spontaneously. In this respect sometimes even parents can be mentors for their offspring – thus,

John Maynard Keynes' principal mentor was his father (Skidelsky, 1978, pp. 73–5) and, in the case of Virginia Woolf, her father, Leslie Stephen, was said to have 'trained her to become his intellectual heir' (Bond, 1986, p. 515). Another reservation is that, when it does become part of the everyday scheme of things, mentoring tends to become caught up in the politics of organizational patronage. Thus, mentors suddenly turn into sponsors, and the material and emotional costs of personality (not to mention gender) mismatches magnify. These possibilities, along with ideological objections to mentoring – that it is an essentially surrogate parental, paternal, elitist and hierarchical relationship, etc. – have fuelled the search for alternative support mechanisms for youthful (especially female) organization members. Shapiro *et al.* (1978, p. 56), for example, recommended the avoidance of mentoring altogether and instead argued for groupings which 'tend to be more egalitarian and peer related, less intense and exclusionary, and therefore potentially more democratic by allowing access to a larger number of young professionals'. More recently Ragins (1989, p. 7) has taken a different line and has observed that, even though women often have very real difficulties in obtaining mentors, they would be ill-advised to turn to peer relations as a substitute, despite the support these are known to give. The reason is that 'peers typically have less power and influence than mentors and may be less able to promote advancement in organizations'. Thus, by relying on peers alone, 'women may be substituting social support for power and advancement'.

Clearly, then, mentoring in the workplace can be tricky. The picture is equally mixed when the dynamics and intricacies of the mentor–protégé dyad are considered. Kathy Kram's (1985) research shows that mentoring relationships typically comprise four developmental stages – initiation, cultivation, separation and redefinition – but without any rigid or fixed time frame being observed. The depth of emotions experienced during mentoring often includes intense feelings of identification and transference by protégés, and sometimes even unconscious oedipal and narcissistic urges (Baum, 1992). Given the possibility of these kinds of psychological recesses being penetrated, the depth of intimacy undergone when a relationship blossoms may well be experienced as stifling and intimidating, particularly when the mentor in whose hands one's developmental welfare lies also happens to be one's superior. Such a possibility amounts to double jeopardy: dependence on a boss as a kind of *de facto* mother or father confessor, and dependence on that same superior for promotion and career development. On the other hand, the coat-tail effect, as it is sometimes known, can work to a protégé's advantage because, by virtue of their association with powerful organizational personnel, protégés may well become members of the dominant group or coalition. One result of this is that (Whitely and Coetsier, 1993, p. 436):

> As the coalition rises within the organization, the protégé receives additional developmental help from other mentors in his or her coalition. Hence career

progress and career mentoring may be reciprocally related in a spiralling 'success syndrome'.

As will be seen shortly when I consider the recommendations of the recent Karpin Report (Industry Task Force on Leadership and Management Skills, 1995) in Australia, mentoring is now receiving official endorsement as part of continuous learning in the workplace. Yet this brief summary is sufficient to indicate that, despite the best of intentions, there are still a number of problems to be resolved with mentoring in organizations.

Returning to our main theme, there is a similar kind of division of opinion over the advantages and disadvantages of a public school education. Broadly speaking, most historians who have criticized the schools have, until recently, confined themselves to highlighting particular shortcomings in the overall machinery which were thought to have yielded negative cultural outcomes. Examples here would include claims that an entire system of upbringing – but particularly the public school component and the ethos of public schooling – encouraged the kind of mindless cult of athleticism we touched on earlier, that it fostered imperialism, and that it bred a militaristic outlook (Parker, 1987, pp. 281–4) and military incompetence among generations of the English high command (Dixon, 1983, p. 395). It has also been alleged that a public school education produced a rather orthodox, conventional way of thinking (Gathorne-Hardy, 1979, p. 416) or, as Wilkinson (1964, p. 80) expressed it, 'mental flexibility rather than imaginative foresight'. The cohorts of public school products who eventually came to head important elite sectors in twentieth-century Britain mostly put a premium on loyalty, were extraordinarily conscientious and hard-working, and had good memories but were invariably hostile to abstract reasoning and theorizing. These kinds of qualities are deemed to have bred complacency and an arrogant superiority – typified, perhaps, by the comment with which the pipe-smoking, headmasterly prime minister, Stanley Baldwin, is supposed to have dismissed a delegation of union leaders during the General Strike in 1926: 'Now run along' (Gathorne-Hardy, 1979, p. 221).

At some point, however, complacency becomes a shackle, and shackles breed national decline. Since the early 1980s the attack on public school education has sharpened significantly. The dispute between historians has now become recast as the relationship between English cultural values and long-term national economic performance. In particular the argument is about the extent to which the persistence of alleged temperamental deficiencies among entire generations of English elites and leaders – and the claim that these have been especially detrimental to recent international competitiveness – can be sheeted home to the agencies I have just been describing. It was the publication of Corelli Barnett's (1972) *The Collapse of British Power* which inaugurated this dramatic turn of events. Barnett pointed out that Cyril Norwood (who was himself educated in a grammar school) had devoted only 10 pages of his book, *The English Tradition of Education*, to Britain's technological backwardness and lack of managerial talent, and yet had included three chapters on religion. Barnett took this order of priorities to be symptomatic of how ill-adapted the public school outlook was to modernity. Norwood, of course, became the chairman of a key government advisory committee whose report in 1943 laid the foundation for the post-war tripartite system of secondary schooling which persisted in Britain until comprehensivization got under way in the 1970s. According to Annan (1988, p. 66) the Norwood Committee's report 'opposed the teaching of any course that might be considered vocational'. The most telling, indeed heinous, omission in the curriculum of the public schools legitimated by this anti-vocationalism was, Martin Wiener (1982, p. 18) claimed in his highly contentious book, *English Culture and the Decline of the Industrial Spirit*, the neglect of science until well into the twentieth century. With a few exceptions (Repton was one) science was rarely taught in the public schools. It was seen mostly as anti-religious, godless and vulgar. The price paid for this attitude was large: a significant lag for a long time in British scientific and techno-logical progress and, as a consequence, in material prosperity.

The most important criticism by Wiener and Barnett was that the balance sheet of more than 150 years of recent English history amounted to national betrayal by the education system. Thanks to the cultural treachery of the public schools, a robust and lively entrepreneurialism – exactly the kinds of values of know-how and foresight which had made Britain the 'first new nation' and 'the workshop of the world' – had receded into the shadows behind a rather dull and dreary, father-knows-best, paternalistic guardian-ship. Cautiousness, instead of risk-taking and innovation, Barnett (1972, p. 37) noted, was a prescription for national stagnation. Not only were these characteristics the wrong ones at the wrong time, critics claim, but the funnelling of the careers of intelligent boys, with or without such outlooks, away from industrial pursuits and into such spheres as public administration, largely denied the commercial and industrial sectors access to the pool of national talent. It was this Wiener–Barnett thesis – i.e. culture-caused-economic-decline – as it has become known, which, during the Thatcher years, was 'seized with glee by the yuppie generation of Conservatives as an excuse no longer to listen to the dons' demands for money raised from taxes' (Annan, 1988, p. 68). More recently it has been the trigger for a wholesale reappraisal of entrepreneurialism and its role in long-term national eco-nomic performance.

The leading opponent of Wiener and Barnett is an Australian economic historian, W.D. Rubinstein, who, in a succession of scholarly papers, and latterly in his book, *Capitalism, Culture, and Decline in Britain, 1750–1990* (Rubinstein, 1994), has sought to rebut every major argument in the arsenal of the British disease-and-decline school. To list them all would mean straying well beyond the confines of the present discussion but, in brief, Rubinstein rejects the conception of the wealth of the British economy as emanating primarily from industry and manufacturing as fundamentally misconceived. Britain's economy 'was *always*, even at the height of the industrial revolution, essentially a commercial, financial, and service-based economy' and the alleged industrial decline 'was simply a working out of this process', coincidental with a continuing rise in the average standard of living (Rubinstein, 1994, p. 24, original emphasis). From there he works his way systematically through a number of key cultural components to show that these were anything but ill-conducive to any so-called industrial spirit. More particularly, Rubinstein undertook a detailed analysis of the occupational destinations of the sons of old boys in a sample of 1,800 entrants to eight public schools – Eton, Harrow, Rugby, Winchester, St. Pauls, Cheltenham, Dulwich and Mill Hill – between 1840 and 1900 which showed that while 'there *was* an intergenerational shift into the professions . . . it affected only a minority of businessmen's sons: the majority followed the family pathway' (Rubinstein, 1994, p. 120, original emphasis).

If for no other reason than the fact that this brief sketch of the contours of one important contemporary debate – the resolution of which turns in part on evidence about the quality and origins of national leadership – demonstrates the relevance and significance of leader formation, then it will have served its purpose. A considerable proportion of the differences between scholars just referred to hinges on events that transpired during the period *c*. 1870–1914 to transform Britain from being the sole world economic superpower to a position in which her rivals had caught up with and even overtaken her. By 1914, far and away the biggest economic power, on every indicator of productivity, was the USA. And it was in that nation, indeed during this same period in dispute by historians, that the earliest initiatives were undertaken in higher education to utilize explicitly defined bodies of management knowledge to make and form managers and leaders. Business education boomed in the USA, so much so that after World War II the approaches adopted by leading US business schools became the very models transplanted back into Britain (particularly in London and Manchester) and in Europe (especially in France) to transform the quality of European management. It is to some of the main features of this second historical trend in leader formation that I now turn.

Achievement: Formal provision through management education

For there to be organized bodies of knowledge for transmission to trainees or students of management and leadership, there has to be in existence already an acknowledged and defined set of operations to which, and a recognized category of people to whom, such material refers. Those functions and that particular group only emerged in public administration, and in the commercial and industrial spheres, towards the end of the nineteenth century in England and the USA. When family capitalism began to break up in the USA during this period (although it lingered on in Europe) the modern corporation was born: property was separated increasingly from the ownership of the family, and control passed to a new class of professional,

salaried managers (Chandler, 1984, p. 496). This transition to the hierarchical, bureaucratized firm – for which the US railway companies during the
westward expansion across the prairies served as the prototype – is often
known as the managerial revolution (Burnham, 1962); and one of the ways
in which this rising class of organizational functionaries sought to legitimize
its new-found status was to frame ideologies and theories of management.

Because different managerial traditions took root in the major industrial
nations different emphases in preparation through management education
emerged. Chronologically, the needs of the productive process were initially
paramount and later on those of product distribution. In the USA it was the
shop-floor engineer who was influential at first and afterwards the cost
accountant, in France it was the highly mathematically skilled engineer, then
in Germany the academic business economist, and in England – which
industrialized before the revolution in transport and communication rather
than after it, as in the USA – it was the self-taught technician. Of the massive
industrial changes under way in England between 1750 and 1830, Pollard
(1965, p. 251) has noted 'the strange absence of management theory'. Apart
from isolated instances among firms there was apparently neither consciousness of its utility nor any expressed need for it. Only much later did
businessmen begin to forge links between industry, science and higher
education, as well as economics and commercial education, in what were
known as the civic universities, such as Birmingham and Manchester. Unlike
their peers then reading classics at Oxbridge, many of the students at these
civic universities came from industrial backgrounds and later went into
industry themselves (Sanderson, 1988, pp. 97–8).

In the USA, where management professionalized itself very quickly, one of
the key influences was the modern business school. The Wharton School
of Commerce and Finance for undergraduates began at the University of
Pennsylvania as early as 1881, for example, on the initiative of a Philadelphia
Quaker industrialist, Joseph Wharton. It was quickly followed by the establishment of business schools at both the University of Chicago and the
University of California in 1899, and at the University of New York in 1900. In
that same year the Amos Tuck School of Administration and Finance was
founded at Dartmouth and the famous Harvard Business School opened in
1909. All the trappings of professionalism – societies, journals, university
courses and consultants – were flourishing by the 1920s, according to the
eminent business historian, A.D. Chandler (1977, p. 468). Those US businessmen born during 1870–1920 were increasingly better educated than
their pioneering, heroic robber-baron forebears had been, and more and
more of them attended college. As graded and salaried career structures
emerged with the bureaucratization of industry, increasing numbers of
managers began to seek credentials to facilitate their mobility: higher
education fast became a means to career advancement. Moreover, the
ideologies and creeds by which US managers were legitimizing themselves
socially began to shift gradually away from Victorian virtues such as self-help

towards doctrines intended to bolster the supremacy of management and managerial control over workers, particularly when under challenge by trade unions (Bendix, 1956, pp. 254–74).

In Europe the picture was different. Nowhere was management taught as a subject before the Great War (Locke, 1985, p. 236). In France higher education was offered by two major sectors: the universities which provided education for the professions and the *grandes écoles* which specifically prepared leaders for commerce, industry and state service. Most of the *grandes écoles* were engineering schools with stringent entry requirements and produced higher mathematical generalists. Many of them had been founded during the French Revolution or later by the Emperor Napoleon and, until well into the twentieth century, were generally thought to be quite useless for management preparation (Locke, 1984, pp. 104–5). A network of commercial schools providing lower-level technical skills had been in existence since the 1880s, but it was not until the 1950s that recognition of the need for a professionalized managerial cadre generated sufficient pressure for management education to be offered in institutions of higher learning. Symptomatic of the eventual acceptance by the French business sector of the significance of US business attitudes and techniques was the founding in 1958 of what has since become probably the most prestigious of French business schools, INSEAD (l'Institut Européen d'Administration des Affaires). In its curriculum structure and teaching methods INSEAD was directly modelled on the Harvard Business School (Whitley *et al.*, 1981, pp. 59–80). At about the same time, across the Channel, the idea that, like British gentlemen, British managers 'were born not made', and that management was 'an art learnt by long years of practical experience in the workplace, rather than in the groves of academe' (Whitley *et al.*, 1981, p. 31), was slowly eroding. The Administrative Staff College had been founded at Henley in 1948 and then, finally, in 1965, after an inquiry commissioned by the National Economic Development Council and chaired by Lord Franks two years before, new university business schools – 'the two "British Harvards"' – were opened in London and Manchester (Whitley *et al.*, 1981, p. 48).

Australian developments mirrored those in Europe for, unlike the USA, formal training for managers emerged slowly. As in the USA there had been something of a heroic age of *laissez-faire* capitalism in colonial Australia, but with only a few pockets of genuine entrepreneurialism and fortunes to be made (and then mainly in pastoralism, woollen exports and retailing) but on nowhere near the scale of the robber barons – in fact there were only 30 Australian millionaires in the 150 years of European settlement to 1939 whereas in the USA there were 7,500 in 1914 alone (Rubinstein, 1983). Furthermore, apart from a handful of founder owner-managers, such Australian career managers as existed were for a long time to be found mainly at the higher levels of the major public instrumentalities – e.g. Peter Board and Frank Tate as state directors of education, and Sir John Monash at the State Electricity Commission and William Calder at the Country Roads Board, both in Victoria – and they largely learnt their craft on the job in a robust 'practical man' or 'school of hard knocks' tradition. Signs that the era of meritocratic management, especially in the business sector, had reached the take-off point, as it is often known, were evident between the two world wars. Frederick Winslow Taylor's theories of scientific management and efficiency were circulating before 1920, for example, and employer groups and peak associations were invoking these in their lobbying of governments. A number of these interest groups, including the Victorian Employers' Federation and the Victorian Chamber of Manufacturers, had been instrumental in having a Faculty of Commerce established at the University of Melbourne in 1924. The first Professor was Douglas Berry Copland, a 30-year-old New Zealander – then Dean of Commerce at the University of Tasmania. By the 1930s, a new career managerial type – personified, perhaps, by Staniforth Rickctson, a prominent Melbourne stockbroker – was becoming discernible (Spierings, 1990).

Later developments in the formalizing of management education in Australia included the establishment in Melbourne in 1941 of the Institute of Industrial Management, following the introduction of a popular course on foremanship at the Melbourne Technical College in 1938. The Institute – the forerunner of the national body, the Australian Institute of Management (1949) – functioned as a clearing-house for discussion and provided short courses on various aspects of management. A handful of major companies had already begun to undertake their own internal staff-training programmes, but in the 1950s there were moves in Sydney and Melbourne 'to provide something more prestigious than the technical college programmes and the evening courses at the Institutes of Management and other professional bodies' (Byrt, 1989, p. 82). The University of Melbourne began six-week residential summer schools in business administration in 1956 and in the same year Professor Copland was appointed as foundation Principal of the new Australian Administrative Staff College at Mt Eliza, near Melbourne – a provider of advanced management courses and modelled on the original staff college at Henley. Only in the early 1960s were Master of Business Administration degrees – the structure and delivery of which, as in Europe, were influenced by existing US models – provided by a handful of Australian universities (Byrt, 1989, pp. 87–92).

A parallel process of the professionalization for educational administrators and managers got under way throughout the world as well. It borrowed heavily on theories and approaches dominant in business and general management, and followed a similar pattern of knowledge diffusion to that of management education – i.e. from the USA, where it was known as 'the Theory Movement', to Britain and the Commonwealth countries, and beyond. (Ironically, of course, this spreading influence gathered momentum at about the same time – the mid-1970s – that Greenfield began launching his intellectual salvos against it.) The first university programme in Australia, the Diploma of Educational Administration, had commenced at the University of New England as early as 1959 (Cunningham and Radford, 1963, p. 20) but, in the absence of many prestigious postgraduate research degrees in Australia until the late 1970s, waves of senior systems administrators and research students had flocked to North American campuses (particularly the University of Alberta, Canada) to undertake advanced study. In 1977 the Government of Victoria established its own statutory provider of short-course, residential in-house programmes for schools and systems personnel, the Institute of Educational Administration, which was partly modelled on the Australian Administrative Staff College (Andrews and Moyle, 1986).[2] As was the case in the bulk of the English-speaking world, postgraduate courses in educational administration had finally taken off in Australia by the early 1980s following the massive expansion of the higher education sector in the previous decade or so.

This long process of the professionalization of management which I have just outlined, however, can now be seen as nearing its end. Changed economic imperatives leading towards an integrated and globalized world economy have prompted a redefinition of the role and workplace needs of managers, and of the leadership expected of them. An important consequence is that management development is currently undergoing a fundamental rethink, particularly in business management but increasingly in education and the school sectors as well. In broad terms, the emerging view of the most appropriate way in which to develop managers emphasizes the outputs of management rather than inputs to it, the interests of the users rather than the producers of knowledge, learning rather than teaching, and modularized and flexibly delivered content and skills rather than esoteric, discipline-based knowledge. A good illustration of this third trend is to be found in the blueprint outlined in the recent Karpin Report – *Enterprising Nation* (Industry Task Force on Leadership and Management Skills, 1995) – currently being implemented in Australia.

Customization: Training in and for the workplace

The three-year-long and 12-member Industry Task Force on Leadership and Management Skills, under the chairmanship of David Karpin (CEO of the resources conglomerate CRA Ltd), was commissioned by the Commonwealth Government to investigate ways of improving Australian managers' performance to secure enhanced industry productivity, consistent with the government's commitment to micro-economic reform. The overall thrust of *Enterprising Nation* is to discredit as outmoded the kind of extended campus-based programmes whose evolution I have just reviewed, and which were designed to facilitate personal professional development and to better equip students to accelerate through predefined and predetermined career roles. Management is claimed to be moving away from 'a structural model of organizations' and there has been too much emphasis on 'the more analytical areas of business' in existing programmes (pp. x, xvii). Instead, a new focus is needed on strategic management skills for medium-size business units – i.e. entrepreneurialism, a global orientation, soft skills, strategic skills and management development, and teamwork skills. The reason given for this new emphasis is that 'Australia is sliding down the league table of economic performance' (p. xii). In order to enhance international competitive advantage, therefore, enterprise and entrepreneurship subjects should be taught in the education sector in order to 'promote the need for individuals to proactively take charge of their own future, including their own economic future' (p. xxii). Even secondary schools (government and non-government) are seen as having a role to play in fostering entrepreneurialism – a complete about-face from the days when the production of gentlemanly dispositions was almost their entire *raison d'être*: 'the Task Force has come to recognize the role of school education in laying the foundation for managerial careers', in particular 'in fostering the values of an enterprise culture but also in teaching self-management and interpersonal skills' (p. 153).

The findings and recommendations of *Enterprising Nation* are focused on improvements at the enterprise level. The Report promotes the idea of a desired manager profile for the year 2010 – the 'Leader/Enabler' – and recommends that 'the seeds of change, and the imperatives of the new paradigm [of management], have to be *inculcated* in the generation of managers who are undertaking postgraduate education and/or holding junior management positions' (p. xi, emphasis added). Such is the flavour of the new thinking: continuous learning, role adaptability, mobility, flexible styles and workplace diversity in ostensibly downsized and flattened organizational structures (p. xxxviii). Of an estimated 900,000 managers in Australia in 1994, the overwhelming majority work for enterprises employing fewer than 50 people; very few of them have been formally trained in management and few undergo additional management development. In this respect the Report notes 'a lack of depth' in the ranks of managers (p. 67) and an anti-intellectualism in Australia which has hindered advanced education and training (p. 71), but it asserts that 'excellence in management development is a major factor in international competitiveness' (p. 77). The Report commits itself to the idea of continuous improvement for all managers – including mentoring as part of effective workplace management development (p. 119) – in contrast to previous course- and programme-based training and development which was 'provider led training and not learner driven, learner centred and enterprise owned' (p. 147).

The Karpin Report's priority for continuous improvement is the frontline manager or supervisor, of whom there are an estimated 400,000 in Australia. Of these about 180,000 have not received any formal training. The Report proposes the establishment of a new national workplace-based leadership programme – the National Certificate in Workplace Learning – to ensure that these frontline managers meet nationally determined minimum competencies (p. 282). In response to this recommendation, the Commonwealth

Government established a National Reference Group, under the auspices of the Australian National Training Authority (ANTA),[3] to implement the new FMI. A new set of national, generic, cross-industry Frontline Management Competency Standards was endorsed in June 1996. These comprize 11 units (five core and six elective) – the completion of four core plus two electives leading to the attainment of Certificate 3, five core plus three electives to Certificate 4 and all 11 units to the acquisition of a diploma. Leadership in the workplace is specifically identified as the focus of the second core subject, but leadership tasks are sprinkled throughout every unit. Having identified a willingness to develop their managerial competencies, and to have these formally acknowledged, frontline managers are first assessed against the competencies to establish their current levels of attainment. Gaps in attainment are identified and an individual learning plan is developed and worked through until all the required competencies are achieved. This tailoring of learning to the needs of the individual learner represents the essence of the principle of customization: competency acquisition takes place within the workplace, with other managers providing coaching, mentoring and support, and in accordance with the principles of self-paced, work-based learning in accordance with preferred individual learning styles (Australian Competency Research Centre, 1997).

This brief consideration of customization completes the opening section of this book devoted to a framework for understanding leadership. The three models outlined in this chapter have represented historically contrasting approaches to institutionalizing the preparation and development of leaders. Institutionalization in respect of leadership means the making of at least minimal provision by formal agencies and authorities to ensure that the production of cohorts of leaders, in organizations and across entire social systems, is not merely a random process or something left to chance. It should be clear from the above discussion that each approach documented was predicated on different sets of implicit assumptions about leadership, about the width or narrowness of the boundaries drawn around the pool of potential leadership recruits and about the extent to which leadership is something that is taught or caught through learning. The trend documented is a movement from a position in which, beginning with the gentleman, leadership was seen as something in-built and instinctual, and the monopoly of high-status males, through one in which leadership was potentially available to all – regardless of gender, status or other background factors – following the attainment of specialist, credentialled knowledge, to one in which no assumptions at all are made about background factors, in which leadership is available to any employee and in which leadership is given a specific vocational focus as part of a macro-level view of enhanced international competitiveness. In each of the three approaches various educational agencies were shown to be central to processes of socialization, and teaching and learning about leadership in one form or another. Ascription, however, was the only one of the three in which there was any recognition of the role played by other formative bodies and groups, and to that extent was significant for highlighting the personal endowments which individuals desirous of exercising leadership brought with them to the role.

I turn now to examine in detail the three particular attributes – identity, values and style – which, I suggest, constitute the personal foundations, or givens, which any potentially customized programme (if it is to succeed) would have to take account, and which – from the perspective of self-understanding should any prospective candidate for leadership undertake a detailed personal self-assessment – will be crucial subsequently in winning acceptance from followers and thereby help to assure the successful exercise of leadership.

Notes

1 As a matter of record, Armstrong (1973, pp. 20–1) also identified a third elite selection model – which aligns with recruitment in the former USSR – but which is not considered here: progressive equal attrition, in which 'at each of several equal time intervals the same proportion of the male cohort is eliminated from eligibility for top administrative posts, until just the requisite number to fill available posts remains when the appropriate age level is attained'.

2 The Institute was abolished by the Government in 1993.

3 ANTA was established following an agreement in 1992 between state and federal governments to rationalize funding to the Technical and Further Education (TAFE) sector – the alternative route to the university sector for students desiring post-secondary education – and has become the policy-making body for national education and training. A further ministerial agreement in late 1996 established the National Training Framework under ANTA auspices. The TAFE sector is playing a major role in the delivery of workplace training and the FMI.

The identities of leaders

In this and the next two chapters the spotlight falls squarely on the prospective leader. At the beginning of Chapters 4, 5 and 6 there is an invitation to aspirants to anticipate the kinds of questions which potential followers might have in their minds about those who would seek to lead them. This stance is in accord with the follower-centric perspective outlined earlier and acknowledges the fact that an aspirant's legitimacy and destiny rest in the hands of those whom she or he would seek to lead. The kinds of questions I have in mind would normally comprise part of the internal conversations most people in organizations hold with themselves, and which are revealed in their gazes of anticipation during their initial and early interpersonal contacts with the new leader or leaders as they begin to mull them over or size them up. Part of followers' watchfulness – as leaders begin to make themselves known – stems from a natural sense of curiosity, but prospective followers, for all sorts of good reasons, may also be experiencing a genuinely mixed bag of emotions. At the same time that new or heir-apparent leaders are endeavouring to anticipate precisely what followers might be thinking they, for their part, are trying hard to be doubly careful about the kinds of signals they are transmitting to those watching them. As we shall see in a moment, new leaders are especially eager to create the right kinds of impressions or to be seen in a desired light. And for good reason: they have invested much psychologically (and materially) in taking up their new appointments or in assuming their new roles, and they fully intend being successful.

These remarks are not intended as a glib set of moves in some elaborate chessboard exercise in gamesmanship. Nor are they an introspective and indulgent angle to be taking on leadership. Far from it. What these suggestions do is to prefigure the kind of perceptual zigging and zagging which goes on constantly throughout an ongoing relationship between leaders and followers, but which is always experienced particularly acutely at the outset of their first encounter. Each, for different kinds of reasons, is in need of reassurance. I shall say more about the mechanics of these initial forays when

I analyse the process of induction in detail in Chapter 9. For the moment the particular questions about their new leaders' identities and sense of self which I suggest followers will probably have in mind are something like: Who *is* this person standing here before my eyes? And, exactly what kind of person is she or he? Going back a step or two in time, to the point at which an aspirant decides to make her or himself a candidate for leadership, similar kinds of questions may also be triggered off in their own minds as well. That is, the realization may well dawn on them that they are going to have to submit themselves to the scrutiny of others and that to do so means that they need to answer convincingly a few important prior questions about themselves. If they are to be candidates then they may well be inclined to ask: What kind of person am I? Why am I the way that I am and know myself to be, and what has made me this way? What are my redeeming features in the eyes of other people?

The point of departure for this discussion of self is Machiavelli's (1967 [1640], p. 101) advice to the young prince which was quoted in Chapter 1. Machiavelli made the important observation that 'men [*sic*] in general judge by their eyes rather than by their hands: because everyone is in a position to watch, few are in a position to come into close contact with you'. It was the fragility of that situation which led him to warn his sovereign about the significance of appearances and results in the framing of judgements about leadership. One implication of this piece of advice is that leaders are judged invariably by the effects of their actions or what, in the eyes of their followers, they are believed to accomplish, rather than solely by their intentions, however noble these may be. But the second and equally important thing is that, no matter what any leader does, or fails to do, frequently it is how she or he appears or seems to be from the point of view of those others – i.e. the impression created for them – which counts in the end.

This chapter does four things. First, it discusses the nature of self, identity and the individual's self-system; second, it shows how a leader's identity is both personally and socially constructed; third, it outlines how leaders devise their own desired public personas, which are expressed in various impression-management techniques and which form the basis of the leadership images attributed to them by followers; and, finally, it shows how and why leaders are susceptible to self-destructive tendencies. A leader's self-system lies at the core of her or his character structure, yet the present state of knowledge is such that it cannot be claimed with any degree of causal certainty why it is that particular facets of individual character take root. The vantage point of the present makes it possible to look back over a leader's life and to attribute any observed characteristics to particular formative agencies – such as linking what appear to be common traits between offspring and their parents to family genes – or to see elements of behaviour as attributable to media or educational influences, but that is about all. This chapter should be read with this caveat in mind, therefore, because while it seeks to elucidate the make-up of the self-system – in which the self-belief that I have suggested is required for leadership is grounded – it remains unclear how and why some individuals acquire that belief in themselves and others appear not to. The best commentators can do is to describe the variety of a leader's selves displayed before different audiences, to try to establish where these come from and who or what controls their definition.

The looking-glass self

These opening remarks are predicated on the assumption that followers – typically organizational peers or subordinates – would be likely to want to know whether the aspirant, or their new leader, is authentic or, expressing it in the vernacular, whether the new appointee is for real. If better self-understanding will assist a leader in projecting a sense of authenticity to others how, then, do prospective leaders go about getting a helpful handle on who they are? I begin by considering some straightforward social psychology about the self which is intended to help us better understand the idea of an identity and its origins. First of all, then, what are the mechanics of the process of normal social interaction by which each of us obtains a sense of who we are? How do we read other people and their actions, and the signals they transmit to us?

An important feature of social interaction is that others serve as mirrors into ourselves. It makes sense to think of the other person as a looking-glass self because we are able to see ourselves through their eyes. Thus, if we picture in our mind's eye two individuals, A and B, A communicates with B and sees something about her or himself mirrored back in B's response – words, perhaps, or a gaze, a look, an expression, or an aspect of demeanour – which is taken by A to be indicative of some aspect of selfhood. Exactly how does that mirroring process work? In any relationship expressed as A<>B, each party reads the other, as it were, and does at least the following things: first, each guesses at what the other's purposes or intentions are; second, each person sums up or intuits the other's attitude and feelings towards themselves, and third, each appraises the other's attitude and feelings towards them as an observer of their actions (Strauss, 1977, p. 59). In essence, then, the other person is a vehicle or means of perception into themselves (Mead, 1974 [1934], p. 138):

> The individual experiences himself [sic] as such, not directly, but only indirectly, from the particular standpoints of other individual members of the same social group, or from the generalized standpoint of the social group as a whole to which he belongs.

The kind of mirroring relationship I am proposing is explicit in the title of Strauss's (1977) book *Mirrors and Masks: The Search for Identity*.

Another aspect of the mirroring relationship is the wearing of masks. For all sorts of reasons – such as protection, insecurity, wariness, bitter experience and so on – the members of organizations learn to be cagey about what they signal to each other and so they often try to construct a desired sense of who they are. That is, while generally we might be conscious that others will be endeavouring better to understand or to read us, we, in turn, try to be very careful about the information we disclose to them on which they might base a possible interpretation (Strauss, 1977, p. 9). ' "A man [*sic*] without a mask" is indeed very rare', according to R.D. Laing (1966, p. 95). Most people, if they are honest with themselves, will admit that, in the privacy of their own minds, they normally take very careful account of what other people think of them, and that they look at themselves constantly in relation to others. 'Mirror, mirror, on the wall; who is the fairest one of all?', asks the wicked Queen in *Snow White*. Thus it is that by engaging in this kind of self-inspection we anticipate others' responses and endeavour to predict how they will see us, and do our best to try and control the perceptions which they have of us as well. The reason why people engage in what seems to be an elaborate display of existential sensitivity is a simple one. They want feedback. This is especially the case in leadership. Valerie Hall (1996, p. 93) remarks that her six women heads were acutely conscious of how other people were interpreting their behaviour: 'reflecting constantly on themselves and their performance in the job was their strategy for facing the demands of headship in the 1990s'. Followers also wear masks, of course, which may or may not reflect accurately what they think of a leader.

Summing this section up, then, two things, specifically, get mirrored back in our interpersonal relations. The first is the image we convey to other people. This is the perception of the sum total of all that we project to them, our desired personas. Image means not only the physical experience these others have of us – although the mental representations they construct are certainly reliant upon this – but also the signs and indications which our physical and bodily attributes convey about the kinds of people we are. Things like our apparel, our physique, our gait and our speech all denote or betray the peculiar attributes of class, gender, status, age, occupation and ethnicity. In a very real sense an individual's image is like a shadow or a tortoise's shell: it cannot be escaped from. The second component of the mirroring process is the evaluation or judgement which people make of our merit or worth. In this respect people's eyes can be very telling, and what gets reflected back may cause us acute self-consciousness or embarrassment. Mirrored reflections can be intimidating. Recall the instance I cited at the outset about the effect of the prying eyes of staff on newly selected leaders in a school, particularly if it is their first appointment. As every pair of eyes inspects them up and down it would be odd if they refused to succumb to some degree of self-consciousness, at least at first.

Self-consciousness is a feeling which is experienced particularly when one is young and far from wise in the ways of the world, or when one is sensitive to what others think and easily embarrassed before an audience. Self-consciousness is something to which leaders are prone but really cannot afford to be afflicted by, for to be a leader means to have, or to be able to develop, a thick skin or hide. Laing (1966, p. 106, original emphasis) defines self-consciousness not merely as nervousness but as 'an awareness of oneself by oneself, and *an awareness of oneself as an object of someone else's observation*'. Unless people are completely insensitive and emotionally impervious then they are liable to be acutely self-conscious, typically in new situations in which they do not know the rules and conventions normally observed, in which they do not know the subtleties of the language codes which others use, for example, and when they feel they are constantly on show and being inspected. Self-consciousness comes early in a career in the workplace, perhaps, when the ropes are being learnt. Heightened self-preoccupation or introspection often leads to feelings of anxiety, shame and guilt – emotions which are very difficult to cope with without losing self-control or flooding out, as Goffman terms it. The self-conscious individual's typical reaction is embarrassment simply because she or he has not got used to anticipating other people's responses to them.

Sense of self and identity

Supposing now that the aspirant leader is willing to engage in the kind of internal conversation which was foreshadowed at the outset and, indeed, sees the need to construct or reconstruct her or his sense of themselves, then there are a number of helpful sets of insights on which they may draw. The first concerns time. If individuals have a sense of who they are – their self – they generally experience that selfhood in at least two ways. At any particular moment they are probably able to represent themselves, or are represented by others, as embodying certain properties and qualities which make them what they are, but they are also likely to be able to define or think of themselves in an ongoing and more durable, and less fleeting, manner. There are, then, two temporal dimensions to the self. The first is a phenomenal, here-and-now sense of who we happen to be at a particular point in time. As we shall see, and as this dialogue between Alice and the caterpillar in Lewis Carroll's *Alice's Adventures in Wonderland* indicates, this is not always as straightforward as it appears:

> 'Who are you?' said the caterpillar. 'I hardly know, Sir, just at present,' Alice replied rather shyly.
> 'At least I knew who I was when I got up this morning, but I think I must have been changed several times since then.'

The second is a developmental, biographical sense of ourselves as constantly becoming and as having been. Thus, we may be aware that in the past we have been, or at least feel ourselves to have been, different, and that in the future there is the possibility of us being different again. This latter sense of self gives us our identities as individuals.

   The second point – as should be clear from the choice of words with which I have been framing this discussion so far – is that there are different senses of self embedded in our everyday speech and these help disentangle the various guises in which individuals are to be understood. The pronouns 'I', 'me' and 'myself' are alternative forms of self-representation. The first-person pronoun 'I' – which is expressed grammatically as the subject of a sentence (as in 'I run') – means the subjective, knowing self and is a reference to the individual's seat or locus of consciousness. 'Me' is the objective case of self and is the entity to which the speaking 'I' refers in acknowledgement of the fact that one is the object of another's perceptions. An example would be the question: 'Is it me to whom you are referring?' 'Myself', lastly, is the self constructed, so to speak, by the knowing self or 'I' when it makes itself the object of its own perception – that is, when it makes itself an object to itself. This relationship is evident in reflexive grammatical expressions such as: 'I flatter myself if I am being really honest with you' or 'I am not myself today'.

The third point is that a person's conception of her or himself may take one of two other forms: a true, real or actual self, as opposed to an ideal, desired and sought-after sense of self. An economical way of describing one's true self is as that which, in her or his heart-of-hearts, if they are sincere and honest with themselves, they know themselves to be. This sense is captured in *Hamlet* (I, iii) – although in this extract it is overlaid with the notion of falsity, which I shall come to in a moment – when Polonius urges Laertes:

> . . . to thine own self be true,
> And it must follow, as the night the day,
> Thou canst not then be false to any man.

One's ideal self, on the other hand, is the self which one would be if one could be, or were one able to be. Thus, when the Queen stands before the mirror and says something like 'Mirror, mirror on the wall . . .', etc., what she really wants the mirror to reflect back is the preferred image she has of herself, viz. that she is more beautiful than Snow White.

A leader's true or real self is hard to detect – as Machiavelli suggested, most people are left with what appears to be the case. Hence the importance of perceptions in leadership: in this sense Machiavelli anticipated the insights of the attribution theorists of leadership reviewed in Chapter 1 by more than 400 years. Every now and then, of course, leaders in the public eye are caught off guard or they drop their masks. On such rare occasions the general public catches a fleeting glimpse of what they might really be like behind the scenes – as television viewing audiences did when Mrs Imelda Marcos's fetish for expensive shoes was revealed to the world after she and her husband, the Philippines President, fled Malacanang Palace in 1987; and as they did, once again, when the stunningly grandiose and opulent lifestyle of Nicolai Ceaucescu, the discredited Romanian dictator, came to light two years later. Occasionally, also, penetrating, in-close pen portraits of leaders appear – such as the one of Joseph Stalin, the Soviet dictator, by Averell Harriman, the US Ambassador during World War II (Urban, 1981). A good illustration of the problems involved in constructing a detailed understanding of a major public figure, using very limited and restricted sources of evidence, is the portrayal of Adolf Hitler by Walter Langer (1973), the psychoanalyst, which was commissioned by the US Office of Strategic Services in 1943–4. The subtitles of Langer's first four chapters are illustrative of some of the distinctions about selfhood being articulated here: 'Hitler: As he believes himself to be'; 'Hitler: As the German people know him'; 'Hitler: As his associates know him' and 'Hitler: As he knows himself'.

Given what was said earlier about being captive of the image others have of us, this real–ideal distinction may be of little consequence, *prima facie*, because what we all are, in the end, depends on how other people see us. That is, our actual selves, in effect, amount to what other people care to impute to us. This is probably what William James (1901, p. 291, original emphasis) was driving at when he wrote at the turn of the century that:

> a man's [*sic*] Self is the sum total of all that he *can* call his, not only his body and his psychic powers, but his clothes and his house, his wife and children, his ancestors and friends, his reputation and works, his lands and horses, and yacht and bank-account.

James (1901, pp. 293, 294) called this social self 'the recognition [a man] gets from his mates' and said that really '[there are] as many social selves as there are individuals who recognize him'. It is the social sense of self which is referred to as 'What I seem to be' (i.e. to others) in this poem 'Esto Quod Esse Videri' (Be what you seem to be) written by Sir James Darling (cited in Gronn, 1986b, p. 40):

> To be or not to be
> This does not worry me,
> Rather to see if I can see
> which of these me's is really me.
>
> Be what I seem to be.
> Fear not lest others see
> What I aspire to be,
> Till that becomes the real me.

These two stanzas written by a noted educational leader reconcile William James's sense of the social with the earlier idea of a real self. The advice they offer is to behave in a way which is consistent with the perceptions – and, therefore, the expectations that these give rise to – which others have of us. This means ensuring that one's real self and the sum of the perceptions which others have of us are consistent and aligned. In addition, however, the poem shows how the real–ideal duality is in fact significant, for the particular aspect of selfhood which is of genuine concern, Darling is suggesting, is the ideal self – 'What I aspire to be' – and the likelihood that it can dominate and become the driving force of an individual's motivation.

This very possibility raised in the last line of Darling's poem forms the subject matter of Karen Horney's (1950) insightful book, *Neurosis and*

Human Growth, in which she articulated a range of typical neurotic personality responses to the internal conflicts generated when individuals try and live according to their ideal self-images: resignation, withdrawal, expansiveness, arrogant-vindictiveness and, the one considered in more detail shortly, narcissism. In essence, everyone, from time to time, asks the same question of the mirror as the Queen does – for the simple reason that they are proud and because occasional bouts of fantasizing feed any delusions about the ideal views of themselves which they may be harbouring. Horney (1950, pp. 113–14, original emphases) cites a poem entitled *Entwicklungsschmerzen* (Growing pains), by Christian Morgenstern, which highlights graphically the internal division and agonizing self-conflict to which people can be subject should their aspirations ever entirely get the better of them:

> I shall succumb, destroyed by myself
> I who am two, what I could be and what I am.
> And in the end one will annihilate the other.
> The *Would-be* is like a prancing steed
> (*I am* is fettered to his tail),
> Is like a wheel to which *I am* is bound,
> Is like a fury whose fingers twine
> Into his victim's hair, is like a vampire
> That sits upon his heart and sucks and sucks.

By contrast, Robert Browning's poem 'Rabbi Ben Ezra' suggests that for those individuals who do manage to contain their self-conflicts, there is some consolation in knowing, perhaps, that they have avoided becoming an undesirable 'Would-be':

> Then, welcome each rebuff
> That burns earth's smoothness rough,
> Each sting that bids nor sit nor stand but go!
> Be our joys three-parts pain!
> Strive, and hold cheap the strain;
> Learn, nor account the pang; dare, never grudge the throe!
> For thence, – a paradox
> Which comforts while it mocks, –
> Shall life succeed in that it seems to fail:
> What I aspire to be,
> And was not, comforts me:
> A brute I might have been, but would not sink i' the scale.

The last dimension of selfhood I want to consider is the idea of a false self – which was captured in Polonius's words about not being 'false to any man'. The idea of a false self represents a denial or the opposite of one's true self (see Winnicott, 1965). Laing (1966, pp. 98–9) gives this example from a therapy session with a little boy in which the boy remarked:

> that he was 'response to what other people say I am'. This consists in acting according to other people's definitions of what one is, in lieu of translating into action one's own definition of whom or what one wishes to be. It consists in

becoming what the other person wants or expects one to become while only being one's 'self' in imagination or in games in front of a mirror.

In this instance the boy was a compliant lad who acted as he did in conformity with the dictates of other people in his life. Behaviour like this is false, however, because the individual becomes merely a creature of what somebody else wants of them or because they impersonate someone else and behave in such a way that they live a lie. Laing (1966, pp. 96–7, original emphases) cites another schoolboy who told him:

> that at school he was fond of mathematics but had a contempt for literature. A performance of *Twelfth Night* was given at school and the boys had to write an essay on the subject. At the time he felt he hated the play but wrote a most appreciative essay about it, by imagining what would be expected of him by the authorities and slavishly adhering to it. This essay won a prize. 'Not one word of it was the expression of how I felt. It was all how I felt I was expected to feel'. Or so he thought at the time. In fact, as he admitted to himself later, he had *really* enjoyed the play, and had *really* felt about it as he had described in the essay.

The lad had not dared to admit this possibility to himself for it would have put him at odds with the values into which he had been socialized and negated his view of himself.

The above examples are sufficient to indicate that when a person either acts in accordance with their ideal self (i.e. how they would like themselves to be and how they would like others to think they really are), or lives out a false self, then they are being deceitful. In the first case they are choosing to be someone they are not, and in the second they are feeling constrained to be inauthentic. In both cases, however, they can be said to be acting knowingly and deliberately – just as spies and double agents do, presumably, when they feign their roles – so that by pointing out how easy it is for deceitful persons to come unstuck, the admonitions in the poems cited are, in effect, recommending the cautious alternatives of sincerity and authenticity. Acting knowingly, however, is one thing. But to act knowingly while at the same time denying the fact to oneself is self-deception or what is sometimes known as acting in bad faith. The final observation to make about the sentiments in the examples is that they all represent forms of self-denial, and to that extent they pose important developmental challenges to potential leaders: the need to be self-aware – or, as one of Hodgkinson's (1983, p. 211) four maxims enjoins leaders, to 'Know oneself' – and the need for self-acceptance. It is a moot point whether in this extract from his diary – which, incidentally, he once referred to as his second self – the young John Monash was giving vent to self-acceptance or to self-denial, as he strove to make sense of just who he really was and wanted himself to become (cited in Serle, 1982, p. 79):

> I have reached the point where I feel disposed to take a new stand. What is the course of my life leading me to? My absurd vanity and brutal self assertion, give me growing cause for anxiety. I feel that ... the occasion has come when I must check those tendencies of character which lead to those frequent outward manifestations which

make me ashamed of and disgusted with myself. I want to try to give the best qualities of my nature the very best opportunities for emphatic development.

From time to time, all persons, leaders included, endeavour to disown who or what they mean to themselves, and the qualities attributed to them by others. But no matter whether our self-pretensions are to be 'both handsome and fat and well-dressed, and a great athlete and make a million a year, be a wit, a *bon-vivant*, and a lady-killer as well as a philosopher; a philanthropist, statesman, warrior, and African explorer, as well as a "tone-poet" and saint' – as William James (1901, p. 309) once outlined the possibilities rather impishly – 'the thing is simply impossible'.

As was suggested earlier, an identity is a more prolonged and enduring sense of selfhood. This is evident if we reflect on the host of everyday ways in which we use identity and associated words. Consider the case of a witness assisting a law enforcement agency with its enquiries. The person may be required to identify a suspect as part of a line-up or identity parade. This entails matching an actual person with an image in their memory. Or, alternatively, a computerized image of a suspect may be assembled with the help of a victim, feature by recalled feature, using an identi-kit technique. In either case the clues may be fleeting or skimpy, but the totality of them from a number of information sources allows for the build-up of an assemblage approximating William James's idea of the social self which, when combined with known details from a suspect's case history and background, reveals to the police a pattern that establishes grounds for a conviction. Likewise, if a socially prominent individual earns a reputation as 'an identity' or larger-than-life character in popular culture it is their noteworthiness or notoriety (because of their public exploits) which makes them a household name. Another telling instance is the currency and trust accorded small plastic ID cards – which rely on minimal identifying details such as photographs, signatures or pin numbers – to capture the unique attributes of an individual's identity. Each of these examples show that the validity of an identity rests on assumptions about continuity and the enduring nature of personal attributes which, if they alter, do so consistently and in an evolutionary way, rather than in an abrupt, about-face manner – which is one reason, presumably, why immigration authorities insist on the regular updating of passport details.

Individuals' identities, however, do not only evolve in non-problematic ways. Sometimes people do experience a *volte-face* or identity crisis. These events signal something about the strain of coping with their sense of who they are, either because internal psychological pressures begin to overwhelm them or because external demands challenge and alter the way they prefer to think of or define themselves. Thus, in *Henry IV, Part II* (V, v), after his father's death, the newly crowned Harry informs Falstaff:

Presume not, that I am the thing I was:
For heaven doth know, so shall the world perceive,
That I have turn'd away my former self;
So will I those that kept me company.

If the change undergone is genuinely swift and far-reaching, and cannot be hidden from people around us, then we are confronted with what is often referred to as a Road-to-Damascus-like conversion. In the terrifying experience of Saul – 'and suddenly there shined around about him a light from heaven ... and he fell to the earth, and heard a voice saying unto him ... ' (*Acts*, 9:3–4) – a spiritual rebirth took place, which has been popularized in the expression to be 'born again'. In secular terms this kind of event or crisis may be the trigger for a fundamental rethink about life goals and an attempted reconstruction of one's public persona. M.K. Gandhi, the charismatic Indian nationalist leader, is a case in point (Muslin and Desai, 1985, p. 129):

> The Gandhi who came to South Africa ... was a man intensely in need of support for a self enfeebled by losses and failures and ... correspondingly vulnerable and reactive to rejections and insults. The deprived masses of Indians in South Africa served an important self-object function for Gandhi's weakened self, and collectively became a source of admiration for Gandhi's self of service. In his virtually instantaneous transformation into a revered presence, the most admired Indian in South Africa, Gandhi experienced a bracing antidote for his flagging self.

This experience, it appears, was the critical turning-point for Gandhi, at which what I have suggested are the two vital components of a leader's self-belief – esteem and efficacy – began to gel and to feed positively off one another.

Impression management and image

The idea of impression management derives from Goffman (1976b) who, in *The Presentation of Self in Everyday Life*, examined how the self-systems of individuals find expression in the institutionally defined roles they are required to fulfil. Impression management is the conscious and knowing act of conveying desired appearances in interaction with other people, which are both convincing and credible. In this next remark from Goffman (1976b, p. 28) there is very close affinity with Machiavelli's point about appearances, because the onlookers here are being invited to take what they see at face value:

> When an individual plays a part he [*sic*] implicitly requests his observers to take seriously the impression that is fostered before them. They are asked to believe that the character they see actually possesses the attributes he appears to possess, that the task he performs will have the consequences that are implicitly claimed for it, and that, in general, matters are what they appear to be. In line with this, there is the popular view that the individual offers his performance and puts on his show 'for the benefit of other people'.

The former US president, Richard Nixon, is often cited by president-watchers as one important leader who was singularly adept at the art of impression management. Barber (1977, p. 357), for example, described Nixon as being so obsessed with self-presentation that for much of his career he was 'a man constructing himself as he goes along'. Another example is

General Douglas MacArthur. Film footage of his early army career shows him to be attired in ways calculated to heighten his already authoritative physical appearance: always photographed in an upward direction – so that he is pictured looking down, Olympian-like, from on high – carrying a swagger stick (rather than the regulation baton), smoking a long corn-cob pipe, and wearing his hat tilted at an ever so slightly rakish angle. Even Florence Nightingale – sanitary reformer, 'Lady with the Lamp' and icon of the Victorian era – has been described in a recent historical reassessment as 'an untiring watcher of herself' and as someone who 'personified the new Machiavelli' (Smith, 1982, pp. 22, 37).

Educational administrators also resort to impression management, a scarcely surprising discovery given that Khleif (1975, p. 375) characterized the case of school administrator preparation he observed first-hand as training in how to become politicians. Candidates were seen to:

> acquire an upper-middle class demeanor, dress, and presentability . . . [to become] more socially polished, masters of small talk, alert politicians with – if necessary – a talent for intrigue and the little arts of popularity.

Martinko and Gardner (1988) investigated the impression-management behaviour of 34 US primary and secondary school principals. They sought to establish whether principals varied the content of their utterances and the manner in which they articulated them according to the status of the audience with whom they were dealing at any one time – whether the audience was known and familiar to them, whether it varied in size and whether it was external or internal to their schools. Principals' verbal self-presentations were designed to communicate desired images of themselves and their schools, and displayed the following linguistic features: verbal ploys such as excuses and justifications for their actions; apologies; entitlements – expressions 'designed to maximize an actor's apparent responsibility for an event'; enhancements – expressions 'designed to maximize the favorability of an event itself'; flattery and favours – 'doing something nice to gain that person's approval' (Martinko and Gardner, 1988, p. 44). This sample of principals was found to resort to 'organizational and self-descriptions more frequently and for more time than they used other types of verbal self-presentational behaviors' (Martinko and Gardner, 1988, p. 61).

The portfolio of personal qualities on which leaders may draw in order to project their desired personas is extensive. Two features are mentioned briefly for illustrative purposes only: presence and coolness. Presence is nominated principally because of its historical significance – part of the prototype of the great headmaster, on which the success of the public schools was thought by its apologists to depend, was the commanding physical and moral presence he projected. Presence is still part of common usage, although euphemisms like gravitas – i.e. the dignifying of an office with importance, seriousness and solemnity – are becoming more common.

Presence poses a conundrum for leaders, for its purpose is to attract and to appeal, by virtue of the mystery and awe it evokes. Yet these are fragile notions which signal the need for the maintenance of a requisite distance. As Benjamin (1977) noted in regard to works of art, the greatness of a visual masterpiece depends in large measure on its rarity and uniqueness. To mimic or reproduce it (by copying), so as to make it more accessible, better known and more common, however, is to tarnish its aura, and to rob it of its magical appeal. If Benjamin is right, then perhaps this explains why leaders and authority figures are careful to try and regulate and control the conditions of access to themselves, and why they are so keen to involve themselves in controversy on some occasions but to be seen to remain well above the fray on others.

The second feature is coolness – a bowdlerized version, perhaps, of poise. This is the feeling of being at ease and assured in the company of others which, from a leader's vantage point, can readily be seen as a desirable trait. To be poised is a reference to an individual's carriage or bearing – which suggests its close affinity to presence – or the capacity to remain unflappable when under duress or extreme provocation, as in the injunction to 'keep your cool'. Emotions like anxiety and fear of ridicule, should they be felt, do not appear to be in evidence when someone is poised or has gathered themselves together. Instead they are contained – all part of what Hodgkinson (1983, p. 210) refers to as the leader's canon of self-knowledge. Coolness or poise can be understand as a kind of studied iciness, and its particular significance for leadership is not hard to find (Lyman and Scott, 1968, p. 95):

> Formal leaders may be thrust from their posts because they panic, and unknown persons raised to political heights because of their publicly displayed ability to remain calm. Much popular folklore perceives calamitous situations as those providing just the right opportunity for a person otherwise unqualified to assume a dominant position. Indeed, if his acts are sufficiently skillful and smooth, the displayer of coolness may be rewarded with future rights of charismatic authority.

On this point about the need for containment, Sir James Darling recalled that on the Western Front in 1918 he learnt very quickly that one of the worst things a young officer could do was to show fear in front of the ranks (Gronn, 1986b, p. 37).

Impression management, as Goffman (1976b, p. 14, original emphases) was careful to point out, is an elusive two-edged process: it controls at the very same time as it affords the scope for control. The reason is that the impressions individuals convey are of two sorts: intended and unintended. An intended impression is one which an individual deliberately '*gives*', whereas an unintended impression is one which an individual '*gives off*' inadvertently. This possibility makes the construction of a public persona to convey a desired image doubly difficult. Every now and then leaders' conscious attempts to charm and seduce can backfire. (It is such indiscretions, of course, which have political cartoonists rubbing their hands with glee.) Thus, when endeavouring to cultivate presence and poise, for example, leaders can easily transmit a sense of arrogance or haughtiness. A classic, even egregious, example of this is the observation attributed to a former British prime minister, Herbert Asquith, to describe the smug air which 'Balliol men' were said to project in their dealings with others: 'tranquil consciousness of effortless superiority'. On the other hand, some leaders – like the former French president, Charles de Gaulle – display all the hallmarks of poise and presence, along with a lofty indifference or aloofness, and manage to get away with doing so. Still others prefer to project themselves as sincere and as a kind of 'real me', as did President Jimmy Carter, with his glittering toothy smile. Still others, blessed with few endearing features, make do with the meagre personal resources at their disposal in projecting a public persona. A good example is *Richard III* (I, i):

> I, that am not shap'd for sportive tricks,
> Nor made to court an amorous looking-glass;
> I, that am rudely stamp'd, and want love's majesty
> To strut before a wanton ambling nymph;
> I, that am curtail'd of this fair proportion,
> Cheated of feature by dissembling Nature,
> Deform'd, unfinish'd, sent before my time
> Into this breathing world, scarce half made up,
> And that so lamely and unfashionable
> That dogs bark at me, as I halt by them;
> Why I, in this weak piping time of peace,
> Have no delight to pass away the time,
> Unless to spy my shadow in the sun,
> And descant on mine own deformity.
> And therefore, since I cannot prove a lover
> To entertain these fair well-spoken days,
> I am determined to prove a villain,
> And hate the idle pleasures of these days.

No matter what their particular physical and other endowments, however, organizational leaders have little choice but to attend to their public personas by seeking to foster desired impressions to their followers and other audiences.

There is some evidence from recent research into leadership in higher education of the extent to which the images of leaders perceived by others match the personas constructed by those same leaders. The perceptions of US university presidents by faculty, for example, have been found to be shaped by the extent to which presidents' gestures take into account the latter's definitions of reality, in particular their expectations and situations. To the extent that presidents were perceived to take the role or standpoint of faculty then their images were seen as positive, and as strengthening the bonds between the two parties. To take the other's role – a stance known technically as altercasting – meant they shared key values, beliefs and thinking patterns to the extent that presidents recognized and empathized with faculty's concerns (Bensimon, 1991, p. 641). In particular, new presidents assumed a non-presidential stance by 'giving the impression of joining the faculty, of becoming one of them', by 'strict adherence to consultation procedures', by 'giving due recognition to criticism and frequently acceding to requests' and by 'acting as an advocate for the institution to powerful external agencies' (Bensimon, 1991, pp. 643, 644, 645, 646). Mention has already been made of Spaulding's (1997) study of the potentially disastrous consequences of negative perceptions of school principals and Bensimon (1991, pp. 648–50) discovered similar images amongst new US university presidents. Negative perceptions were fuelled by their failure to communicate, to consult and to acknowledge faculty governance.

A key assumption underlying the discussion to this point has been that a healthy regard for oneself – or what I have summarized as a robust sense of self-belief – is an important component of the preliminary audit to which aspirant leaders might be expected or encouraged to subject themselves. On the other hand, there is likely to be a level at which that preoccupation with oneself becomes excessive, so much so in fact that the image the mirror reflects is one with which the leader becomes almost totally self-absorbed, and with which – like Narcissus in the Greek myth – she or he falls in love. Should that possibility eventuate, then it is likely that a person will have succumbed to the syndrome known as narcissism.

Self-destruction

The last two decades have seen a burgeoning interest in narcissistic leaders. This has been stimulated by two main developments: first, growing evidence from documented clinical case histories of increasing numbers of patients displaying symptoms of narcissistic personality disorders and, second, a greater tolerance for the expression of individualism as part of a wider shift in Western cultural values. In this latter respect, because of the illusion of intimacy, frankness and candour created by its roving camera lens, television – in particular – has both bred and fed an urge on the part of mass viewing audiences for psychological closeness with their leaders and public figures. Such a desire fosters a focus on leaders' feelings. So intense has the scrutiny of political leaders, in particular, become that in the USA, for example, the president-watching segment of the overall political science and psycho-biography-writing community now engages in an unrelenting personality profiling and psychological assessment of the character structure of incumbents of the White House to an extent never before witnessed (see e.g. Renshon, 1994).

For purposes of the present discussion, narcissistic individuals – according to the *Diagnostic and Statistical Manual of Mental Disorders* (3rd edition) of the American Psychiatric Association – display, *inter alia*, the following characteristics: grandiose self-importance; fantasies of unlimited success, power and brilliance; exhibitionism and the need for constant attention; cool indifference; a sense of entitlement; self-aggrandisement and an inability to empathize. Consideration by leadership commentators of the significance of these kinds of narcissistic traits has focused on two main questions: first, the developmental origins of narcissistic personalities and the extent to which the manifestation of narcissistic symptoms represents a mainly neurotic or a borderline psychotic personality disorder and, second, the extent to which narcissism is an individual and social pathology, or whether there are anti- and pro-social forms of narcissism manifested by leaders. Contributors to the debate over the first question take the writings of Freud (who linked displays of narcissism with a propensity to lead) as their departure point and they – mainly Kohut (1978) and Kernberg (1978, 1984) – have been locked in a dispute about narcissism as a phenomenon *sui generis*, and in its particular relation to leadership. The second question was raised originally by Volkan (1980) and has been carried forward most recently by Kets de Vries (1989a, 1989b, 1991b).

If, as I have suggested, a firm sense of efficacy is an important part of a leader's self-belief system then one implication is that leaders are likely to accept that they can and will make a difference or have an impact on their organizational worlds through their actions. Moreover, if they also happen to occupy formal positions of authority, as opposed to exercising leadership on an informal basis, then they have the added weight of office on which to fall back in order to achieve their particular ends. In short, because of the potential strength of a leader's hand in any particular context, there may, over time, turn out to be few inhibiting factors or disincentives to them getting their own way. From that possibility it is but a quick step to experiencing a sense of dominance, and an inflated sense of their own self-importance, as Kets de Vries (1991a, p. 128) explains:

> The need for self-confirmation [on the part of leaders] can turn into what resembles an addiction, so that CEOs [or their equivalents] thus afflicted can never get enough attention. They want to be in the limelight all the time. Some even begin to think they are infallible. As leaders they may come to believe that they have the license to do anything, that the normal rules of conduct do not apply to them. They have lost all touch with reality and have moved into the sphere of eventual abuse of power.

In short, what begins as benign feelings of success stimulates additional feelings of success which, if the confirmatory imagery being mirrored back in the responses of their followers, peers and colleagues is interpreted as adulatory, can, in turn, fuel an unconscious fantasy of invulnerability, or even invincibility. When that happens, leaders tend to become complacent: they attend only to such feedback as confirms what they already know or prefer to believe about themselves and the rightness of their actions, they become error-prone and, as the responses of the emperor's retinue in the fable *The Emperor's New Clothes* suggest, those in their immediate circle soon learn that their own survival depends on feeding their superiors only what they want to hear.

Kernberg's overriding concern is with organizational health and the contribution of a leader's personality to that equilibrium. Any unresolved emotional conflicts – narcissistic or otherwise – in a leader's psychological make-up or amongst the personalities of a leadership group, will generally manifest themselves by distorting rationality and impairing judgement. Yet creative organizational leadership depends upon impulse control and the harnessing of emotions like aggression, in particular, in the pursuit of useful and socially productive ends. Considerable harm is generated when leaders are in so dominant a position that they are able to project their grandiosity onto the organization, and to use other people as mirrors for self-confirmation and psychological nourishment. Part of being a leader means to be prepared to be the object or container of other people's aggressive and destructive emotional impulses, and yet leaders are unable to do this if their own needs continually get in the way: 'this is one reason why severely narcissistic and paranoid personalities make poor task leaders' (Kernberg, 1978, p. 16). At one point Kernberg (1984, p. 21) ponders whether there may be grounds for thinking that 'a small dose of narcissism' just might be felicitous but he shies away, for an excess of narcissism, suspicion and paranoia 'may suddenly trigger regression in leaders'. This, in turn, may bring about organizational regression. Rational task leadership, however, requires high intelligence, honesty and non-corruptibility, a capacity to sustain depth in interpersonal relations, the ability to take a perspective on oneself, caution and alertness, and at best a very limited dose of 'healthy narcissism': merely 'in the sense of being self-assertive rather than self-effacing' (Kernberg, 1984, p. 20).

Kohut (1978), on the other hand, takes a strongly affirmative stance towards narcissism and the narcissistic personality. His view of the self-system of the narcissist – in contrast also to Horney's (1950, p. 154) earlier position, which is that 'the individual is his [sic] idealized self and seems to adore it' – is that it has fragmented. Restoration to wholeness comes not from repression or denial, but through acting out. Yet for Kohut (1978, p. 619) 'the deeply ingrained value system of the Occident (pervading the religion, the philosophy, the social utopias of Western man) extols altruism and concern for others and disparages egotism and concern for one's self'. But instead of instinctual repression, an individual's narcissistic needs should be given free rein (Kohut, 1978, p. 620):

> We should not deny our ambitions, our wish to dominate, our wish to shine, and our yearning to merge into omnipotent figures, but should instead learn to acknowledge the legitimacy of our object-instinctual strivings.

Kohut's point of departure from the familiar threefold Freudian model of the mind – i.e. id, ego and super-ego – is that there is an ontological narcissistic realm quite separate from the instinctual domain fenced off by Freud. In every individual there is to be found an embryonic self striving to burst out of its cage and be free. And if in making this break a child, or an adult, is unable to find adequate parental-substitute figures on which to

transfer its narcissistic strivings, its urges to realize itself and find confirmation of itself in others and obtain strength from them by merging, then it will
likely feel enfeebled, and overwhelmed by the anxiety that is disintegrating.
Denied the opportunity to idealize their parents as role models, perhaps,
and having experienced inadequate confirmation of themselves and who
they are, the individual learns to vent, on those around them, her or his rage,
and narcissistic injuries and hurts.

Discussions of narcissistic leadership display the same ambivalence commentators feel about charismatic figures – i.e. that they may be a force either
for collective uplift or for maladaptive and nihilistic regression. This ambivalence has led to a refinement of narcissism as a leadership category. In an
attempt to retrieve positive aspects of the concept, Volkan (1980) distinguishes reparative from destructive narcissist leadership. On the one hand, a
destructive narcissist leader 'protects the cohesion of his grandiose self
chiefly by devaluing others', whereas a reparative leader – a national saviour
or hero perhaps – uplifts followers 'in order to build his [sic] support on as
impressively high a level as possible' and 'strengthens the cohesiveness and
stability of his grandiose self by idealizing a group of others whom he then
includes in an idealized extension of himself' (Volkan, 1980, pp. 138–9).
Exemplary reparative narcissism, for Volkan, is best exemplified by Mustafa
Kemal Atatürk, the founder of modern Turkey after the break-up of the
Ottoman Empire at the end of the Great War. Three children had died
before Mustafa was born; another died after him and his father passed away
when the boy was seven. The religious and devoted, but psychologically
smothering, mother of this handsome, blond-haired loner believed her son
had claims to immortality and was special; his teacher gave him the name
'Kemal' – meaning perfect – and when he became President of Turkey he
took the name 'Atatürk' or 'Father Turk'. He was a hero at Gallipoli in
combat with the Australians and luckily survived shrapnel wounds, all of
which added to the illusion that he was somehow great and immortal
(Volkan, 1980, pp. 142–5). Atatürk was a man who fought hard to overcome
his country's servile attitude to tradition. He was, claims Volkan (1980, p.
147), a fine example of the congruence or fit between 'a high-level narcissistic leader' and a people having undergone 'narcissistic hurt' due to
national invasion and forced migration. This last point indicates that 'mirror
hunger', as it is known, works by followers feeding off leaders, as well as the
reverse relationship. That is, a leader can be made the mirror for the
collective attributions and fantasies of narcissistic followers. 'We frequently
use the leader to reflect what we want to see', notes Kets de Vries (1989b, p.
610), so that leaders are as much captive as captivating.

In these remarks I have been trying to argue that while the idea of the self,
at any one point in time, is many-layered and multi-faceted the notion of
individual identity – or selfhood thought of through time – while not rigidly
fixed, displays the properties of emergence, consistency and predictability.
But these kinds of assumptions – not unlike those already seen as under-

girding our long-standing conceptions of career – are now being challenged. The latest word on selfhood is no longer narcissism – which, perhaps, was emblematic of the swing to self-centred libertarianism in so many cultural spheres in the 1980s – but proteanism: the idea of an infinitely malleable, adaptable and changing concept of self. In Chapter 2 I provided a foretaste of what was to come with the notion of the boundaryless, protean, do-it-yourself career and Lipman-Blumen's connective, woman- or man-for-all-seasons leader. But the fullest expression of the new protean impulse is to be found in Robert Jay Lifton's (1993) *The Protean Self.* Lifton acknowledges his debt to many theorists – one of whom, interestingly, was Kohut: 'I came to his work late, but found much in common with him during several extended conversations' (Lifton, 1993, p. 27). Proteanism is the motif for the 1990s and the new millennium. It stands for many-sidedness, multiple selves, and an infinite range of options, possibilities and combinations; in short: a do-it-yourself conception of designer-selfhood. Lifton's optimism about the self is understandable. His notion is based, after all, on a long and respected career of research into the extraordinary resilience displayed by the human species – testimony to its amazing capacity to survive the most horrifying and severe forms of deprivation, dislocation, uprootedness, persecution, homelessness, indoctrination and re-education. In this new conception flux, chaos, fragmentation, free-floating detachment and the like are not, as far as Lifton is concerned, mere ephemera but features on the landscape of the self as it strives for renewed authenticity and the attainment of its yet unheard-of potential.

Lifton may be right: perhaps the protean prospect does await us; and maybe the capacity to make connections in the way suggested by Lipman-Blumen is the hallmark of the new millennium leader. On the other hand, proteanism still has to be viewed as a possibility, rather than an actuality. And if I am right about formation, and the degrees of freedom it makes possible between institutional constraint and unlimited human choice, then clearly some individuals will be well placed to undertake the extent of the identity work which proteanism would appear to entail. Others, however, for reasons of lesser degrees of freedom made available by the particular circumstances of their formation will not. Moreover, such protean types will be extremely well positioned to ride the waves of change – for that, in the end, is what proteanism is all about – engulfing the world at every conceivable level: global, national, organizational and local. Like Riesman *et al.*'s (1961) celebrated traditional, inner-directed and other-directed types, which stood the test of time so well for so long, followed by the narcissist, the protean self will no doubt take its place in the pantheon of archetypes which seem to best symbolize the spirit of different eras of societal and cultural evolution. This discussion will have served the would-be leader well by alerting her or him to this latest addition to the universe of possible selves. But the decision as to how much currency and credibility is likely to be accorded the protean self, needless to say, will be in the hands of those with whose prying eyes this chapter began: potential followers and those among their number who made the original selection. In addition to discovering something about their new leader's identity – be this ephemeral or be it enduring – these same people are also likely to be asking other vital questions about their new leader, and it is to the next of these that I now turn.

CHAPTER 5

The values of leaders

The second area of immediate concern to followers on their first encounter with a new leader will most likely be to do with her or his values. They will probably be asking themselves something like: What does this person believe in? What is it that she or he stands for and would be prepared to fight for at all costs? To what extent do her or his values square with those to which I am committed? A leadership aspirant can anticipate being asked questions about their educational values or philosophy at some point during a selection process. Some of those assembled to meet the new leader on their arrival, provided they have been members of a selection panel or have been privy to its behind-the-scenes dealings, will already have an inkling of what is in store for them. Those not so privileged, however – and that is usually the overwhelming majority – will have had to bide their time.

It is quite possible that questions similar to these were passing through the minds of the staff of the Melbourne Church of England Girls' Grammar School (MCEGGS) in late 1957 upon the arrival from England of Miss Edith Mountain, the new headmistress. If indeed the mistresses on the staff were waiting with baited breath they were to be disappointed because Miss Mountain 'had undertaken to remain as an observer for her first year in the school' (McCarthy, 1993, p. 151). It was to be almost exactly 12 months later, on 9 October 1958, that Miss Mountain delivered the result of her year's labour of watching to the assembled staff. The previous evening 15 senior mistresses had sent individual letters of resignation and a combined letter to the chairman of the school council, the Archbishop of the Diocese of Melbourne, Dr Frank Woods. That morning their letters of resignation had also been hand-delivered to Miss Mountain. For the next month or so in public – in the embarrassingly full blare of metropolitan daily newspaper coverage – and for much longer within the bosom of the school, MCEGGS, a pillar institution of the Melbourne establishment, began to rip itself apart. By Christmas that year the total of resignations attributable to differences with the new headmistress had swelled to 33 – about two-thirds of the staff (Connell, 1983, p. 216) – in a school with a pupil enrolment of about 900

(Gardiner, 1993, pp. 128–37). Part of the staff's disagreement was to do with the style and personality of the new headmistress (and is dealt with in Chapter 6), but the major objections to her were philosophical ones. Miss Mountain's educational world view was completely at odds with that of her predecessor, Miss D.J. Ross, MCEGGS's headmistress from 1939 until 1955, and it was that incompatibility which was the trigger for the staff's resignations. Those differences split the entire school community and, for a while, caused irreparable harm to MCEGGS's reputation and standing.

There is much to be learned from this devastating incident in the life of the school about leadership succession and induction. I have chosen to cite aspects of the case at this point in the book because the depth of feeling the division provoked says something about the lengths to which determined people will go to defend the causes and actions which they believe to be right. For those staff who resigned, the new headmistress's policy represented a betrayal of everything for which they, and her predecessor, had stood. An account of an important meeting for parents in late October 1958 attended by about 1,000 people is indicative of the passions that were unleashed (Gardiner, 1993, pp. 139-140):

> The meeting overflowed into the grounds and on to the street beyond. It was addressed, first, by A.A. Phillips [a parent, schoolmaster and noted literary figure] who attempted to give an objective account of events to date, but allegedly only confused his audience. Phillips was followed by Edith Mountain who had prepared the way for her address by sending a letter to all parents outlining her position and her plans for the school. These, in both letter and speech, were a simplified version of the policy speech of the previous week. The archbishop, delayed in returning from [the Church of England Primate] Archbishop Mowll's funeral in Sydney, and consequently under considerable stress, also spoke. He stated the Council's position, reiterated its support for the headmistress, and urged all parents to work with the Council and headmistress to rebuild the school community. Several parents then attempted to ask questions. The archbishop said that there were to be no questions, a decision which outraged a large section of his audience. Feelings ran high, and in an allegedly responsible gathering of respectable and intelligent adults, there was much shouting, name calling and verbal abuse, culminating in minor physical violence as successful attempts were made to disconnect the tape-recorder. Appalled, the archbishop pronounced the Benediction; this produced momentary silence, but was followed immediately by renewed pandemonium. He then ordered the singing of the National Anthem and escorted Miss Mountain from the stage. The meeting dissolved noisily and in bad order.

As can be imagined, the morning press provided front-page reports of the meeting under large headlines.

Such succession-related incidents in schools and beyond are by no means isolated. What is surprising, then – given the steadfastness with which, in this instance, both the new leader and the council which appointed her were to stick to their guns – is that scholarly interest in the values of the leader is only fairly recent in origin. And differences in values formed a significant component of what happened to be at stake in this particular instance. For a long time the torch for values was carried principally by two classic writers in the field of leadership, Barnard and Selznick. In one of his later writings Barnard (1956, pp. 85–6) asserted that the function of a leader was 'to know and say what to do, where to go, and when to stop, with reference to the general purpose or objective of the undertaking in which he [*sic*] is engaged'. Earlier, in the book for which he had already become famous, *The Functions of the Executive*, Barnard had argued persuasively that it was also the leader's job to formulate that same general purpose or objective. In *The Functions* he conceived of leadership as a moral act and claimed that, as a moral agent, the job of the leader was to bind an organization's members to those ethical ends for which their organization stood and which it was the leader's job to define. In fact, in a what now reads almost as a booming utterance delivered *ex cathedra*, Barnard (1982 [1938], p. 282) pronounced that 'organizations endure ... in proportion to the breadth of the morality by which they are governed'. 'This', he explained, 'is only to say that foresight, long purposes, high ideals, are the basis for the persistence of coöperation.'

Selznick (1957) built on Barnard's *Functions* in his book *Leadership in Administration*. There, Selznick made an important distinction (for which he became famous and which continues to be widely cited) between organizations (which were set up to perform technical tasks) and institutions (or enduring structures designed to give expression to important social needs). It was in the transition to institutional status that Selznick believed that leaders performed a critical role, for it was a leader's job, Selznick (1957, p. 60, original emphasis) maintained, to infuse an institution with value, and '*to choose key values and to create a social structure that embodies them*'. Complementing Barnard's image of the moral leader is Selznick's version of the leader as a person who instils an organization with character.

This chapter considers that connection between leadership and organizational values. The approach taken might be best characterized as values-in-action. That is, in keeping with the spirit of the dramatic cameo which I have just cited I confine myself mostly to examples of leaders acting in conformity with and pursuing particular valued ends, a connection, note Hambrick and Brandon (1988, p. 3), on which 'relatively little work has been done'. I eschew, therefore, philosophical analysis as such and instead analyse some of the philosophies or moral codes espoused by leaders. I begin by defining values and then consider a number of increasingly popular terms used by leadership commentators in which values figure prominently. I then say something about the significance of leaders' values and compare two examples of visionary educational leaders, each of which in their respective reform proposals sought to bring about morally desired outcomes. Finally, by reference to one further case example I indicate some of the main features of the character transformation leaders undergo when they experience a formative shift in their values.

The architecture of values

The contemporary theorist who has laboured longest and hardest to deepen the understanding that students of leadership and administration have of values is, of course, Christopher Hodgkinson. No-one else has made a more lucid and compelling case for the claim that the administrator (or leader) is a philosopher-in-action, and that her or his craft is best thought of as an art. For Hodgkinson values are the wellsprings of human action and the motivating force behind everything that people choose or choose not to do. A value, claims Hodgkinson (1991, p. 89, and see Hofstede, 1994, p. 8), is a concept or conception 'of the desirable' – or, in the words of Hambrick and Brandon (1988, p. 5, original emphasis), '*a broad and relatively enduring preference for some state of affairs*'. The phenomena desired may be physical objects, end or goal states which individuals solely and collectively pursue. 'The essential point to grasp', Hodgkinson (1983, p. 31, original emphasis) suggests, 'is that values do not exist *in the world*. They are utterly phenomenological [i.e. constructed in the consciousness of the observer], subjective, facts of inner and personal experience, ultimately only susceptible of location within an individual cranium.' Expressions of value, then, are statements of worth which individuals impute to features of their everyday reality and experience. Thus, for one individual, a particular idea may be adjudged as good or right, and is thereby esteemed as more important, better or significant than a rival notion.

In four important books Hodgkinson (1978, 1983, 1991, 1996) has progressively elaborated on a framework for ordering, comparing and ranking different values which is known as the 'value paradigm' (Hodgkinson, 1983, p. 38). Elsewhere (Gronn, 1993a) I have tried to show how the conception of leadership commensurate with his paradigm embodies traditional attributions of greatness, but here I merely summarize the essential details of Hodgkinson's scaffolding because his paradigm provides a very helpful means of ordering some of the examples of moral leadership considered shortly. The paradigmatic edifice Hodgkinson outlines comprises a fourfold hierarchy embodying a series of different grounds or justifications for valuing something or, as he says, the 'four kinds of answer' to the question: 'Why is an object or action or event deemed to be *good* and *right*?' (Hodgkinson, 1983, p. 37, original emphases). Working upwards from the basest to the most elevated of warrantable reasoning, a type-3 justification for valuing something rests on the simple, primitive ground of subjective preference or desire. At level 2, some kind of reasoned basis normally legitimates value claims. This reasoning takes one of two forms: first, a numerical majority or consensus view can be appealed to, so that a policy or legislative measure, perhaps, is justified as deriving from an electoral mandate. That is, the fact that everyone or nearly everyone likes something might be invoked as a reason for claiming that it is proper, good or right. Democracy is supposed to be an effective system for determining outcomes of this kind, because it is, after all, a system for aggregating preferences. The second form of reasoning is qualitative: the consequences of a particular action or policy being pursued are deemed to be beneficial or detrimental. The ground here is still primitive, or at least pragmatic and utilitarian, as Hodgkinson (1983, p. 39) points out with this example:

> Honesty is right because it makes for a better, more efficient and effective organiza-
> tion or social context.

Or, another ground of appeal at this level, perhaps, would be that a decision or a policy is right because it works, or because it disadvantages fewer people than an alternative measure.

Type-1 values are principles for which Hodgkinson believes their adherents would fight to defend. Such values have a metaphysical character about them and are often grounded in a religious or surrogate-religious cosmology. Thus, 'adultery is [or might be deemed] wrong at this level', says Hodgkinson (1983, p. 39), 'because it was so chiseled into the tablets of stone brought down from Mount Sinai'. Or, to cite another of his examples: 'death on the battlefield for the honor of his [*sic*] regiment and in front of his men is right and good because the ethic of *dulce et decorum est pro patria mori* [it is a sweet and noble thing to die for one's country] has been subscribed to by that particular soldier'. Likewise, film footage from 1961 of the current president of South Africa, Nelson Mandela, depicts him as a political dissident about to be incarcerated and saying that he is prepared to die for the principle of one-man-one-vote for his country. The kind of reasoning represented by these examples is an appeal to God, nature or something beyond reason – hence Hodgkinson labels such values transrational. It is worth noting that other commentators, such as Hambrick and Brandon (1988, pp. 6, 30, n. 2), concede the existence of values hierarchies for individuals but see most people's values in practice as 'jumbled together', in which case a values hierarchy is at best 'a crude contrivance'. For Hodgkinson, leaders and administrators – and, as I suggested in Chapter 1, for him these words mean the same thing – inhabit a world suffused with ethical choices and constant value clashes. The realm of values constitutes a field. It, too, according to Hodgkinson, can be arranged hierarchically with each value context nested in a succession of five levels. From the top these layers are: V_5 : the realm of societal, cultural and transnational value systems; V_4: subcultural and sectoral adaptations of value systems; V_3: the values of particular organizations; V_2: group, subgroup and unit values and V_1: individual values. Always, 'the individual alone has the only real *experience* of value' and 'by force of will or force of preference, has the sole *capacity* to take value action'; but the individual at V_1 'is the constant recipient of values-determining forces beyond his [*sic*] control or even beyond his ken' from the other four levels in the values field (Hodgkinson, 1996, p. 152, emphases in original).

Other schematic attempts at logically ordering and arranging values have relied on multi-dimensions, vectors, axes, polarities and continua rather than hierarchies (see Hambrick and Brandon, 1988, pp. 7–14). Such schemes represent attempts to make meaningful connections between values. The totality of any individual's values depicted by such a scheme forms (to some degree) an integrated pattern or configuration rather than a mere aggregation. Two alternative and synonymous ways of describing sets of values are world views and outlooks, although these terms generally include phenomena other than, but closely related to, values. One of the most ambitious recent attempts to map outlooks was undertaken by Davies (1980, p. 469 n. 1), who chose outlook because he had been searching for 'some inclusive term, with suitably vague boundaries' with which to 'lift us above the aridity of having to consider component ideas, opinions, beliefs, attitudes, values, principles or ideals'. Such a battery of distinguishing components makes an outlook coterminous with something like a temperament or disposition. And that is the sense in which Davies employed outlook in his comprehensive three-dimensional typology of 26 value positions and accompanying personality types.

Explicit or implied uses of the term outlook vary greatly. One restricted sense of outlook is to confine its application to a single social segment or sphere and to consider values as forming part of an individual's social or educational outlook – as with the examples of educational leaders to be considered shortly – or as typical of the collective mentality of a sector, such as the military (e.g. Dixon, 1983). The more common use of outlook is even more global, in the sense that the values of an entire era or of a whole society or nation are typified in a uniform way. Well-known examples include characterizations like the Reagan years, Thatcherism, the Victorian era or, in Australia, the Ming Dynasty, as the long prime ministerial incumbency of Sir Robert Menzies (1949–66) became known. In each case the thinking and values of a particularly long-serving and dominant individual became so institutionalized in the regime of which they were the head that they were believed to permeate entire organizations and larger collectivities. Such dominance is precisely what occurs in a dictatorship and the extreme version of it, of course, is hegemony. In political and social democracies, apart from the normal routes of policy-making and legislative enactment, values – particularly of the type-1 variety – are often diffused by moral exhortation. A good illustration is *A Call to the People of Australia.*

In 1951, to mark the jubilee year of the Commonwealth of Australia, leading judges and religious leaders issued a loftily worded document which was given wide coverage in the media. Nearly 1.5 million copies of this plea for moral order were distributed. The *Call* railed against the evils of moral and intellectual apathy. At one point its authors called for:

> a new effort from all Australians to advance moral standards. We ask for it from individuals in their personal and vocational relationships; in and through the lives of families; in and through our voluntary associations: trades unions, employers' and professional groups, the organisations of women, of servicemen, and all the societies which our people have created to express their cultural, social, and economic interests.

Nearly 50 years later, with the new orthodoxy of libertarianism still in the ascendancy in many Western nations, what strikes one is less the *Call*'s paternalism and its universalistic, absolutist moral pretensions, but its emphasis on the sinews of tribe and community. Its authors were at pains to invoke commonweal values and collective interests, and not guarantees of rights and the sanctity of individual choice. It affirmed nationhood and, perhaps even more importantly, it affirmed a vigorous civil society and culture. The idea which gained ground in the 1980s, for example, that there is no such thing as society, would have been incomprehensible to the authors of the *Call*. In that way, then, the *Call* is a useful indicator of the extent to which type-1 cultural values undergo change.

Values are also central to a number of closely related and popular terms in contemporary discussions of organizational leadership. The four most relevant and important terms are culture, mission, vision and strategy, and each is summarized very briefly to indicate their connection with values.

Culture

Since the early 1980s considerable attention has been given to culture by students of leadership and organizations. Prior to this groundswell of interest culture was mainly part of the intellectual terrain of anthropology. Schein (1992, p. 12, original emphasis), a leading commentator in this relatively new domain, defines organizational culture as:

> *A pattern of shared basic assumptions that a group learned as it solved its problems of external adaptation and internal integration, that has worked well enough to be considered valid and, therefore, to be taught to new members as the correct way to perceive, think, and feel in relation to those problems.*

Schein (1992, pp. 17–27) suggests that the culture of an organization manifests itself in three main ways: in its artefacts (i.e. its various practices, procedures and products); in its espoused values, and in the behaviour which is ostensibly predicated on those values (or is consistent with the actual values-in-use). For Hofstede (1994, p. 8), as well, values lie at the core of a culture. The use of 'its' in respect of Schein's definition, of course, presumes a coherent, integrated, stable and unitary entity, when in fact the reality may well be (and, indeed, invariably is) the exact opposite: fracture, division, diffuse goals and contending values as vested interests struggle for ascendancy. But to the extent that there is coherence then, put simply, an organization's culture is its chosen or preferred way of doing whatever it happens to do, and expresses its commitment to that end.

Just as there may be levels of values in the manner suggested earlier by Hodgkinson, so there may also be similar levels for understanding culture. Likewise, just as values are one of the determinants of individual actions, and simultaneously shape an individual's perceptions of real-world contexts for action, then so too do cultures. Hofstede's (1994) metaphor for this kind of dualistic relationship between culture and action is programming, and on the basis of this idea he has endeavoured to map national cultural differences (and, therefore, national differences in values) on five cross-national dimensions: power distance (expectation of unequal power distribution), collectivism–individualism, masculinity–femininity, uncertainty avoidance (extent of feeling threatened by uncertain and unknown situations) and long-term versus short-term orientation. One of Hofstede's basic assumptions is that different cultures programme their members' values and actions in such a way that, when compared cross-nationally, representatives of different cultures are highly likely to perceive and solve shared problems differently, thereby complicating inter-cultural communication and perhaps thwarting trends like globalization. These kinds of complexities are illustrated in David Halberstam's (1987) *The Reckoning*, which deals with the interplay of national and organizational cultural values (Hodgkinson's V_5 and V_3) in a comparative analysis of the evolution and changing market fortunes of two powerful international automotive manufacturers, Nissan (Japan) and Ford (USA).

Mission

An organizational mission statement is usually a declaration of what an enterprise, agency or body sees as its role and purpose within its sphere of activity, and where it fits within the overall scheme of things. Crudely interpreted, an organization's statement of mission is an attempt by it to justify its existence and to spell out what it claims as its distinctive contribution. Despite its current popularity and corporate associations mission has a respectable pedigree in leadership for it was part of Selznick's lexicon of institutionalization. Indeed, more than four decades ago, Selznick (1957, pp. 65–89) devoted an entire chapter to the notion of organizational mission and said that one of a leader's jobs was to frame missions. Thus, '*he [sic] must specify and recast the general aims of his organization so as to adapt them, without serious corruption, to the requirements of institutional survival*' (Selznick, 1957, p. 66, original emphasis). The current popularity of mission statements derives from the fact that organizations in the corporate, not-for-profit and voluntary sectors which restructure, re-position and realign themselves, and gear up to meet performance output or service targets in conformity with the various quality procedures in vogue, begin to rethink purposes which previously went without saying or were taken for granted. Needless to say, statements of mission will incorporate the values and ends to which those organizations stand committed.

Vision

A biblical passage much quoted, almost hackneyed, in the 1990s has been: 'Where there is no vision, the people perish' (Proverbs 29:18). Vision and visionary are two other popular words used in respect of the role of leadership in transforming and restructuring organizations. Like mission, vision is closely connected to organizational purposes or ends, and therefore values. Visions are usually thought of as authored by individuals but, as the Proverbs quote suggests, visions have collective force. Thus, 'when people truly share a vision they are connected, bound together by a common aspiration' (Senge, 1993, p. 206). A vision is a conception of an outcome or desired future state of affairs for an organization which, to be accepted and endorsed, has to be 'consistent with values that people live by day by day [or else it will] fail to inspire genuine enthusiasm' (Senge, 1993, p. 223).

Like mission, vision is not a new leadership word either but simply one that has become fashionable in the changed contingencies that confront leaders. An Australian historian, Greening (1964), for example, used it some three decades or so ago in a study of Dr Mannix – the famous Roman Catholic Archbishop of Melbourne – and his educational aspirations for working-class Catholics during his long episcopate from 1913 to 1963. Greening (1964, p. 290) described Mannix as, in 1917, '[looking] forward to the time when Catholics would share his vision of the place of higher learning in public life'. The essence of the Mannix vision (or thesis) for Melbourne Catholics was (Greening, 1964, p. 292):

> not secondary education for all, but opportunity for the growth of talent regardless of class. From the talented youth would come a group of Catholic intellectuals who would benefit the university by the 'leavening of living, active Catholicism', and who, from their university training, would gain a prestige that would make their ideas more acceptable in a liberal society.

Sectarian and sectional Mannix's values may have been, but this was a vision no less and in Hodgkinson's terms amounts to a policy grounded in type-2B values (i.e. a measure justified as producing desired social benefits) in the pursuit of a type-1 outcome (i.e. safeguarding the interests of the faith).

Strategy

A strategy is the plan adhered to by an organization in order to realize its mission and to secure the implementation of its vision, in which case a strategy plan operationalizes a mission and vision and, therefore, the attainment of organizational values. In *Leading the Way*, for example, Monash University has committed itself to the pursuit of three core values (or 'The three defining themes of Monash University' – p. 4): innovation, engagement and internationalization. If, therefore, organizational mission and vision are thought of as the 'what' and the 'why' then strategy represents the 'how'. Strategic plans comprise an analysis and evaluation of, and decisions about, all of the relevant information and data from internal and external sources related to implementation (Fidler, 1992, p. 22). The focus of strategic thinking in leadership concerns the re-positioning and realigning of an organization in projected and anticipated future environmental circumstances consistent with a declared mission and vision. To the extent that strategic leadership and planning require choices to be made between options and alternative futures, then values come into play in the scanning and analytical processes involved in strategy formulation, as well as in the articulation and implementation of the desired ends.

I now turn to consider in detail two examples of educational reformers. My purpose is twofold. The first case, Darling's proposal in 1951 to establish Timbertop, a campus of the Geelong Grammar School in a remote mountain setting in Victoria, Australia, has been selected because it permits a detailed analysis of the connection between visionary thinking and values. Darling's plan for Timbertop is also of interest because it was articulated with the avowed intention of creating a regime for moral leadership in a democratic society. The other example is the internal reform measures undertaken by Darling's contemporary Miss Ross at MCEGGS. Ross's reforms were also geared to better equipping girls for citizenship in a democratic society, but eventually had to endure the conservative backlash witnessed at the beginning of the chapter. The second purpose is to compare both leaders' efforts with a view to highlighting the importance (in each case) of the conjunction between organizational changes and the wider climate in which they were undertaken (once more the interrelationship of, or a collision between, Hodgkinson's V_5 and V_3).

Moral leadership for a democracy

From the many published statements about Timbertop at the time of its foundation here I analyse just two: a pamphlet entitled 'Timbertop' authored by Darling and extracts from the 'Headmaster's Speech Day Report, 1951', both of which were reproduced in the December 1951 edition of the *Corian*, the Geelong Grammar School magazine. Darling's proposal is a good illustration of what would now be considered as strategic leadership, albeit from an era in which it would have occurred to very few people – least of all Darling – to have thought of or expressed what he was doing in such terms. As well as being statements of his personal vision, the documents articulate Darling's sense of his school's mission, and provide numerous indicators of the school's distinctive cultural ethos and the desired moral ends at which Darling sought to direct the energies of members of the school community. To many people the new educational venture has probably become best known for the fact that Charles, the Prince of Wales, spent two terms there on exchange from Gordonstoun School, near Inverness, Scotland, in 1966. The campus is located about 2,000 feet above sea level on the slopes of Mt Timbertop, 140 miles north-east of Melbourne, and about 180 miles from the main school at Corio near Geelong. To the immediate east is the Mt Buller alpine village, Victoria's premier skiing resort. Timbertop opened in February 1953 when the site comprised about 500 acres with an additional leasehold.

As the prototype of an educational vision Darling's 'Timbertop' pamphlet comprises two key elements. The first is its content and the second is the rhetoric of justification which enshrines the evaluative statements that undergird or legitimate what is proposed. The nub or essence of the content of Darling's plan is summarized in the opening paragraph (p. 160):

> The School Council has made arrangements to acquire a country property upon which will be built accommodation for about 120 boys. To this new auxiliary part of the School will be sent all boys during the calendar year, generally known as Middle Dormitory year, that is, the second year in Senior School, when the ages (at the beginning of the year) will be between $14\frac{1}{2}$ and $15\frac{1}{2}$.

The paragraph concludes by invoking three values which it is anticipated Timbertop will achieve (p. 160):

> First, it will be in a locality and environment in which largely the physical and moral development of the boy will be encouraged through the challenge of the natural conditions; secondly, it will be planned in such a way as to make it easily run by the boys themselves without dependence upon a large supply of employed domestic and other labour; and, thirdly, it will be as nearly as possible self-supporting, or, at least, planned in such a way as to become so.

Darling concluded his introduction by carefully aligning the new scheme with such highly regarded precedents as the Salem and Gordonstoun schools founded by Dr Kurt Hahn (from whom he later quoted directly), and the Outward Bound movement in Britain. The effect of doing so was to anchor his innovation in a legitimate historical context.

The next three main headings in Darling's text offer various educational, administrative and financial justifications (in that order of priority) for Timbertop. In marshalling his educational arguments Darling moved from a series of general deficiencies in the school's current operations to a number of new possibilities opened up by the proposal. Although the deficiencies cited were internal ones they derived from external pressures on Geelong Grammar, especially the grind of the examination system and the consequent failure of what Darling describes as the 'machine' (p. 160) to develop boys' characters due to the implied comfort and security afforded by a daily academic routine. But the new plan would lift boys out of their comfort zones and 'throw the emphasis back upon the individual' (p. 160). After all, 'boys are sent to school in order to fit themselves for their lives as men' (p. 160), he said, in which case during the year at Timbertop they will be expected to (pp. 160–1):

> learn to look after themselves, to find their own occupation, and develop their own capacities. The rather harder conditions and the challenge of the environment will convince all boys, even those who are physically undeveloped, of their capacity to surmount difficulties and overcome the weakness of their bodies. The absence of paid assistance will teach boys to be independent and give them the confidence derived from the knowledge that they can be so. It is believed that this self-confidence will be transferred into all departments of their lives, giving them courage in tackling difficulties in school work and, later, to take the responsibility of leadership in all sorts of public opinion.

Besides these developmental advantages, the added benefit of living close to nature would provide boys with pleasures and joys (such as fishing, bird-watching, mountain-climbing and hiking) normally denied them in an urban environment, and thereby enrich their lives.

This reasoning in this summary statement of the case is interesting because Darling has mostly couched his arguments in type-2 values terminology. While this is understandable, given that the pamphlet was probably intended to be read for background information by parents and old boys (and to that end had been distributed on speech day just before Darling's address), its structure and content indicate that visions, while opening up and exploring possible desirable futures, are more likely to be seen as credible if they provide workable solutions to practical problems. It was in his headmaster's address, with which he actually launched the scheme, that Darling genuinely began to invoke the rhetoric of Hodgkinson's type-1 values. The text displays a slightly different argumentative structure from the 'Timbertop' summary pamphlet and the vision itself contains a much lengthier and more elaborated justification. The speech itself is the most extended and detailed illustration provided in this book of what I described in Chapter 1 as the core activity of leadership: a leader's attempt to frame meaning for followers. The proposal he outlined was new (not only at Geelong Grammar but in Australia and beyond), bold and financially expensive. More importantly, because it was a dramatic departure from parents' and the old boys' conventional expectations of schooling Darling had to craft his words and choice of symbols very carefully to secure the school community's commitment.

He began by aiming his sights high and made a direct reference to the *Call*, which had been broadcast a month earlier, and said that in every sphere of the nation's life 'we have a right to expect from this School men who will take a lead' (p. 148). It had been part of the tradition of the school for the boys to be told by visitors that they 'were the future leaders of Australia' (p. 148) and Australia was not so strong yet that that leadership could be done without. True to the traditional public school spirit of *noblesse oblige*, Darling intoned that leadership was not a right but a privilege. Now more than ever, he continued, it is (p. 148):

> moral leadership which is required; that is, a refusal to accept the low judgment of the many in matters of right and wrong in conduct, of good and bad in taste, and in the willing recognition of national and social duty. Far from being undemocratic, this is the only way in which democracy can survive. Things being as they are, we can in no way deny or refuse our privileges, but we can and must accept them as responsibilities.

In Australia during the early 1950s, just as in a number of Western countries, there were fears held for the future of democracy in conservative opinion circles because of an alleged threat of communism. A national referendum to ban the Communist Party in Australia had just failed to pass barely three months before Darling's speech. As we shall see shortly, this shift in the climate of opinion began to erode acceptance of the reforms first established by Miss Ross during the more congenial immediate post-war years and strengthened the hands of those of her opponents who sought a return to more orthodox schooling arrangements. Darling's way of dealing with communism in his speech was to reject its status as society's genuine enemy. Instead, the real threat was the spirit of materialism that lay behind it. The educational antidote for these ills was the better delivery of traditional ingredients like the pursuit of knowledge, love of scholarship and a willingness to work together. Yet something was missing from that prescription for, while 'the tightly-packed machine of school organization grips us' and boys emerge from it as 'disciplined, decent and comfortable', they still lack some of 'the most necessary qualities of leadership' (p. 149).

He was convinced, he told his audience, that genuine intellectual and moral courage could only come from experience. Indeed (p. 149):

> [courage] is a habit formed as a result of testing oneself, of learning to master bodily weakness and fear, of stretching tired muscles beyond the temptation of fatigue, of facing intellectual and moral error in oneself, of acknowledging faults and ignorance, of pursuing a line of thought logically to its end however unpleasant, of sticking to one's own ideas of right and wrong regardless of the persecution or the mockery of one's fellows, of loving devotedly, even sacrificially, Honour, Truth, Beauty and Goodness.

To this point, then, as in the 'Timbertop' pamphlet summary, Darling had sought to demonstrate how current school practices were falling short of his noble idealist prescriptions, and that the remedy for rectifying the short-fall could only ever in part be more-of-the-same-done-better. It was at this point in his delivery that he raised an exciting new possibility as the other part of the solution, but he did so very shrewdly and carefully by characterizing it as an extension of the school's long-standing nature and outdoor pursuits. From the point of view of strategic leadership, Darling can be seen as building on the virtues of an existing organizational culture. At this point he mentioned Hahn and the Outward Bound schools: 'our scheme is along these lines; its originality lies in the fact that we are making it part of the ordinary life of an ordinary school' (p. 150).

He then announced the acquisition of a property near the small town of Mansfield, on which a new part of the school known as Timbertop would be built. His intention was that Timbertop would be (p. 150):

> simpler in organisation and administration, freer in life, and as independent as possible of domestic labour. Ordinary school work will be done, and for various reasons we think better done, but outside activities will take their colour from the natural surroundings, and in all things emphasis will be placed upon self-dependence and initiative.

Extensive tree-planting was proposed, along with expeditions in the mountains, first-hand education in biology and 'the pursuit of all those natural pleasures of country life, which urban civilisation is tending to crowd out of our lives' (p. 150). This new branch of the school would be self-supporting, but it was not intended to be a farm (p. 150):

> the main idea is different, and is directed more towards the development of individual self-dependence and initiative and to the spreading amongst all boys of that love of the land which can come only from those who, in some degree, are capable of understanding it.

Darling then clinched all of the high-minded and nuts-and-bolts value claims he had so far made by saying that 'in one glorious hit we really solve in the only possible way' (p. 150) all of the immediate intolerable problems pressing in on the school. Having reached the climax of his appeal to his listeners, he then asked them for a financial commitment and welcomed the guest speaker for the prize-giving that day, Sir Russell Grimwade, a leading Melbourne businessman and public benefactor, whom he hoped would endorse the scheme.

As the first head of Timbertop Darling appointed E.H. Montgomery, a master at Corio since 1941, and his general factotum whenever practical matters needed attention. Until Darling's retirement in 1961 he and Montgomery forged – mainly through correspondence and occasional visits back and forth between the two school sites – a form of dual leadership that might best be described as an odd-couple relationship. Each man shared substantially the same values but they displayed contrasting operational styles and were temperamentally different. Between them they shouldered the burden of building in virgin bushland a thriving educational community in which the 100 or so boys annually acquired invaluable leadership training as part of an experiment of self-governing boy democracy (Gronn, 1999, forthcoming). Meanwhile, a slightly different democratic experiment, this time for both girls and their teachers, was taking place back within the confines of that very urban environment which Darling had decried as ill-conducive to the development of autonomy and self-reliance.

The school as a democracy

Unlike Darling, Dorothy Ross was a progressive educationalist, in the then New Education Fellowship sense of that word. While the judgement of one of her biographers is that she 'became progressive only in a modest way' (Connell, 1993, p. 103), she was by nature 'an anti-authoritarian liberal' (Gardiner, 1993, p. 131). Miss Ross made no secret of her support for the Australian Labor Party, for example, and employed several left-wing women on her staff. In a school with a very large conservative component amongst its parents (Connell, 1993, p. 97):

> it was not to be wondered at, therefore, that with such a staff in such a social environment, the Council was reported to have received letters from parents complaining that the girls were learning subversive political ideas and that a number of staff and the headmistress herself were believed to be communists.

Yet, as the following brief catalogue of her reforms throughout her 16 years as headmistress discloses, Miss Ross proceeded gradually. It became quickly apparent to her staff that she was prepared to consult them painstakingly on matters to do with the running of the school, although in doing so she was really only acting in conformity with an expectation which had grown up under her predecessor, Miss Kathleen Gilman Jones. As chair of the monthly meeting of staff Miss Ross likened her role to that of an orchestra conductor: ' "The orchestra", she explained, "knows a lot better than the conductor how to play an oboe, but the conductor knows the sorts of sounds that he wants to come out of the oboe" ' (Connell, 1983, p. 217). Ross was convinced that if an innovation was to succeed then it had to be accepted widely. This kind of commitment necessitated lengthy deliberation, a source of frustration to far less committed people: ' "Why don't you just say you'll *do* it?" ', a new staff member is reported to have once said, but 'that was not her way' (Epstein, 1981, p. 72, original emphasis). The other virtues of wide consultation were that it facilitated personal development and promoted critical thinking, as Ross later explained (cited in Connell, 1983, p. 218):

> I had to make them [the MCEGGS staff] think below the surface ... I question everything before I do it, I question everything I do myself, I analyse everything I've done after I've done it ... If you can get below the surface of yourself like that, then you can get below the surface of other people. I think it was an attitude of questioning that the staff meetings were really for.

Ross always maintained that the overriding criterion whenever staff meetings made decisions was whether or not the proposal in question was the right one for the girls at that particular time.

She soon introduced other more far-reaching changes to the administrative machinery of the school. As early as her appointment year, 1939, for example, Ross had inaugurated a school advisory committee – the first of a number of significant changes to school organization. Initially this body comprised seven girls and four staff, but was soon expanded to 17. It acted as a forum for school opinion and, in 1941, when a student became its chair, a written constitution gave it the power to appoint secretaries in charge of various school activities as well as the editors of the school magazine, to control sports awards and various other arrangements, to test the feelings of the school on matters nominated by it, and to advise on discipline and matters of general interest. Miss Ross always retained a veto over its actions. 'The subsequent history of self-government at the school was essentially that of the extension of the executive powers of the council and the absorption of the prefect system into it' (Connell, 1983, p. 219). A year later in 1942 the prefects – elected from that year on by all senior school girls, the staff and Miss Ross – were permitted to elect the school captain. There were 20 prefects at MCEGGS and they formed a body known as the Prefects' Executive Committee. Eventually in 1948 the executive and advisory committees coalesced after a vote by the staff, prefects and senior students. A new elected body, the Executive Council of the School, comprised five staff and

25 students, and was presided over by a senior girl. Its jurisdiction covered school uniform, clubs and school committees, tuckshop, cloakroom and school assembly. Ross exercised a veto over matters of finance, religion, health, curriculum and general behaviour (Connell, 1983, p. 220).

Within the confines of a school structured on traditional church governance lines Ross had encouraged about as much self-government for staff and girls as was possible. Interestingly, three decades later in the mid-1970s, when the educational climate was again more receptive to liberal ideals – although the two proposals were not directly related – the Victorian Secondary Teachers' Association (VSTA) adopted as policy the establishment of staff executive committees in state secondary schools. The VSTA's proposal was lampooned by its critics for subverting the managerial prerogative of the principal and reducing her or him to a cipher on a kind of works'-council-style body. Compulsory local administration committees were eventually implemented in 1982 as part of an industrial agreement between the incoming state Labor Government and the VSTA, but with the abolition of that agreement in 1992 by a conservative state coalition government the formation of such consultative bodies has been left entirely to the discretion of principals. Miss Ross justified her radical innovation at the time as an exercise in learning for the staff and the girls (cited in Epstein, 1981, p. 70):

> Such meetings gave pupils a chance to express through a legitimate channel their ideas for the improved running of the school ... It gave opportunities to learn techniques for conducting meetings, to acquire tolerance in reasoned discussion, to learn the unsuspected difficulties often involved in making changes, to respect and value minority opinion – in fact to acquire the art of carrying out an official job in a responsible and creative way.

A former pupil, the noted Australian composer Helen Gifford (1982, pp. 182–3), recalled that the introduction of the school executive 'softened the standard divisions within the school hierarchy', so that 'staff and students were more on a level, and the girls, collectively as well as individually, were expected to be responsible for their own behaviour':

> When I was at MCEGGS there was a complete absence of the repressive atmosphere that could be observed in some of the more conservatively run schools, and so it seemed then all the more extraordinary that the school should be under criticism for its lack of conservatism, and more specifically, for some of Miss Ross's innovations, the external signs of a more liberal concept of education which aimed to lessen the formality of dress and procedure and to discourage the hyper-competitive attitude that invades most areas of school life. Berets had been added to the uniform, and slacks could be worn within the grounds; there were no school prizes other than the valedictory books issued to all girls on leaving school: instead of a prefect system there was an executive council composed of senior girls and staff; and sports day was replaced by 'field day', where the accent was on demonstrated rather than competitive abilities.

Gifford (1982, p. 183) found the vehement opposition which Miss Ross's reforms aroused hard to credit, but even harder to credit was the fact that 'a successor should have decided to change it all back again'.

But change it Miss Ross's successor did. Lack of knowledge of all of the inner workings of MCEGGS at the time make it difficult to know precisely why what has been aptly termed the 'moral order' of a school (Greenfield and Ribbins, 1993, p. 225) shifted so dramatically in the manner and direction that it did after Miss Ross's departure. The stance of the school council in backing Miss Mountain appears to have been decisive. The *Call*, which Darling had been able to invoke to help legitimate his new scheme, symbolized the growing conservative mood of early-1950s Australia, and while the *Call* itself was irrelevant to what happened at MCEGGS to destroy Miss Ross's innovation, the mood of which it was a part was clearly not. It became apparent that the moral order at MCEGGS of which Miss Ross's school self-governance measure formed the centrepiece had not, given the occasional rumblings against her, been a unanimously acclaimed one. Indeed, an MCEGGS historian notes that 'there was more support for Miss Mountain than is generally supposed' (McCarthy, 1993, p. 152) and gives as evidence the 400 or so letters of support for her from parents, old girls and friends of the school. Another historian cites a demographic shift in MCEGGS's enrolments away from the daughters of the professional families who had patronized the school before World War II towards those from business backgrounds. This transition bred increased intolerance for an education which gave less emphasis to 'the business virtues of competition, examinable results, firm direction and clear-cut discipline' (Connell, 1983, p. 216). In the face of such an undercurrent, the appointment of Miss Mountain – whom, ironically, Miss Ross (then in England at the time – 1956), as well as the London interview panel, had recommended – gave the school council the opportunity to 'bring the school back into line', as Archbishop Woods was later quoted as saying (Gardiner, 1993, p. 134).

Consideration of both of these examples of Darling and Ross might suggest that mere exposure to a moral order of values is sufficient to ensure their endorsement and adoption by impressionable young minds. Sometimes it is and that may partly account for the concern of some of the MCEGGS parents. The risk of exposure may also explain why other experiments in educational liberalism within mainstream schooling – such as the one already mentioned which so deeply influenced Darling himself at Repton (Gronn, 1990) and the one with which he had had to deal at Geelong Grammar in 1942–3 (Gronn, 1991) – create headaches for administrators and often founder or are aborted. At other times exposure to particular values, like the attempted inculcation of them, can produce a reaction or counter-revolution against the moral order. These possibilities bring us to the matter of the acquisition of values by aspiring leaders. Exposure and inculcation, along with role modelling and the influence of mentors, suggest *how* one's values might be shaped, and the kind of biographical examination of careers recommended in Chapter 2 provides clues as to *when* that shaping occurs. But exactly *why* leaders adopt the values they do, however, remains a mystery. Sometimes if students of leadership are fortunate enough to have evidence of a leader monitoring phases of her or his journey through life then that is as close as we can ever get to an answer. There is evidence available of a shift in Darling's values framework, just over two decades before he unveiled his plans for Timbertop, and it provides a useful illustrative case of values formation.

A leader's formative odyssey

In the 1920s, when he was a history master at Charterhouse, Darling (1978, p. 96) was also a socialist and an active member of the British Labour Party. In 1929, a year before he took up his appointment as headmaster of Geelong Grammar School, he accepted an invitation to lead a party of 45 English public-schoolboys on a tour of New Zealand. This trip, under the auspices of the School Empire-Tour Committee, was important for Darling because it was his first direct experience of the British Empire. Until then imperialism and imperial bonds had always been things to which he paid lip-service. Yet, during the four months of the tour (January to May, 1929), a subtle but significant shift took place in his outlook. A sequential examination of some of his reflections in his diary alongside the daily newspaper reports of the speeches he was required to make as tour leader discloses the restlessness of his mind (Gronn, 1989).

New Zealand at this time was a predominantly white dominion and almost totally dependent for its livelihood on the export of primary produce. Its economy was extremely vulnerable to world commodity price movements. These had begun to tumble just as Darling's party arrived. Because they were desperate to attract Britishers with financial capital, New Zealanders lavished attention on English public-schoolboy visitors in the hope that they or their fathers might be persuaded either to invest or to settle. From the moment of their arrival, the tour party was lionized by the New Zealand press, and editorials in all of the major city papers commented on its significance. 'Model English gentlemen', 'profound men', 'a Solomon of 17', the obsequiousness ran (Gronn, 1989, p. 53). Darling found this praise and attention lavished on the boys hard to stomach. They were not, he felt in his own mind, the best of what England had to offer, and yet he knew that the public appearances which had to be sustained for the sake of the tour necessarily disguised or papered over all their foibles and idiosyncrasies. Given Darling's cheek-by-jowl knowledge of the party and some of the tensions to which the pressures of touring inevitably gave rise, the ambivalence he felt about the public schools and his leftish sympathies, it is small wonder that such concerns intruded into his diary. He was oppressed by the need to please his hosts but refused to be taken in by all the hero worship of the boys.

The fact of having to cope with the public and private faces of the tour wrought a change in Darling. In speech after speech he felt it incumbent upon him as tour leader to assert the need for a strengthening of the imperial bonds – which, of course, was what the tour was aiming at. Almost as soon as he had spoken, however, his words were staring back at him that same afternoon or the very next morning in the newspapers. They provided a mirror image of his publicly perceived self. The effect on him was that he began to take seriously the words which he had spoken. The first cracks in his anti-imperialism appeared. It was at a war memorial in New Plymouth that the full import of what he was doing on the tour finally hit him. The advance agent who arranged the tour's sightseeing had insisted on wreaths being placed at town cenotaphs in memory of the war dead. The plan was that each time Darling would be required to speak, but he 'strongly objected' (Gronn, 1989, p. 54). Against his better judgement, Darling agreed to deliver just one address and, because it was to be the only one, he worked very hard at it and tried to learn it by heart.

His speech was taken very seriously. At least two newspapers carried the text and the *Otago Daily Times* gave it editorial space, calling it 'a graceful tribute' to New Zealand's fallen. His words achieved the requisite solemnity and it was a worthy panegyric. When Darling read the report of it, he could scarcely believe what he had said, as he reflected later in his diary (Gronn, 1989, p. 54):

> The boys seemed fairly good and I myself was, I think, the only person whom it struck as odd that I ... should be standing in so pompous a fashion, uttering a funeral oration. Often in the tour, I have wanted to laugh at myself, but never more than then, when I should have so completely collapsed to see my brother or my friends amongst the audience .... Yet I was quite sincere in what I said. The model of the English cenotaph standing there by the sea in the Antipodes, and standing for the memorial to those who had died so far from home, for the place that they called Home, did touch me and nothing which I said do I in any way depreciate. It was only odd that I should be the central figure doing this serious thing.

He experienced the same affinity of sentiment and spirit between the two countries at church the next morning when 'listening to the words of the English prayer book' (Gronn, 1989, p. 54). It seemed to him that there may be something to be said for the Empire after all. In short, then, because the circumstances of the tour demanded that he respond in a way he would not otherwise have had to, his previous beliefs began to erode under the pressure of the responsibility and his experience of a new world society.

With the needs of the aspirant leader in mind, the two main case examples in this chapter were chosen with a view to illustrating some of the problems and possibilities inherent in the process of institutionalizing values. As a bare minimum expression of their commitment to a valued standpoint, at some point or points in their careers leaders can expect to be required to articulate or defend what they stand for. Should they happen to be more proactive in relation to their values and educational philosophies, however, as Darling and Ross clearly were, then they will be seeking to win the allegiance of followers' hearts and minds to an existing, reconstructed or desired moral order. Commitment, in either of these two ways, but especially the second, can be personally taxing and costly. Although it was not possible to convey any sense of personal struggle in Darling's and Ross's attempts to bed down their reforms, some indication of the individual consequences of having to be clear about one's commitment as a neophyte leader were to be seen in the example of Darling wrestling earlier on in his career with his personal values (and understanding of himself) amidst the press of circumstances not of his own making and in entirely new surroundings. What is not certain is whether the pursuit and defence of values by educational leaders becomes any easier with experience and age – although, notably, Ross was approaching, and Darling had just turned, 50 years of age when they initiated these major educational reforms. What would be anticipated, however, is that most educational leaders at an equivalent stage in their careers would have a reasonably firm understanding of themselves as persons, a fairly good idea of what they stood for and the directions in which they wanted their schools to go, and also a knowledge of their own personal resources and attributes, and tried-and-true methods on which they could call to achieve their aims. It is this final stylistic component of a leader's make-up which remains to be considered in the next chapter.

CHAPTER 6

The styles of leaders

The third and final batch of questions about an incoming leader which I have presumed will be of interest to her or his new colleagues and subordinates concerns matters of style and approach. These deal with the way in which a leader – particularly if she or he is in an executive or head role – is likely to want to run a school or college, or a major campus, section, unit or department within it. Is this new person going to be someone who offers more of the same, more of what staff in this school are used to? Or, is this person going to be a new broom and bring in an entirely different way of doing things? And, what if she or he does – what effect is that going to have? What, then, is this person's preferred way of operating and how is this going to make a difference in this place?

Most discussions of leadership styles assume that they are relatively fixed ways of behaving which would only ever be important during the incumbency phase of the career leadership framework. One of the few dissenters from that kind of view is the US political scientist and president-watcher James Barber (1977, p. 10, original emphasis) who has argued that styles take root in early adulthood. For Barber it was this period in the lives of each of the men who became US presidents in which – on the evidence in most biographies of their lives – 'the young man found himself':

> I call it his first independent political success. It was then he moved beyond the detailed guidance of his family; then his self-esteem was dramatically boosted; then he came forth as a person to be reckoned with by other people. The *way* he did that is profoundly important to him. Typically he grasps that style and hangs onto it. Much later, coming into the Presidency, something in him remembers this earlier victory and re-emphasizes the style that made it happen.

Thus, the way in which the commander-in-chief in the Oval Office is likely to behave has been prefigured in the first glimmerings of style during this crucial formative period. A future incumbent's first political success, therefore, is held to be a predictor of his future behaviour in the White House (Barber, 1977, p. 99). In the career leadership model I have allowed for this kind of possibility as regards educational leaders, but the furthest that I was prepared to go in Barber's direction was to suggest that the mere rudiments of a later working style might become manifest during accession. I make no claims about the predictive value of early-discovered ways of doing things, although that is not to say that when an aspirant leader becomes a candidate for selection, selectors would be averse to making those kinds of connections. The main reason I link style to the accession stage of a career is that if someone has aspirations to lead and they begin to think of themselves in candidate terms, then they are very likely to begin pondering their preferred way of doing things.

On the other hand, critics who take a more deterministic view of human agency are likely to be dismissive of Barber's entire predictive enterprise and to be sceptical about any account of the activities of organizations which accords key individuals so much untrammelled volition. In short, individual style would make precious little, if any, difference to the attainment of educational outcomes. That, however, is not what the staff at MCEGGS thought while they waited for Miss Mountain to declare her hand (Gardiner, 1993, p. 129):

> They waited because they assumed that any newcomer with D.J. [Ross]'s recommendation was bound to share her educational philosophy; they waited because they were fair-minded enough to allow a new headmistress time to find her feet, to make mistakes, and, as was her prerogative, to make some changes; they waited because they were extremely busy with their teaching and pastoral duties.

In the end they gave up waiting because attributes of Miss Mountain's style had begun to grate on them (Gardiner, 1993, pp. 129–30):

> Numerous small incidents began to rankle. They found the headmistress unapproachable; attempts to talk with her, even by senior form and subject mistresses were usually rebuffed; the girls, too, found the previously always-open door of the head's study now shut. Attempts at social familiarisation were brushed aside or neglected; the head no longer mingled informally at morning and afternoon tea, or at lunch time in the common-room. On the rare occasions when a formal interview was granted, the new headmistress heard staff advice, made no comment, and often took a different course of action.

It is not known what the equivalent of Barber's notion of first political success might have been in Miss Mountain's case – which, if his argument is valid, might have helped predict this pattern of aloofness – except that she is known to have harboured 'a long-held ambition to become a headmistress' (McCarthy, 1993, pp. 147–8). What is certain, however, is that the MCEGGS mistresses believed that the style of Miss Ross's successor was calculated to undermine the Ross philosophy and approach, and that outcome for them was anathema.

Without unduly prolonging consideration of the MCEGGS case the transition from Miss Ross to Miss Mountain touches on a number of important style-related issues to do with roles and the performance of roles by particular role incumbents. These matters are not peculiar to MCEGGS but go to the heart of a series of difficulties invariably experienced during role turnover and replacement and include the following questions: Does style matter? What makes it possible for what is, ostensibly, the same role to be performed quite differently by two successive incumbents? Are there particular attributes and properties, for example, which different individuals bring to an incumbency that might account for differential role performance? And is there any evidence that these differences in performance styles make a difference to organizational outcomes? The realist stance taken in this chapter in respect of the relationship between the individual and the role she or he occupies has been well summarized by Margaret Archer (1995, p. 187, original emphasis):

> A person occupying a particular role acquires vested interests with it and is both constrained and enabled by its 'dos and don'ts' in conjunction with the penalties and promotions which encourage compliance. Yet these are not determinants, because there is always leeway for interpretation, especially given that they are only partial in their coverage and clarity. Even the small print of my university contract is silent on whether I can offer my students a drink or my political opinions. Thus, far from roles being fully scripted and their occupants as comprehensively programmed robots, it seems more useful to think of people *personifying* them in different ways, thus making [in this example] for different lecturers.

In this realist perspective both roles and the personal properties incumbents bring to their performance of roles are emergent – i.e. they permit the realization of divergent (but not unlimited) possibilities through time – and are revealed empirically in the interplay between self and role.

This chapter, then, addresses the problem of explaining 'different "performances" of the same role and how this simultaneously leads both to role re-definition and personal development' (Archer, 1995, p. 186). I begin by defining style and I then review a range of different style types constituted by a variety of personal attributes and properties, and the effects of dominant, upper-echelon leadership styles. Finally, I review some of the normative possibilities currently being propounded by advocates of style types devised in response to the pressures of globalization.

Styles and roles

The overwhelming bulk of the current knowledge of style in the field of leadership has originated from two major sources: president-watching and clinically derived, psycho-dynamic studies of organizational executives. Developments in both these traditions are considered in this and the following section. The clearest rationale for the significance of US presidential styles has been given by Barber (1974, p. 450, original emphasis):

> I think presidents are important mainly because of the effects they have on the actual human beings who make up polities ... Presidents in my scheme of values are overwhelmingly more important as political forces than as individuals. Presidents are *dangerous*: they can and do hurt people, just as they can and do contribute to social progress.

That kind of reasoning led Barber (1974, p. 456) to summarize the focus of his research into the character and style of US presidents as: 'How and why did they do what they did to people?'. One of the main methodological problems which Davies (1972, p. 133) believed would frustrate first-hand research into styles was obtaining direct, on-the-hoof access to leaders – i.e. of 'establishing sufficiently sensitive students at posts where they might make the sort of observations required'. This difficulty was overcome to some extent by Neustadt (1961), a pioneering president-watcher, who had worked closely with President Truman as a member of his staff, and was later a consultant to President Kennedy.

In *Presidential Power*, Neustadt (1961) contoured the different political styles of three US presidents – Roosevelt, Truman and Eisenhower – to which he later added a cameo of Kennedy (Neustadt, 1964). The contrast between the styles of these three men was dramatic – even allowing for the differing external circumstances surrounding their incumbencies. Roosevelt, president from 1932 to 1945, for example, was distinctive in his highly competitive management of information (Neustadt, 1961, p. 150, original emphases):

> 'He would call you in,' one of his aides once told me, 'and he'd ask you to get the story on some complicated business, and you'd come back after a couple of days hard labor and present the juicy morsel you'd uncovered under a stone somewhere, and *then* you'd find out he knew all about it, along with something else you *didn't* know. Where he got his information from he wouldn't mention, usually, but after he had done this to you once or twice you got damn careful about your information.'

Neustadt's (1961, p. 151) explanation for Roosevelt's resort to competing sources and jurisdictions was that it was his formula for putting pressure on himself and for ensuring that his subordinates pushed choices up to him which they could not make themselves. 'It also made them advertise their punches; their quarrels provided him not only heat but information. Administrative competition gave him two rewards. He got the choices and due notice, both'. Eisenhower, the former Supreme Allied Commander, by contrast, was 'a sort of Roosevelt in reverse' (Neustadt, 1961, p. 156), a man who wanted to be president, not so much for personal power but as a hero with a reputation to crown and as a victor who sought national unity.

Styles are a matter of interpretation, no matter what the sphere or level of leadership in question, and later observers have challenged Neustadt's image of the fatherly Eisenhower. Lerner (1985, p. 39), for example, notes of Eisenhower that he was:

> a leader of useful contradictions. He seemed unambitious, yet he twice captured the presidency. He seemed above politics, yet his adversaries knew him as a subtle manoeuvrer and a master of indirection. Preoccupied with prestige and credibility, he hoarded his popularity, declining to spend it even for a just cause. The result was what one historian called a 'hidden-hand presidency.' Behind a protective screen, Eisenhower called the plays, laid out the strategy, and enjoyed the gap between his seeming and actual roles in human events.

Different interpretations of leaders are no doubt accounted for in part by the different vantage points from which assessments are made and by new evidence which comes to light. For this latter reason Greenstein (1983, p. 162) has also taken issue with Neustadt's portrayal of Eisenhower:

> in the mid-1970s presidential library archives yielded evidence that Eisenhower's advising system was neither formalistic nor collegial but rather made systematic, coordinated use of both modes.

Ronald Reagan's presidential style has also been the subject of ongoing debate. Biggart (1981, p. 295), for example, claims that, when he was Governor of California, Reagan 'reigned but did not rule over government' and delegated to an extent rarely seen in politics. This strategy quickly became the received wisdom of Reagan's presidency, yet Greenstein (1983, p. 167) insists that Reagan was a very emotionally secure individual who fostered a very strong sense of collegiality amongst his staff.

These conflicting but fascinating and incisive perceptions of the styles of very powerful office-holders are interesting for a host of reasons, yet they beg at least two important methodological points which apply not just in the case of presidents but to any other form of leader-watching. The first key question is: What, in the observation of leaders, is the appropriate unit of analysis? As I suggested in Chapter 1, the traditional working assumption made by commentators is to treat the stand-alone individual leader as the principal object of analysis. One instance in which this was clearly inappropriate was provided in the last chapter – the interdependence of Darling and Montgomery as a leadership couple in endeavouring to implement Timbertop. Another (in the psycho-dynamic tradition considered in the next section) is the painstaking two-year field study by Hodgson *et al.* (1965) of the executive role constellation formed by three US medical executives, Cadman, Suprin and Asche. The recent emergence of the study of so-called top groups – senior management teams, upper echelons and strategic elites (see Pettigrew, 1992) – instead of just top individuals, is a belated recognition that leaders are rarely solo performers. What, then, is the justification for placing so much emphasis on the styles of individual executives like US presidents instead of on collective entities such as 'the Clinton administration', for example, which comprise veritable armies of advisers, assistants, spokeswomen and -men, consultants and minders? Barber's justification was that, despite the division of powers under the US constitution, presidents are very powerful individuals who are located at the end of a long chain of decision-making and advice, and in that capacity give or withhold the final sanction for decisions. Moreover, during a four-year incumbency a president's entire administration would inevitably take on the character desired by the particular individual at its apex because his staff (desirous, no doubt, of the retention of their jobs) are appointed to gear their advice to his expectations.

Supposing it is conceded that the appropriate unit of analysis is the individual leader, the second key question to do with style which is still begged by the tradition of president-watching concerns what I term a leader's zone of discretion. This idea, following the lead given by Hambrick and Finkelstein (1987, p. 371, original emphasis), may be defined as the extent and scope of a leader's capacity to define, and not merely choose from, the range of opportunities for action confronting them, within the particular demands and constraints of their roles. Thus, in my terms, presidents are accorded a wide zone of potential discretion by their watchers in the belief that their personal styles not only find expression but carry important consequences. Yet to properly understand the role performance of organizational leaders, and the extent of the possible causal effects attributable to their actions, we need to be clear about the relationship between style and zone of discretion. Such clarification is crucial for those contemplating leadership roles for the very first time if they are to make informed and accurate appraisals of possible styles they may embody and if they are to form realistic expectations of their own potential for achieving desired outcomes. After all, the siren call of the traditional archetypes of greatness and heroism considered earlier – and of some of the prototypical models and styles currently in popular favour – is that leadership is a sphere of virtually unlimited possibility for making a difference as an individual.

What, then, is meant by a leadership style? The idea of style concerns the incursion of the personal attributes of a role incumbent into the enactment of her or his role. For Davies (1972, p. 118) there are two perspectives from which to understand an administrative or leadership workstyle: style *of* work and style *in* work. Style of work emphasizes the agency of individual leaders and refers to 'a person's characteristic way of handling given tasks' or, expressed in the vernacular, her or his distinctive way of going about things. In an aside Davies suggests that 'we encounter a fringe of it subjectively from time to time in a realisation, usually rather unpleasant, of being unable to change what seems to be the one way we can do certain parts of our work'. Presumably, in relation to the other parts of our work we do have options and can change our ways because of our capacity to learn. This sense of style suggests that part of a leader's zone of discretion is defined *by*, rather then solely *for*, her or him. Some choice in their approach to leadership is based on a range of personal characteristics (e.g. cognition, affect and previous experience). Davies's notion of style in work, on the other hand, focuses on the properties of the task to be performed, rather than on those of the performer, and refers to 'that part of the way a job is done which is not standard, which does not go without saying'. For the reasons already given this chapter concentrates on styles of work, but the notion of style in work has a bearing on Archer's point about the leeway for role interpretation and indicates that a second sense of discretion concerns the degree of freedom of choice inherent in a task. With most administrative roles, for example, an ambit of discretion is usually available for two main reasons. First, role descriptions purport to provide a list of duties to be performed yet – as with the earlier example of Archer's drinks and political opinions – they also leave a number of things unsaid. Sometimes this is deliberate. Second, apart from any strictures about broadly unethical or unacceptable conduct, duty statements rarely prescribe the fine detail of the means by which it is intended that work responsibilities will be performed. Yet it is precisely these aspects of role task definition which permit variations in styles of role performance.

Apart from the ambit of discretion inherent in the task and the discretionary characteristics of the incumbent, the third factor determining a leader's zone of discretion is a range of contextual elements, one of which is the strength of follower expectations. For some commentators who attach very little significance to the expression of individual differences in role performance (e.g. Jaques and Clement, 1995) the idea that followers' perceptions might play a part in shaping a role is abhorrent. Nonetheless, Constance de Roche's (1994) two case studies of General and St Martha's – two hospital-based nursing schools in Nova Scotia, Canada – illustrate how it is that, when leaders' perceptions and followers' expectations are aligned, the same role can be performed by two individuals in dramatically different ways. General and St Martha's were each part of 'equivalent hospital bureaucracies' (de Roche, 1994, p. 212), yet the differences in the styles of their two female directors and the work cultures in each school could not have been greater. Caroline Manley at General displayed a working style consistent with her espoused philosophy of care, as one informant commented (cited in de Roche, 1994, p. 214):

> [Caroline] is exceptional. She doesn't take a lot of credit for her abilities. She's a terrific, caring person. It comes through in everything she does. She's very democratic. She expects people to be professional, to make decisions. She gives us credit for being professional people who can make decisions … She's exceptional in making people feel valued. She has high expectations, mind you, but you're up there doing for her because you want to.

Diane Parsons, on the other hand, 'varied markedly from her counterpart', for 'order and control aptly summarize the principles by which St Martha's was governed': ' "That's the way it should be" ', Diane was reported as saying, ' "decisions from the top" ' (de Roche, 1994, p. 215). One staff member confessed to de Roche that the director was:

> very autocratic, that's a good word to describe her. She loves to have power. Everyone of us are intimidated by her. I told myself I wasn't going to be, but I am.

Parsons was even known to enter the staff room and look at a nursing instructor and say: ' "You, see you in my office" ' (de Roche, 1994, p. 216).

This idea of a zone of discretion can be seen as the obverse or flipside of Barnard's (1982 [1938], pp. 168–9) classic notion of a zone of indifference which described organization members' willingness to accept a superior's actions as legitimate and to obey without question. Jaques and Clement (1995, pp. 97–9) see discretion solely in terms of time-span, but discretion is a socio-politically grounded phenomenon in organizations. That is, it does not come readily defined and leaders have to search for its limits by probing for the bounds of their followers' tolerance or by trying to determine how far they can encroach into their comfort zones. Inevitably, on some issues, followers will dig their heels in. Thus, the scope and extent of a leader's zone of discretion is usually ill-defined and uncertain but is likely to become known by being honoured in the breach when various subordinates and vested interests suddenly cease to be indifferent to a leader's actions (Hambrick and Finkelstein, 1987, p. 375):

> It is in the manager's own loss of influence that the acid test of discretion may exist, because generally, when a manager exceeds his or her discretionary bounds, a major loss of influence occurs – removal, demotion, creation of board watchdog committees and so on.

A zone of discretion, then, is a domain in which leaders' preferred styles find expression. Discretion is always contingent and is determined by the relative strength and combination of the variety of personal, task, and contextual factors prevailing at particular points in time. In each of these three categories there are numerous elements which can shape discretion (see Hambrick and Finkelstein, 1987, p. 379). From the multiple combinations of these contingent elements emerges a universe of possible style types, some of the better-known examples of which I know consider in more detail.

Individual and organizational styles

For explanatory purposes I have classified the following examples into two broad style groups: functional and dysfunctional. I am aware, having done so, that in some quarters during the 1980s, as the battle between the proponents of competing paradigms of organizations rolled on, words like functional and dysfunctional fell from grace for many commentators. Indeed, so ill-chosen did functionalism become that to some eyes it was rivalled only by positivism in the race for bogeyman status. With the emergence of relativist epistemologies in the 1980s and 1990s the litmus test for the use of such words has become something like: 'Functional or dysfunctional for whom?' Generally it is presumed that the use of functional signals the existence of latent sets of competing interests. In this discussion functional and dysfunctional are taken to mean, respectively, styles which have been shown, empirically or clinically, to have been broadly benign, on the one hand, or detrimental in their consequences, on the other, to both the leaders manifesting them and the followers having to endure them. Thus, to take a literary example, only the most perverse of readers can come away from the text of Herman Wouk's *The Caine Mutiny* and not concede that the style of the paranoid Captain Queeg was clearly dysfunctional for himself and his crew, especially in respect of their safety, morale and tactics when under enemy fire.

The Queeg case raises the question of whether one is justified in referring to the existence of an organizational or systemic style, as opposed to an aggregate of individual styles. Based on their extensive clinical, consultancy and research work in the corporate sector, Kets de Vries and Miller (1984, pp. 18–24) in *The Neurotic Organization* suggested five conditions – that transpose readily to human service areas like education – which account for a greater likelihood of a dominant individual style embedding itself across a significant proportion of an organization's activities and operations (and see Hambrick and Mason, 1984):

- the strong personality of the leader;
- the centralization of power and decision-making processes;
- the longevity or founder status of CEOs (or their equivalents);
- the degree of synchronicity between the recruitment and selection of personnel and a dominant coalition's values (and the reinforcement of sympathetic outlooks in promotion and reward mechanisms); and,
- legitimating myths, legends and organizational stories.

To this list may be added two more: a role description which confers wide, even sweeping, powers on a particular incumbent and a sympathetic climate of follower expectations. This expanded list of seven conditions would more than justify the concentrated focus of president-watchers on the activities of incumbents of the White House.

The examples that follow by no means exhaust the entire range of possible leader styles. As with adherence to values, few watertight causal reasons can explain why particular individuals develop the leadership styles which they do. The standard modes for the diffusion of styles are much the same as for values: first-hand observations of colleagues, superiors and mentors who embody them; second-hand knowledge of them through textbooks, case histories, biographies, and other print and visual media; and hearsay verbal reports, stories, folklore, gossip and mythology. Nor are the examples discussed with any intention of recommending them as desirable models for emulation by aspiring leaders. Rather, that purpose is furthered admirably by the vast promotional literature of training and development programmes which recommends various normative and desired approaches to leadership. Barber may have been right about the importance of a first-time political success for presidents as a style predictor, but the experience of most leaders is probably that styles evolve randomly through a combination of trial-and-error, hunt-and-peck and two-steps-forward-one-back experimentation until finally they become comfortable with something that seems to work for them. To the extent that styles are learned by systematic reflection on experience then the advantage of the following cases is that they are all grounded in real-world contexts in which their effects have been publicly tested.

Functional styles

The pioneering study in the psycho-dynamic tradition of leader-watching is Hodgson *et al.*'s (1965) *The Executive Role Constellation*. Scholars in this approach to styles have tended to focus on the character structure of organizational executives and highlighted what is known as the inner theatre of the mind: i.e. internal personal psychological conflicts and the ways in which these intrude into the performance of role tasks. In elucidating these character struggles, studies have drawn extensively on Freudian and object-relations psychoanalytic theories. Hodgson *et al.*'s idea of a constellation denoted an upper-echelon management group in which a division of labour operated both in respect of the formal managerial work performed and the emotional needs of the three men concerned, Drs Cadman, Suprin and Asche. Each man performed a dual role of administrator and psychiatrist, and was responsible for his own specialized task area in the clinic, the Memorial Psychiatric Institute (MPI). While each of them performed these tasks differently, their individual approaches were found to complement and balance one another. The similarity between this triad and the familistic one of father, mother and uncle was 'unmistakable' (Hodgson *et al.*, 1965, p. 482) and the role types embodied by Suprin, Cadman and Asche were, respectively, paternal-assertive, maternal-nurturant and fraternal-permissive.

The documentation of each man's role performance in *The Executive Role Constellation* is extensive and includes their self-concept and identity, their values, their own individual interpersonal styles, their one-on-one relations with each other and their complementary relations and transactions as constellation members. Moreover, the study documents each man's perceptions of the other constellation members and the perceptions which their subordinates had of them, and analyses extensively detailed slices of their interpersonal and meeting interactions using samples of spoken dialogue. Briefly, Suprin – the superintendent – was a no-nonsense, direct and open administrator, and was perceived frequently as being blunt to the point of brutality, even with patients. In his interpersonal dealings, by contrast, Cadman – the clinical director – tended to identify with the suffering, the grief-stricken, the sad, the lonely and the disappointed. Asche – the assistant superintendent – finally, was more like the charismatic teacher, John Keating, in the film *Dead Poets Society*: enthusiastic, excited, creative, exhilarating to be with and physically demonstrative. Davies's (1972, p. 132) comment that the portraits of the three men in this evolving relationship 'are simply the fullest and most acute clinical studies of administrators-at-work we have' is still the case more than 30 years after the publication of the *Constellation*.

One of the great strengths of the *Constellation* study is its emphasis on role complementarity, a phenomenon which has been investigated to a limited extent in instances of leadership couples. Sometimes a couple's two-step dance-style pairing can be disabling, as in the bickering relationship between the passive, sullen and inept US corporation vice-president, Al, and Sarah, his overbearing and punitive superior (Krantz, 1989). In relationships like theirs, it is as if the twosome creates 'unconscious [but perverse] agreements in order to maintain mutual misperceptions as a defence against recognizing the underlying problems, conflicts or differences' (Krantz, 1989, p. 167). In a suburban high school in Melbourne, on the other hand, the dyad formed by Prinn and Deprinn – the principal and her male deputy – was found to be an entirely complementary one with Prinn behaving in a very person-centred manner and Deprinn being highly task-focused. Their close working relationship had developed against the backdrop of a climate of suspicion fostered by Prinn's predecessor. The reciprocal understanding between them was evident in the way in which the two of them reflected on the revised managerial flow-chart (Gronn, 1986c, p. 33):

> Originally we had a little separate box for the deputy-principal. She didn't like it that way and she wanted them put together ... that was quite significant.

True, Prinn noted: 'When I'm hit by the [proverbial] bus Deprinn should be able to understand and take over completely.' She had also been keen during a recent prolonged absence that Deprinn should be referred to as the principal, rather than as the acting principal, of the school.

Like Prinn, Mandire, the managing director of a Melbourne consultancy firm, had also succeeded a predecessor who was thought by staff to be ill-fitted for the role. Aloof, sarcastic, ageing, hierarchical and distant was the description of the previous incumbent provided by Admiss, Mandire's personal assistant, and yet teamwork was essential, given that most of the firm's tendering work involved assembling cross-functional task forces to collaborate on developmental projects. Mandire, however, with his 'Okay team!' catchcry, embodied the requisite style. His leadership exemplified Kaplan's (1990b) expansive type executive: focused, productive, success- and achievement-oriented, standards-driven and forceful. Moreover, Mandire was an extrovert with a good sense of humour who succeeded in fostering a strong atmosphere of camaraderie and banter in the firm's project teams (Gronn, 1986c, p. 36). In a third example, a private Melbourne charitable agency, a relationship paralleling the familial archetype at MPI existed between Cheefex, the chief executive, and Deppex, his deputy. Their dyadic relationship comprised a tough–tender blending of personalities. Cheefex was a self-confessed perfectionist in his battle for scarce welfare dollars and a man who maintained a controlled distance from the social workers on his staff. For his part Deppex commented that his superior 'provides a lot of instrumental functioning and I provide a lot more of the expressive'. Indeed, 'I think that's the reason he employed me ... if he wanted to play the public arena then he needed somebody else to keep the ... domestic scene under control' (Gronn, 1986c, p. 38).

These latter examples reflect the gradual movement away by commentators during the 1980s from their exclusive preoccupation with styles evident in commercial or political settings (an exception being the MPI study). Ramamurti's (1987) analysis of leadership in state-owned enterprises (SOEs), for example, was indicative of a growing interest in the restructuring of public-sector agencies along entrepreneurial lines. For the first time in that decade public-sector executives began to experience considerable lat-itude and flexibility in their roles. Ramamurti (1987) found four sets of typical style responses to these changed environmental conditions: first, a conventional low-profile, play-it-safe, controversy-minimizing cautiousness – best typified, perhaps, by Sir Humphrey Appleby in the television series *Yes Minister*; second, a market-oriented, financially autonomous, upbeat, make-a-buck, commercial-good maximizer; third, a wheeling-and-dealing, favour-currying, political-gameswoman or -gamesman; and fourth, a public-interest-oriented, politically neutral statesmanlike figure. Another increasingly commercialized sphere over the last decade or so has been academe, and Ralston (1990) discovered an emerging organizational games-man type in a case study of an Australian university which she labelled an academic entrepreneur (AE). This person was a senior academic in charge of a free-standing centre or administrative unit known as Intrachange, which cut across conventional faculty and departmental structures, who pioneered a previously unheard-of boosterish, can-do style of academic leadership. Ralston's (1990, p. 333) period of entrepreneur-watching disclosed AE to be a hard-driving, organizational mission-oriented evangelist with boundless energy; an 'up-front man' immersed in a multitude of projects, 'mingling with men of affairs, raising grants, negotiating with large companies, and gaining commitment from others to follow him'.

Yet not everything in AE's Intrachange garden was rosy for, like other individuals in the entrepreneurial mould, he lacked any managerial system and chaos tended to follow in his wake: 'I'm going crazy', a bewildered staff member once complained, just before AE departed on an overseas flight, and who then exclaimed upon his return: 'He's going to have a heart attack. How many things can one person do at once?' (Ralston, 1990, p. 331). Clearly, then, there was a downside to AE's seemingly endless reserves of energy and enthusiasm, and these features were thought to be dysfunctional, which suggests that all styles are seen to have their pluses and minuses, and that an overall distinction between wholly functional or dysfunctional styles may be difficult to sustain. On the other hand, if the line to be drawn between the positive and negative consequences of styles is a fine one, then the cases which follow fall mainly on the negative side of it.

Dysfunctional styles

Kets de Vries and Miller (1984) studied organizational leadership in ailing firms in which there was a concentration of power in the hands of leaders whose styles manifested neurotic personality symptoms. This meant that an individual executive's character traits impaired her or his own capacity to make effective judgements, their reasoning capacity and their ability to attend to reality, and were found to contribute significantly to the poor performance of the organizations for which they were responsible. Kets de Vries and Miller distinguished five typically defective style types: dramatic, depressive, schizoid, paranoid and compulsive. Some of these clinical terms (e.g. paranoid) have begun to slip into common usage during the last decade or so.

Taking each type in turn, the word dramatic is a euphemism for the recently emerging phenomenon of narcissism already discussed in Chapter 4. In dramatic firms the pace of work is frenetic, and the dominant decision-making style tends to be hyperactive, impulsive and non-reflective. Projects and ventures often turn out to be self-serving vehicles for the expression of the leader or leadership group's grandiosity. Ken Lane of Lane Corporation, for example, had purchased a limping fire equipment manufacturing company and, in the familiar entrepreneurial jargon, turned-it-around by a series of acquisitions, mergers and the streamlining of various product lines. Eventually Lane sat at the head of a sprawling but complex commercial conglomerate yet he resisted all attempts to rationalize and regularize its operations. Instead (Kets de Vries and Miller, 1984, p. 34, original emphases):

> he continued to make all the key decisions himself. It was *his* company and *his* strategy, so he would take the credit for its achievements.

As Lane made more and more off-the-cuff decisions, his mistakes increased and company profits fell. Lane's creditors finally managed to eject him but were forced to sell off many of the firm's assets to secure their investments. An organization and its leadership which can be characterized as depressive, by contrast, tends to be listless, insular, lacking in purpose and inert. Its preference is to rely on well-tested, tried-and-true bureaucratic routines. There is a leadership vacuum and pessimism is pervasive. In a world of turbulent environments the depressive organization is analogous to a dinosaur or a beached whale: incapable of helping itself. Roderick Kent, the head of a dairy company, was typical: a don't-rock-the-boat mentality, fastidious with trivial details and a man longing for the simple life.

Schizoid organizations also suffer from leadership vacuums, except that in the face of indecisiveness and withdrawal effective leadership passes to a second layer or level of lieutenants who compete for the ear of the chief. The result is 'a fertile breeding ground for opportunists who are adept at catering to the leader's insecurities' (Kets de Vries and Miller, 1984, p. 39), so that envy, favouritism and politicking tend to be rife. At best there is incremental change. Selma Gitnick, head of the Cornish Corporation, a ladies' apparel manufacturer, was a case in point. The recent victim of a family tragedy, Gitnick is described by Kets de Vries and Miller (1984, p. 40) – in a way that echoes some of the complaints levelled by her critics against Miss Mountain – as someone who 'rarely left her office or had other managers visit her there. Instead, everything was done through written memos.'

Paranoid, the third type, denotes suspicion. This translates, in leadership terms, into an obsession with control, and with the constant sifting of and scanning for information. Threats, wariness, competitive challenges, anxiety and fear tend to preoccupy the mind of the paranoid leader. Distrust breeds cautiousness and a reactive, rather than a proactive, leadership stance is the result. Closely related to paranoia is the compulsive style. Here enormous reserves of energy tend to be expended in trying to nail down every detail, to anticipate every conceivable contingency and to pre-programme organizational operations. Once again there are sophisticated controls in place along with elaborate regulations, rules and procedures. Kets de Vries and Miller's (1984, p. 31) example here is David Richardson, the engineer-founder of the Minutiae Corporation, a roller-bearing manufacturer. Richardson's quality controls were extremely strict and elaborate, and for a long time Minutiae's product was top class. In the face of increased competitiveness, however, Richardson refused to adapt to new materials and technology. His older product became too expensive and Minutiae finished up losing significant profit and market share.

Recently, Kets de Vries (1989c) has documented another style type: the organizational alexithymic. This type is a rather emotionally impoverished individual who is an updated version of the rather faceless, dispassionate, man-in-the-grey-flannel-suit functionary bemoaned by Whyte in *The Organization Man*. Alexithymia denotes an inner emotional void or an inability to find words for moods. Alexithymics are extraordinarily detached and indifferent to the needs of others. They are believed to lack the usual internal reference points, in the form of fantasies or dreams, and use other people as external benchmarks or mirrors to generate the symbols of which they themselves are bereft (Kets de Vries, 1989c, p. 1085):

> Whatever the exact percentage of alexithymics in the general population may be, this construct is used to describe individuals with an extreme reality-based cognitive style, an impoverished fantasy life, a paucity of inner emotional experiences, a tendency to engage in stereotypical interpersonal behavior, and a speech pattern characterized by endless, trivial, repetitive details. This last characteristic seems to be the outcome of the need to find some kind of foothold in the external world due to the difficulty these people experience internally in describing what they feel. Whatever feelings they may have tend to be of a vague, diffuse nature.

Impersonal details count above all else for alexithymics – along with abstractions, inanimate objects and systems of varying kinds – who lack spontaneity and whose interpersonal contacts are mechanical. Alexithymic executives, according to Kets de Vries (1989c, p. 1091), are rather wooden people who need 'to discover or re-discover the ability to "play", learn how to use humour and how to engage in flights of fancy'. A good example might be Millie, one of the young lawyers in the English television series, *This Life*.

If commentators on styles are agreed about one thing then it is that there is no one approach to leading which qualifies as a style for all seasons. In fact virtually every leadership style has its day. From time to time, therefore, either as the outcome of research or as a response to changed macro-level environmental circumstances which leaders have to address, new approaches to role performance emerge. These often begin life as new types or models or, more flimsily, as rudimentary impressionistic tendencies observed by somebody, somewhere but which soon metamorphose into a sturdier conception for everyday application of a more desirable way of doing things. Three currently popular examples are charismatic, transformational and connective leadership.

Styles to suit the mood of the times

Charisma, as the discussion in Chapter 1 suggested, originated with the German scholar Max Weber, for whom it was a foundation for authority grounded in the person of a leader. As was also suggested, Weber stipulated that charisma was a quality attributed to leaders by followers and only in that highly contingent sense could it be thought of as a property which leaders possessed. Since Weber, charisma has come to mean many things to many people – inspiration, spell-binding and captivating oratory, infectiousness, a sense of being on fire, being uplifted, transported to a new realm, magnetized, transfixed and so on. Until about the late 1970s, however, charisma was a phenomenon confined to the margins of political and organizational analysis, mainly because the credentials of those leaders believed to exemplify it – principally European dictators of the inter-war period and early post-colonial nationalist movement leaders – were thought to be dubious. An important publication by House (1977), which suggested that the effects of charisma could be measured, proved instrumental in removing charisma's rather shadowy image. At last, it seemed, the connection between charisma and leadership in organizations had been made. Some commentators (e.g. Schein, 1992, p. 229) now view charisma as the vital ingredient in communicating an organizational leader's values to followers. Indeed, because of the magnitude of the follower effects listed above, charismatic leaders are often spoken of by their followers and by proponents of charismatic styles as heroic or great in stature. In this way, charisma has come to serve as a proxy for the two age-old and time-honoured prototypes of leaders.

The same proxy status applies to Bass's (1985) model of transformational leadership. Indeed, charismatic and transformational leadership bear a particularly close relationship to one another and some commentators use them interchangeably. Four criteria distinguish transformational leaders. Known as the four Is they are: inspirational leadership, individualized consideration, intellectual stimulation and idealized influence. The promise of transformational leadership for its proponents is that it will assist organizational leaders to add value and to secure peak performance from their subordinates. The antecedents of transformational leadership differ from those of charismatic leadership and stem from Bass's transposition of the first of two types of leaders originally distinguished by Burns (1978), transforming and transactional leaders, into transform*ational*, in keeping with the scope of the changes thought to be desired in the new world order of organizations. In this borrowing Bass sacrificed the notion of ethical uplift which was central to Burns's idea of transforming leadership – unlike Jill Graham (1991), who retained it as the core of her model of the servant leader. The overlap (and confusion) between charismatic and transformational leadership results from the inclusion of charisma as one of the four Is in some versions of Bass's model. These two popular styles of leadership come together in an important longitudinal study of a female school superintendent in Mid-west, a US school district, conducted by Nancy Roberts (1985).

Inspired like many of her contemporaries by precisely the same need for 'a special kind of leadership in today's society to revitalize our institutions and organizations', Roberts (1985, p. 1023) tried to broaden the understanding of Burns's transforming type by concentrating on 'the major structures and contextual elements of transforming leadership' as well as on the person of the leader. What circumstances gave rise to transforming leadership?, Roberts (1985, p. 1024) enquired. What form did it take and how was it sustained over time? Mid-west – a largely middle-class, mixed suburban–rural district of 13,000 students in 10 elementary, three middle and two high schools – was undergoing a crisis of contraction, caused by a dramatic loss of revenue to the state, resulting in a 10 per cent cut-back in the district's budget. Barely six months in office, the new superintendent immediately launched a highly innovative approach to crisis management (Roberts, 1985, p. 1027):

> Rather than rely on additional levies to compensate for the loss of revenues (one had recently been passed), or allow retrenchment to undermine morale and promote adversarial relations between teachers and administrators, schools and the communities they served, she instituted a program to revitalize the district. Her goal was not only to survive the budgetary crisis, but to prepare people for the educational challenges in the future.

Measures implemented included a new statement of mission and a vision, a temporary restructure and the introduction of a participatory management process.

For about five months, budget preparation meetings were held in public forums all over the school district. These involved a plethora of task forces of teachers, administrators, pupils and citizens, all of whom tried to frame a united response to a reduction of $2.4m in as painless a way as possible. The superintendent's strategy of galvanizing support through 'open yet structured participation' was successful and the school board adopted her proposed measures. Budget reductions were made 'without acrimonious debate', for which teachers awarded the superintendent with a standing ovation, 'despite the recommendations to cut support jobs and funding for programmes' (Roberts, 1985, p. 1033). Three factors in the minds of Mid-westerners account for her success: alignment, attunement and energy. People felt aligned because their personal goals were focused and in accord with a common purpose; attuned, because they were relating to others on the basis of mutual respect and care, and energized, finally, because they were optimistic and excited by the prospect of change. Roberts (1985, p. 1036) noted that it was a sense of crisis – an occasion which Weber had originally suggested was ripe for the emergence of charismatic leaders – which motivated the district and 'set the tone and shaped the setting by giving leadership its raison d'être and momentum'. Finally, Roberts observes that charismatic status was attributed to the superintendent because of her extraordinary personal qualities, but that this attribution was only made after Mid-west had successfully weathered its troubles. The transformative process, therefore, 'was *not* dependent on the charismatic qualities of the superintendent' (Roberts, 1985, p. 1042, emphasis added).

After a mere two years in office and widespread media publicity, an impressed state governor appointed the superintendent as his commissioner of education. She now presided over 435 school districts and, as part of the same fourfold strategy she had used in Mid-west, visited every single district jurisdiction in her first year in order to make herself visible and to develop an extensive network of support (Roberts and Bradley, 1988, p. 263). Did the commissioner's charisma 'transfer', second time around? 'Thus far', Roberts and Bradley (1988, p. 264) concluded, 'there is no evidence of charisma associated with the commissioner at the state level.' Hundreds of hours of interviews and observations with informants yielded not one link between the commissioner, her behaviour and charisma. She was described as hard-driving, creative, innovative and committed, but not as manifesting extraordinary abilities nor the 'awestricken' characteristics perceived during her earlier superintendency (Roberts and Bradley, 1988, p. 265). These conclusions suggest that charisma is far from being a formula-driven phenomenon, so that it makes little sense, from a leader's point of view, to being committed to trying to make oneself charismatic. They also suggest that what is perceived to be the case in one leadership context may well be perceived differently in another, no matter what one's own view of oneself happens to be. On this last point, Berg (1996) uncovered a match between another new US school superintendent's perception of his style and those of his immediate district staff, but this time a gross mismatch with the perceptions of school-site personnel. Gil Traynor, the superintendent, saw himself as a hands-on leader, a visionary and as consultative, and he made a series of important personnel changes designed to streamline his district's operations. While interview responses from district personnel displayed a kind of reverence (Berg, 1996, p. 86) for Traynor's political skills, administrative personnel in the schools could rarely be found to put in a good word for him. Three years after his appointment Traynor was believed to be far too political and his consultative committees were dismissed as charades. When Berg (1996, p. 82) confronted Traynor with these contrasting perceptions he was 'completely taken aback'. The intended Traynor style had failed to take root across the district.

Another important issue which emerges from Roberts's study – but which, given its magnitude, can only be touched on here – is the question of whether or not there are gender-based differences in leadership styles. After all, perceptions of women school leaders' styles, for example, have been affected for a long time by stereotypical, binary masculine–feminine attributions. Thus, 'the one immutable, enduring difference between men and women', says Felice Schwartz (1989, p. 66), 'is maternity', and it is that biological fact which for so long has shaped perceptions of the roles thought to be appropriate for women and the socialization arrangements required to facilitate the assumption of those roles. In addition to trying to remedy a range of structural impediments which discriminate against women by narrowing their employment and career opportunities, many reformers have also been critical of traditional patterns of women's socialization for creating psychological barriers to their advancement and success. Recently, however, some commentators (e.g. Rosener, 1990) have argued that women who have succeeded in breaking through occupational glass ceilings have done so because of, rather than in spite of, experiences unique to their socialization. In short, what may once have been a disadvantage has now become an advantage. The particularly favourable attributes acquired through socialization are largely interactional qualities including a strong predisposition in favour of participation, a more conversational approach in women's dealings with their colleagues, a willingness to share information and a refusal to covet power for themselves. Moreover, Rosener claims, successful women endeavour to make other people feel important, they refrain from projecting themselves as superior, they enthuse others and communicate excitement about the ways in which their own work is important to them. Thus, upwardly mobile women in the traditional macho cultures of many organizations have succeeded by making the best of the resources which they have had available to them (Rosener, 1990, p. 124):

> As women entered the business world, they tended to find themselves in positions consistent with the roles they played at home: in staff positions rather than in line positions, supporting the work of others, and in functions like communications or human resources where they had relatively small budgets and few people reporting directly to them.
>
> The fact that most women have lacked formal authority over others and control over resources means that by default they have had to find other ways to accomplish their work.

In short, those ways of behaving which came naturally to women or were seen as socially acceptable for them have proven to be highly successful in at least some managerial settings.

The other claim advanced recently is that organizations are also thought to be increasingly sympathetic towards those qualities traditionally considered to be feminine. This trend is known as the feminization of work. It stems partly from the sheer weight of numbers of women in many (but by no means all) sectors of the paid labour force in many countries and also from claims that the de-layering of organizational hierarchies, the decoupling of work units, the dis-aggregation of organizational conglomerates, the adoption of less rigid work scheduling and increasingly boundaryless work careers favour female sensibilities ahead of those of males (Fondas, 1996, p. 288):

> Traits that are needed in this more fluid context are not those culturally ascribed to men – rationality, self-interest, toughness, domination – but, rather, are traits traditionally held to be feminine ones.

These include personal attributes associated with cooperation, shared influence and relationship-building across traditional divisions, lines and command chains. As was suggested briefly in Chapter 2, it is these very interactional properties which form the basis of Lipman-Blumen's (1996) model of connective leadership for a new world order comprising two global trends, diversity and interdependence. These are thought to be at odds with each other: 'even as diversity evokes independence, separatism, tribalism, and individual identities, interdependence pulls in a different direction' (Lipman-Blumen, 1996, p. 6).

In this kind of context connective leadership commends itself as an empowering style designed to transcend traditional gender-based stereotypes, and to strengthen the links and networks already existing between people. Its prominence also reflects an increasing emphasis on androgyny in discussions of leadership. Marie Coleman's (1996, p. 168) transcripts of her interviews with five UK women secondary heads – who, incidentally, saw themselves as transformational – for example, yielded perceptions of their own styles which 'could have been made by any headteacher, male or female'. And in *Dancing on the Ceiling*, Valerie Hall's (1996, p. 153) six UK female heads fly high 'for reasons relating to their own formative experiences':

> the women heads in the study developed the confidence to enact their own interpretation of management and leadership, based on characteristics that are neither exclusively masculine or feminine.

Fairhurst's (1993) analysis of the spoken discourse of female organizational leaders in a variety of one-on-one exchanges with their subordinates (male and female) has a bearing on this point. Her transcripts reveal a wide range of linguistic ploys and strategies adopted by women leaders – e.g. disagreement, coaching, role negotiation and the framing of choices. A close inspection of each strip of talk reveals few if any attributes which mark them as distinctively and uniquely female. Fairhurst (1993, pp. 345–6) equivocates on this point when addressing Rosener's (1990) celebration of feminine leadership models and asserts that gender contributed in two ways to the conduct of the chosen exchanges: the women leaders displayed a relationship orientation in their verbal exchanges – by attending to their subordinates' concerns first, rather than privileging their own interests – and they were reluctant to engage in typical male hairy-chestedness; instead they relied on so-called feminine wiles to get their way. The appropriate response to those sorts of claims is that such interactional strategies may in fact be further evidence of Hall's point that the socialization experiences of individual leaders – be they female or male – predispose them to behave in ways consistent with those experiences and that the responses are nothing more than that, rather than being evidence of gender category-based responses.

There would seem to be little merit, then, in claiming that there are gender-derived styles, when in actual fact the leader style differences *within* gender categories – recall Caroline Manley and Diane Parsons, and Miss Ross and Miss Mountain for that matter – are likely to be at least, or more, significant than those thought to exist *between* categories. This point should not be taken to mean, however, that gender does not count for or against an aspirant leader fulfilling her or his ambition to lead for, as will be seen in Chapter 8, it may well prey on the minds of selectors. In respect of the notion of a zone of discretion advanced earlier one's gender and one's feelings as a prospective leader about that gender will be part of a number of personal characteristics, central also to one's sense of identity and values, which come together to shape one's image of a preferred style of leading. Personal attributes, it will be recalled, comprised one of the three categories of factors which it was suggested together determined the precise texture and contours of a leader's discretionary domain. The second category of factors was concerned with the tasks required by a forthcoming role vacancy. As candidates for such appointments there is clearly considerable latitude within the collective capacity of a pool of aspirants to construct their desired personae in respect of the first category of factors and much that they can also do by way of preparation to sharpen their foreknowledge of position descriptions and requirements in respect of the second. But it is the third set of factors – to do with the particular context in which they will have to perform their much-sought-after roles – which represents the most daunting of the three. This contextual category is made up of a whole set of unknowns and givens which, despite all their best endeavours to get to grips with them, elude them until they are notified, perhaps, that they have been short-listed and are invited to be interviewed, all this time having been spent wondering just what has been going on at their possible future places of employment. In the next three chapters I show how the members of those organizations have been adjusting to a former leader's departure, while preparing themselves for somebody new, and the extent to which aspirants have strategically groomed themselves for what lies in store.

Succeeding leaders

'*Who's Next?*' was the headline above a full-page picture, taken from behind, of the bowed head of Pope John Paul II, which appeared in a supplement in the *Guardian*, 15 January 1998. 'We've had nearly 20 years of Pope John Paul II', the accompanying caption read, and 'Madeleine Bunting examines the discreet struggle for succession.' Perhaps nothing encapsulates better the essence of the process of succession than that image and those words. Indeed, succession in any organization or system is invariably experienced by those directly involved, and perceived by those who are spectators looking on, as a struggle, as the MCEGGS example indicated. And struggles, by definition, are rarely, if ever, discreet. Moreover, the picture of an ageing spiritual leader, head forward and neck exposed, tantalizes *Guardian* readers with a number of possible meanings. Interpreted in the most benign way the image signifies, and dignifies, the Vicar of Christ at prayer – as befits the reverence and solemnity of his office – or, because his head of hair is sparse and white, and he is bending forward, it may be taken as meaning frailty. A slightly more sinister way of understanding the picture, however, would be to see it as a leader exposed and vulnerable, his head positioned in a way that suggests his leadership is about to come to an inglorious end by being cut off – accentuated, perhaps, by the reddish mark on his neck left by the imprint of his collar. An even more sinister possibility would be that, because the Pope's bowed back is to the camera, the image is suggestive of betrayal as when a leader is about to be 'stabbed in the back'.

Without pressing such possibilities any further here, the article typifies the speculation that nearly always surrounds the changing-of-the-guard – as succession is sometimes known – between leaders who are the incumbents of formal offices and positions. To the president-watchers mentioned previously there need to be added two other well-known species of commentators with an interest in the character of public figures, and who are constantly on the look-out for early signs of leadership transition and help fuel the accompanying speculation: Royal-watchers and Vatican-watchers (or Vaticanologists, as the *Guardian* article calls them). Thankfully, most educational leaders, and certainly those in schools and colleges, are not required to run the entire gauntlet of media scrutiny to which bigger fish like spiritual leaders, monarchs, politicians and celebrities are relentlessly subjected. Nevertheless, within the confines of the particular educational communities and contexts they inhabit, the same kinds of pressures, speculative possibilities, guesswork, rumour and techniques for exacerbating or containing such things can be seen at work in precisely the same way that they operate at the grander level. The only differences are that in the smaller arenas of education the scale and visibility of the actions involved, and the significance of the outcomes, are much less.

Succession in any complex organization, educational or non-educational, brings to the fore three closely interrelated aspects of personnel management and leadership: first, how best to recruit and utilize its actual and prospective pool of human talent; second, how to mitigate and diminish the detrimental effects of the turnover consequent on the loss of that talent; and third, how to retain structural continuity and minimize disruption during occasions of transition in the life-cycle of organizations which mark the arrival or departure of that talent. Those three aspects make succession a highly politically charged phenomenon because, as one early commentator (Zald, 1965, p. 52, original emphases) pointed out, the wholesale changes which take place as part of succession are really to do with 'the *process* and *consequences* of the transfer of power'. For these reasons it is little wonder that Gouldner (1965, p. 662), the pioneer of research into organizational succession, once claimed:

> succession may be conceived of as a universally 'traumatic' experience of all social organizations, impairing lines of communication and authority, disrupting extant patterns of informal relations, and portending or resulting in alterations of policy.

In short, succession is a potentially highly destabilising process which 'occurs frequently' (Hart, 1991, p. 451) in every type of organization. Some idea of the extent of this instability and the ubiquity of succession can be obtained by recalling the proportions of unfilled headship vacancies in the UK in 1997 mentioned in the Introduction: one in four primary schools and about one in seven secondary schools with successions unresolved.

In this chapter I consider the major elements in the process of leadership succession. This choice of topic might seem slightly odd, from the point of leadership aspirants, because most of the activities comprising the early part of a succession process go on behind their backs: a successor to the incumbency of a formal role – certainly if she or he has been recruited from outside the organization – remains largely ignorant of what went on before her or his accession to the role. Yet some awareness and understanding of what Gabarro (1988, p. 258) has labelled the 'prearrival factors' would seem to be essential for aspirants because details of what did go on beforehand usually come to light afterwards and have to be confronted and dealt with. More important, however, is the fact that pre-arrival factors shape both the parameters and the conduct of the selection phase (to which aspirants have to submit themselves) which lies at the heart of the succession process, and the induction of the new leader – the subject matter of the next two chapters. In each of these three phases a new process of attribution-formation is under way. Attribution-making begins in the pre-arrival phase of succession with the weakening of prevailing attributions of the departing predecessor (Heller, 1989). A process of attribution-transfer to prospective successors begins for selectors during the selection phase. In a case study in the UK of the selection of a primary school deputy head (Gronn, 1986a, p. 5), for example, the female head's preference for a new male deputy, and the governing body's willingness to defer to her, legitimated a key part of the framework within which the qualities attributed to successor candidates would be perceived. Finally, the induction of the successor can be understood as the period when attributions of the new appointee solidify and diffuse amongst colleagues, peers and subordinates. As will become clear, the circumstances of an incumbent's departure, the emotional and other responses these evoke, and the psycho-politics of her or his replacement together shape the kinds of assumptions that are fed into the selection of the successor and also determine whether the reception she or he is accorded is hostile or friendly.

I begin by considering the pioneering research into succession reported in Gouldner's (1954) classic study, *Patterns of Industrial Bureaucracy*, and the early research conducted in its wake. There are two reasons for this starting-point: first, to provide an appreciation of the heritage of research on this topic and, second, to provide a narrative feel for what is entailed in succession. I then analyse the various constituent elements of a succession process, the aim being to confront aspirant leaders with the intended and unintended consequences of the machinations of the various parties to their succession which, because they inherit them, constrain their early leadership. While the remarks which follow are written primarily with the first-time leader in mind, a point made earlier bears repeating: every time an existing leader takes on a new set of role responsibilities – through promotion, transfer, appointment or selection – she or he revisits the same experiences and pressures negotiated during the attainment of their initial leadership appointment.

The significance of succession

Shortly after their marriage, the young, shy and new Mrs de Winter accompanies her husband Maxim to Manderley, in Daphne du Maurier's novel *Rebecca*. She is Maxim's second wife – the first, Rebecca, much beloved by the entire household, has died in mysterious circumstances – and as the two of them pass through the iron gates and motor down the long drive she becomes nervous and apprehensive:

I saw faces peering through the dark windows of the lodge, and a child ran around the back, staring curiously. I shrank back against the seat, my heart beating curiously, knowing why the faces were at the window, and why the child stared.

They wanted to see what I was like. I could imagine them now, talking excitedly, laughing in the little kitchen. 'Only caught sight of the top of her hat,' they would say, 'she wouldn't show her face. Oh well, we'll know by tomorrow. Word will come from the house'.

Maxim reassures his new wife that the staff are understandably curious:

'Everyone will want to know what you are like. They have probably talked of nothing else for weeks. You've only got to be yourself and they will adore you.'

These extracts communicate one aspect of succession: the newcomer's apprehension about whether or not they will measure up in the eyes of others to their predecessor. The other is the nostalgia felt by the onlookers for what has been taken away from them.

The anxieties experienced if a succession process is to be successfully negotiated, from the vantage points of all the parties involved, are captured admirably in the imagery of this vignette. Gouldner (1954, p. 79) also drew on du Maurier's novel and pointed out how and why it is that new managers and leaders invariably have to confront a 'Rebecca myth', especially if their predecessors have been idealized or esteemed. It was on the basis of his observations at the General Gypsum Company, in Oscar Centre, near the North American Great Lakes, that Gouldner analysed the effects of succession. At Oscar Centre there was a mine employing about 75 men and a surface operations section of factories employing a further 150. In the first year of Gouldner's research, a new plant manager, Vincent Peele, was appointed along with other supervisory and middle-managerial personnel. Following these changes, a wholesale pattern of instability, disruption and strikes set in at the plant. These were the outcomes of Peele's attempts to alter existing workplace customs and practices, a combination of factors which had resulted in what Gouldner characterized as an 'indulgency pattern' being accepted as normal on all sides – or what might be referred to in the language of the present-day industrial relations and micro-economic reform climate as inefficiencies, perks or even rorts.

At Oscar Centre this indulgency pattern was a system involving lenient supervision by management or the turning of a blind eye in the making of all sorts of concessions to the workers in a bid by management to appease them and to retain their loyalty. This entailed tolerance for employees who helped themselves to gypsum wallboard for their own private or domestic purposes, flexibility or even laxity about when to clock on or off work shifts, ease in deploying men around the plant to different jobs, a reluctance to fire workers who were not productive or did not shape up, and so on (Gouldner, 1954, p. 56). A similar pattern of teacher prerogatives was evident at Valley Elementary School in the USA and was visibly exposed when Mr Brown, the principal, announced his retirement: 'I was real disappointed [at the news] because the status-quo is safe, especially when we don't know what is coming', one 6th grade teacher commented (Fauske and Ogawa, 1987, p. 37). And in her reflections on her own succession experiences as a US high school principal, Hart (1988, p. 338) recalled how at an early meeting with teaching staff she heard them joking nervously about 'wanting to be "left alone in their classrooms to do their own thing" '.

Given the General Gypsum Company's wish to achieve new efficiencies, Peele's response to indulgency after his appointment was to try and eradicate the workers' privileges, an approach which earned him their undying animosity and contempt (Gouldner, 1954, p. 61, emphases added):

> Mourning for the past, workers began to contrast the favours now allowed them with those once bestowed under the previous plant manager, 'Old Doug.' If you wanted any gyp board from Doug, they explained, 'he'd let you have a truck-load. But *now*, if you want any board, it will be delivered to your home – *with a bill*!'

A corollary of this sense of outrage, Gouldner claimed, was a predilection on the part of the newly disenfranchised workers to view their past life through rose-coloured spectacles. Indeed, 'almost to a man, workers in the plant were in the spell of a backward-looking reverie. They overflowed with stories which highlighted the differences between the two managers, the leniency of Doug [Peele's predecessor] and the strictness of Peele' (Gouldner, 1954, p. 80). Thus it was that Old Doug functioned for the grieving workers in much the same way as du Maurier's character Rebecca did for the staff at Manderley.

Patterns of Industrial Bureaucracy, then, describes a new-broom manager at work and the effects of the changeover. As part of the new order of things Peele made a series of key appointments – or 'strategic replacements' – instituted regular checks on the workers, issued warnings and disciplined employees for so-called shirking. The import of all these measures, comments Gouldner (1954, p. 69, original emphasis), was that they 'may be seen as evidence of increasing *bureaucratization*' – the establishment of formal rules and prescriptions to replace or eliminate tacit understandings. Gouldner christened this transition between old and new regimes as a switch in leadership styles from representative to punishment-centred bureaucracy. His case study stimulated the research hypothesis that executive succession necessarily leads to the resort to increased formal means of control by new incumbents – especially the imposition of rules in the form of orders and directives – in order to ensure employee compliance. Thus, 'Peele intensified bureaucracy not merely because he wanted to, not necessarily because he liked bureaucracy, nor because he valued it above other techniques', observes Gouldner (1954, p. 98), 'but also because he was constrained to do so by the tensions of his succession.' Gouldner also speculated about the effects of the appointment of an internal or external successor, and believed that an internal appointment would generate tensions of a different type – a point investigated by Carlson (1961–2) in the earliest study of succession research in education.

In a study of the effects of a change in superintendency at Eastern State Hospital – a large US mental hospital with over 1,000 staff – Kotin and Sharaf (1967) modified some of Gouldner's findings. Kotin and Sharaf documented the transition between Dr Smith – the superintendent for 17 years – and his replacement Dr Lattimore. During his leadership Smith had forged a major breakthrough by instituting a psychoanalytic regime of clinical treatment. Lattimore, however, was more medically and psychiatrically inclined and made a number of strategic appointments which reflected this particular professional orientation. Predictably, some key staff resigned. Those who stayed adjusted psychologically by engaging in the practice familiar to psychoanalytic commentators known as splitting: proponents and opponents of both Smith and Lattimore thought of them in either positive or negative terms. Kotin and Sharaf (1967, p. 241) also demonstrated that succession need not necessarily trigger an increased reliance on rules and regulations. Instead, what a successor chooses to do reflects both the particular situational pressures confronting her or him, and the new incumbent's own personality. At Eastern State Hospital this shift was, broadly, away from a tight bureaucratic style towards a looser, more circumventive one. In contrast, therefore, to Gouldner's hypothesis about succession effects (Kotin and Sharaf, 1967, p. 246):

> A successor's loose style permits him [*sic*] to avoid the Charybdis of premature direct confrontation with his recalcitrant lieutenants and the Scylla of institutional paralysis stemming from the resistance of the old lieutenants. To some extent he can impose his will on the organization by working around the recalcitrant lieutenants without forcing a showdown.

Looseness, on the other hand, seems to have proven dysfunctional in this particular instance for, by performing his role in a vague, ambiguous and fluid manner, in the hope of maximizing his own advantage, Lattimore merely succeeded in triggering off complaints about lack of proper procedures being established and maintained, and inadequate lines of communication being utilized.

The next issue addressed by the early succession researchers concerned the kinds of enterprises which institutionalized regular succession processes. In one early study, Trow (1961–2) examined succession in more than 100 small manufacturing plants (i.e. five or six managers in family-owned firms employing fewer than 100 employees), particularly in the metals and machinery manufacturing markets. Only about half of these had formal succession plans in place – that is, provision for a designated successor, or a crown prince or princess – a plan for the training or preparation of such a person and acceptance of the need for it by the company personnel responsible for the anticipated changes. Most small firms were found to delay making provision for change – if they made any at all – until very close to the point of retirement of the top woman or man. The availability or non-availability of an heir apparent was one major consideration here as, of course, was the capability of such a person. In fact, ability was the one factor, Trow (1961–2,

p. 236) claimed, which 'appears to make the difference' between planning and lack of planning for a change-over. One final observation from the work of the first generation of succession researchers was that even though succession was disruptive, it was not necessarily experienced by everyone concerned as unpleasant. Thus, not every successor who followed a popular incumbent like Old Doug had as difficult a time as Peele. Cooley, the automotive plant manager studied by Guest (1962), for example, found himself in a similar position of having to tighten up work practices but he got a far better reception from his men than Peele had done. The reason was that Cooley resorted to representative rather than punishment-centred bureaucratic arrangements, and worked informally and consultatively with his men rather then legalistically.

Subsequent research from the 1970s through to the 1990s into succession effects on performance – most of it quantitative – has concentrated on the market position of companies (relying on measures of investment return and levels of risk incurred attributable to CEOs) and the winning percentage of sporting teams (attributable to coaches). It was only in the 1980s that a later generation of researchers turned from an exclusive preoccupation with organizational factors to examine how the various parties with a stake in the outcome of succession perceived and interpreted the overall process (Fauske and Ogawa, 1987, p. 24; Heller, 1989, p. 67). Finally, with the exception of the aforementioned Carlson (1961), until the mid-1980s there was virtually no research undertaken on any aspect of succession in educational settings (Johnson and Licata, 1995, p. 395). Field research into superintendent succession in two North American school districts – Mossville and Desert Flats – conducted by Firestone (1990) is the only educational study to directly amend Gouldner's original thesis about succession effects. Unlike Gouldner, Firestone (1990, p. 371) concluded that 'there is no necessary relationship between succession and bureaucracy': while the changes initiated in Mossville did emphasize discipline and bureaucracy, those set in train in Desert Flats by the successor superintendent were to do with teacher professionalism and career development.

Standing aside

There are four main perspectives from which to consider succession – the organization, the predecessor, prospective followers and the successor – and this analysis of the pre-arrival components moves back and forth between them as appropriate. For the organization or system a succession process is triggered whenever monarchs abdicate, whenever a military rebellion is mounted by rebel officers, whenever an incumbent government calls an election, whenever shareholders vote in a new board of directors or whenever a leader departs abruptly. While it is possible to be fairly clear about the point in time at which a succession phase gets under way in an organization, it is difficult to be precise about when it ends and, therefore, to say exactly how long a succession lasts and its effects endure. While it is in train, however, a succession is something which, because it disrupts normality and upsets an existing balance of interests, can re-activate or bring to the surface a variety of emotions to do with material and psychological loss or gain, and security and change of personal and organizational identity. The outcomes of succession, however, need not be solely negative, as Miskel and Cosgrove (1985, p. 88) suggest, for:

> Changing leaders can represent a psychological impact of a new personal style, a new definition of the situation, a new communication network with the environment, or a jolt to the system that opens its members' minds. When members are recruited, particularly principals, teachers, and other professional personnel, new bodies of knowledge, skills, and behaviours are imported, which often serve as sources of new ideas in schools.

Despite this optimism, succession is rarely ever as smooth and uncomplicated a process as is suggested in the biblical examples of Elisha requesting a double portion of Elijah's spirit just before Elijah is swept heavenward by a whirlwind (2 Kings 2:9-11), and in the commissioning of Joshua by Moses (Deuteronomy 31:7-8):

> Then Moses called unto Joshua, and said to him in the sight of all Israel, Be strong and of a good courage: for thou must go with this people unto the land which the LORD hath sworn unto their fathers to give them; and thou shalt cause them to inherit it. And the LORD, he it is that doth go before thee; he will be with thee, he will not fail thee, neither forsake thee: fear not, neither be dismayed.

Few other organizational processes have provided as rich a source of popular expressions as succession, such as: passing on the mantle, the baton in the knapsack, grooming an heir, handing over the reins, jumping ship, abdication crisis, putsch, bloodless coup, bloodletting and others, as will become evident.

These two biblical accounts just cited do not make clear what the immediate stimuli or triggers for Elijah's and Moses' actions were, but in most organizations there are normally two kinds of departures of heads and leaders which inaugurate a succession: voluntary and involuntary. From the point of view of the subsequent good and well-being of the organization, the immediate and longer-term effects of both forms of disengagement vary both qualitatively and quantitatively. These effects will be determined by four sets of factors: the precipitating circumstances, the prevailing performance of the organization, the characteristics and power of the predecessor, and her or his longevity. Moreover, the effect on the organization of the longevity of the departing leader will be compounded if the position to be vacated is the final leadership engagement in her or his career because – harking back to our four-stage model – the action of standing aside marks the predecessor's transition to divestiture. The relinquishment of leadership influence, as some of the instances to be considered in a moment indicate, is something about which many ageing organizational leaders and heads are far from sanguine. Needless to say, the manner in which the reins are let go, whether that letting go is voluntary or enforced – and whether all formal and informal links with the organization are severed – may or may not cruel the pitch for their replacement. As Farquhar (1995, p. 62) comments on the acrimonious departure of Ed Morehouse, the head of Greenwood School in the USA, 'the live wires of his administration crackled through the school for months'.

Triggers for voluntary departures take a number of forms but they share the feature that the exit from office or a position of influence occurs at a time nominated by the incumbent. An unforced decision to resign or retire – consequent, say, upon the acceptance of a severance or voluntary departure package – is a good example. Voluntary departures have the advantage of making for a relatively clean break. On the other hand, if they occur without warning and take immediate effect, their unanticipated and unscheduled timing catches colleagues unawares until such time as, having come to terms with the meaning and implications of an incumbent's decision to leave, they are able to galvanize themselves into seeking a replacement. Obviously there are various significant others such as family, friends and colleagues to be consulted, and informed about one's pending departure, but it is doubtful whether there is any preferred sequence of disclosure (Austin and Gilmore, 1993, p. 49). The swiftness and tidiness of the organization's response will be determined in part by whether or not it has engaged in succession planning. Should a pending departure be announced, but without it taking immediate effect, the remainder of the incumbency is likely to be interpreted as an on-hold or seat-warming period. It is during such times that predecessors are treated as lame ducks. A good illustration is second-term US presidents towards the end of their four-year tenure in the run-up through the primaries to the election. The reason for this change in status is that colleagues and subordinates have begun counting down the days and perceive a weakened superior's diminishing authority – a phenomenon labelled by Farquhar (1995, p. 56) as a 'who cares?' mentality. They are also likely to have begun redefining their expectations of the office and to have been caught up in intrigue about potential replacements. On the other hand, a forthcoming departure deadline can buy time for a predecessor and be the spur to complete unfinished business so as not to burden a successor or to ensure that pet projects and procedures are bedded down and put beyond a successor's reach (Austin and Gilmore, 1993, p. 53).

At one level this kind of behaviour is indicative of followers' intolerance for leadership vacuums and of their desire to transfer their leadership allegiances quickly. But given the way the act of leadership was defined in Chapter 1 these responses may also be seen as evidence of followers' reliance or dependence on leaders for framing meaning, and their readiness to transfer attributions to alternative authority figures as part of a process defined by Heller (1989) as conversion or substitution. Conversion takes the form of a polarization of views about a previous and a future leader, the movement from the former to the latter being accomplished by a variety of cognitive mechanisms, including: segregation, repudiation, annihilation and the rewriting of history. Hart's (1988, p. 335) data on her own succession experiences charted a relatively benign follower conversion in which initial scepticism and repudiation eroded over time: 'a gradual replacement of preconceived perceptions, expectations, and speculations about [her] intentions with a social network of interaction and support (and pockets of resistance) in the school'. In the instance of the transfer of allegiance to a new development corporation director and his revised plan for a community project examined by Heller (1989, p. 75), followers projected substantially more enmity on the departed leader than teachers did in Hart's case: they first discerned differences between the views of predecessor and successor; they next repudiated the former – to the extent of demonizing him with the familiar attribution of villain (for an alleged con job) while idealizing the latter as a hero – and then rationalized previous organizational events in keeping with their new leadership loyalties. Part of this idealisation, Gilmore and Ronchi (1995, p. 19) suggest, involves responding to the new leader as though she or he is equivalent to 'a projective screen onto which many of the hopes and fears of the staff get placed'.

Conversion, then, represents the antithesis of the Rebecca myth, or a direct reversal of the treatments accorded Old Doug and Peele. Moreover, the repudiation of former leaders emphasized by Heller has strong empirical support: in a study of 43 legal service agency head transitions Farquhar (1991, p. 207) claims that one of the most consistent findings was 'the degree of negativity toward the departing executive'. A particularly potent form of repudiation is the discrediting of a predecessor by resort to humiliation. This is often experienced in cases of involuntary departure and in one of two ways: privately, or publicly by degradation. Privately experienced shame or humiliation occurred for Waters, a lay Catholic principal in an order-owned school in Victoria, Australia, when his employer refused to renew his appointment (Burns, 1991, pp. 43–4):

> When I was told that my contract would not be renewed I felt a complete failure. I rang a few people to ask for advice but I found it very difficult to face staff at the College, students and parents. I was embarrassed and staff, especially, seemed to want to avoid talking to me. Perhaps I had been given a job I was not ready for, or not suited to, but I feel I should have been treated with more dignity, and allowed to keep my self-respect.

On some occasions a predecessor's loss of self-respect consequent on removal from office is compounded by being stripped of their rank and status, as Gephart (1978, p. 566) – 'RG' in the following dialogue – who documented his own removal as chairman of a graduate students' committee, has noted:

> 37. IM: If RG resigns, we need a temporary chairman.
> 38. LB: GRC [Graduate Representatives Council] can reaffirm you or reappoint you. Will you resign or do we have to move you resign?
> 39. RG: I'm not resigning.

40. DA: I'd hoped you'd resign and avoid this distasteful procedure. I move the chairman be removed.
41. RG: You can't vote me out. You can only recommend it to GRC.
42. LB: I'll turn the chair over to IM and call the question.
43. IM: All in favor? (Members in favor raise their hands – three of five members vote in favor, thereby passing the motion in accord with majority rule.) I guess the motion is carried.

With this simple act of denunciation RG's status as predecessor was effectively scapegoated and he was summarily degraded to a lesser level.

The experience of involuntary departure need not be as stressful as in these instances. Normally such departures include scheduled, pre-planned occasions such as the mandatory retirement of an office-holder by a required age or, as in the above instance of Waters, at the cessation of an employment contract. These events can be relatively minor in their effects on both the predecessor and the organization, in that within the imposed deadline there is usually some scope for her or him to depart at a time of their own choosing or at least to make the public announcement of their proposed departure date when it suits both parties to do so. On the other hand, such desires can be thwarted by rumour and innuendo: Mr Brown at Valley Elementary School in the USA, for example, was forced to go public when his secret was leaked to staff by a friend (Fauske and Ogawa, 1987, p. 35). On the other hand, involuntary departures can also be sudden, as in the case of the death of the incumbent or when a leader is dismissed from office – although the timing of the latter possibility is always uncertain because it is mired in psycho-political contingencies (Fredrickson *et al.*, 1988, p. 267). Both of these occurrences create an organizational authority vacuum. In the case of dismissal a predecessor may have been given the opportunity by a governing board (or its equivalent) to go quietly – perhaps through an agreement to resign or to be paid out of a contractual obligation – but she or he has chosen instead to be ejected from office, perhaps in a fit of pique to generate maximum damaging publicity for the purposes of vindication. In this latter respect, controversial, scandal-wracked departures in the commercial sector are quite common and make good media fare (Farquhar, 1995, p. 52).

Letting go

Considered from the point of view of incumbents and soon-to-be predecessors, and assuming for the moment that they have some freedom in the choice of the time at which they will stand down or aside, the question which they have to answer for themselves at some point in both their overall career and in their particular incumbency is: When is it best for me to go? For those still young enough to move on to another leadership appointment the question of whether to stay or go is likely to be determined by an overall career plan and the availability of a desired opening or post. In such cases the question is merely one of calculation and timing. For those leaders faced with divesting themselves of their entire leadership responsibility in the twilight years or late phase of their working life, however, the force of such an apparently innocuous question is vastly more difficult to acknowledge let alone answer. If death is one of the few certainties in life – as it is often claimed to be – then one certainty of leadership is that all leaders have a best-by or use-by date. Yet for reasons that are perhaps partly tied up with the narcissistic and grandiose predispositions noted earlier, not every leader realizes or is willing to confront this ineluctable fact. Their refusal to accept their own mortality, and their unwillingness to let go power gracefully is often a major contributor to the disruptive problems encountered during succession transitions. Apart from rare occasions in which leaders might fall dangerously ill, it is only at the point of possible retirement that what they have previously taken for granted for so long – their potency and power – seem as though they are going to slip away. US business heroes, suggests Sonnenfeld (1988, p. 284), 'believe they have earned their stature through their deeds and sacrifice. Thus, they do not realize until their retirement that their position is, in part, a social creation.' Only at that point in their lives does the realization finally dawn on them with full force that what they have striven so hard for and struggled to build up – their leadership legacy or monument to their immortality – might just be put at risk by whoever succeeds them.

Letting go, then, is difficult to come to terms with because of the intensity of a leader's commitment to, or identification with, what she or he has achieved. The greater the magnitude and scale of this achievement in their own and others' eyes the greater the impact of the anticipated loss of what has to be foregone (Sonnenfeld, 1986, pp. 307–8). Thus it is that leaders face not only the loss of control over their material achievements, and their emotional attachments to them, but also the prospect of loss of recognition and the confirmatory mirror provided by an audience of followers and supporters. This is doubly burdensome because (Sonnenfeld, 1986, p. 311, emphasis added):

> while any public figure can lose an audience and the recognition that audience provides of one's image or identity through retirement, the retired leader also loses the power *to shape* that audience.

Should these impulses be experienced strongly, or acutely even, then there will be a strong tendency for leaders to refuse to get the message and to want to hold on rather than to let go. The founders of companies or firms, 'who see their companies as symbols of their success and extensions of their own personalities' (Kets de Vries, 1988, p. 57), provide a particularly good example.

Whenever leaders are reluctant to plan for their succession and try to hang on to office, a range of potentially disastrous effects of longevity are likely to ensue. Political figures are notorious for wanting to cling on to power and for succumbing to their vaulting ambitions. In 1987 Australia witnessed the rather indecent spectacle of an ageing leader, Sir Johannes Bjelke-Peterson, then the Premier of Queensland for just under 20 years, projecting himself as a kind of saviour of the nation by trying to assume the national mantle of Liberal–National Coalition leadership as part of a 'Joh for Canberra' campaign. This initiative succeeded in wreaking havoc in Queensland and nationally at the federal election in that year, and may well have cost John Howard, the then Leader of the Opposition (and now the current Prime Minister), victory. Another effect of seniority and long incumbency is to discourage potential heirs. By the time Sir Robert Menzies retired as Prime Minister in 1966 he was so dominant in his party and so adept at disposing of potential rivals that there was no-one of comparable stature left to replace him. This latter phenomenon is known as 'jealousy by the old'. It amounts to the virtual killing-off of crown princes and potential successors and 'is translated [or interpreted] by the intended protégés as selfishness and stodginess'. On the other hand, a departing generation of leaders is likely to view its own disappointment as 'a partial casualty of another generation's greed' (Sonnenfeld, 1986, pp. 312, 319).

Four typical CEO departure styles are: monarchs, generals, ambassadors and governors (Sonnenfeld, 1988, pp. 292–4). Monarch-style leaders usually have to be ejected from office while generals depart reluctantly and remain hopeful of being recalled. Examples of these two types in education do not spring readily to mind, but ambassadors, who retain some kind of informal elder stateswoman or statesman connection with their former employing organizations, and governors, who exit gracefully to other pursuits, are more likely to be recalled (e.g. former principals lay foundation stones or open new buildings and their families endow memorials or scholarship funds after their death).

The interregnum

One unanticipated but frequent result of a leader standing aside – whether performed voluntarily or involuntarily, and in one of Sonnenfeld's suggested ways or not – is the creation of a buffer or time-out period of temporary or caretaker leadership. Provided organizations have a formally designated heir or second-in-command waiting in the wings, however, then this interim period between departure and replacement is more likely be experienced as smooth. D.T. Hall (1995) – proponent of the protean career idea considered earlier in Chapter 2 – found himself thrust into the role of acting dean of the School of Management, Boston University, at very short notice. There had been rumblings of the dean's departure but one day Hall (who was one of two associate deans) was summoned by the provost and informed that the dean was resigning (of his own volition) in 48 hours time, and would Hall care to act as caretaker while a national search for a replacement was conducted? '*This* was a big-time surprise' (Hall, 1995, p. 72, original emphasis) and acceptance of the offer meant that Hall, at 50 years of age, had to reinvent himself quickly in an unanticipated role in mid-career.

In his temporary new leadership capacity Hall was lucky enough to be able to enlist the support of his fellow associate dean, and the two of them oversaw a major faculty restructure and nominated members of the dean search committee during a period of crisis for the School (Hall, 1995, p. 79):

> Because the organization had done no preparation for this sudden transition, much intelligence (in the head of the former Dean) was lost, and we spent months playing catch-up.

Hall, himself not a candidate for the deanship – a fact which he and the president and provost were careful to make public at the outset, and which was signalled by the use of the designation acting, rather than interim, in his title – successfully weathered this hiatus period of nine months, and his successor was entirely comfortable in their subsequent collaboration.

A common form of interim leadership in schools, especially in Australia, is the resort to relieving school principals during an incumbent's absence for reasons of extended recreation leave, illness and the like. Because they comprise a kind of reserve army or roving cadre of trouble-shooters who are used by employing authorities to plug administrative gaps for short, intensive periods these people owe no school site allegiances to any person or group and are thereby immune from many of the normal routine constraints. As a consequence they often turn out to be square pegs in round holes, as this chairman of a school council in a Melbourne technical school in the late 1970s explained (Gronn, 1979, p. 418):

> As a relieving principal [during the incumbent principal's illness] he knew all the lurks and he used all the lurks ... But by the same token he went through the [principal's] files and he pulled things out of those files that we were interested in that nobody had even brought to our notice before, and so really was ... a breath of fresh air.

Anderson (1982, pp. 78–9) – himself a relieving principal – interviewed 11 of his Victorian primary school relieving peers. Three attributes were seen as essential to cope with constant changes in work venues: flexibility in approach and style, capacity for quick situational assessments and the ability to cope with social isolation. A closely related species of interim leader is the acting school principal – usually a senior and experienced teacher or administrator appointed from within a school to take over during a principal's absence. Unlike a reliever, who is an outsider, the dynamics of the acting role for an insider will be different, as Rowles (1990) found when she took charge, at very short notice, of the Melbourne state primary school in which she was teaching. Rowles (1990, p. 49) logged her learning experiences in a journal over a three-month period and found herself growing in the job, in a similar kind of self-actualizing way to that described by Hall (1995, p. 78):

> At the commencement of my term as acting principal I was most conscious of my ignorance of routine processes; what information was required on a given return, which files to use, where to find particular records, what new information had to be

documented, what procedure should be initiated in order to achieve a desired outcome. My perception of my learning needs at that time focused on the deficiencies in my factual knowledge.

Later, however, Rowles's learning changed and her journal entries began to deal with such considerations as organizational strategies, coping mechanisms, ways of relating to people and dealing with situations.

There are two other, slightly rarer, types of interregna to be found in schools. The first is similar to Sonnenfeld's (1988) ambassador sub-type who retires as CEO but then becomes a board member, only this time in reverse, when a school councillor steps in as an interim principal. After the untimely death of the headmaster, Charles Fisher, in late 1978, R.B. Ritchie, the chairman of the council of Geelong Grammar School, 'was asked by the council to take on the running of the school'. This he did for over 18 months until mid-1980 because of the unavailability of Fisher's deputy who had left to take up a headship elsewhere and because the newly appointed headmaster, John Lewis (the current head of Eton), was still subject to existing contractual arrangements. Geelong Grammar School had just undergone an important amalgamation and had also become co-educational. Ritchie, notes the school historian (Bate, 1990, p. 276), 'was determined to take stock' and wanted to 'consolidate the amalgamation, look closely at management structures and review the use of material and human resources'. In order not to create difficulties for Lewis, his successor, Ritchie (1980, p. 1) chose not to rejoin the school council. The second example is relatively new in schooling and is of interest because it illustrates how an officially sanctioned and externally imposed interim leader operates with virtually unlimited authority, and a wide zone of discretion in relation to the fortunes of a school. This is the recent UK practice of principal appointments to schools requiring special measures following an OFSTED inspection. Linda Turner (1998, p. 97) was given two years to help Roundthorn County Primary School 'demonstrate that it was becoming effective'. On her own admission Turner succeeded in lifting morale and securing staff commitment to a level sufficient to warrant the description of a turnaround during this short period. This was accomplished by a series of structural changes and staff development measures, but also by ensuring that everyone was empowered by sharing in the overall managerial responsibilities.

All of these examples suggest that interim leaders, whatever their particular guise, are clearly more than mere placeholders – to borrow Farquhar's (1995, p. 51) term – or time-servers. The appropriate analogy is with what the psychoanalyst Winnicott (1965, p. 150) terms a 'transitional object': a person or object with which a child forms an attachment but which is a substitute for something else (e.g. a doll or toy, or thumb-sucking). So appealing is interim leadership to some individuals, such as the relieving principals, that they make a career out of overseeing leadership transitions. These roles have their equivalents outside education as well – such as those clergy who are known as *locum tenens* appointees in parishes pending the induction of a new priest, or accountants who are appointed as administrators whenever firms are put into receivership prior to liquidation. Sometimes temporary leadership produces strange and unexpected outcomes. In the previously cited case of Greenwood School, following the resignation of Morehouse after two decades as head, the board appointed a trustee, Trowberry, as acting head – a situation not unlike that of Ritchie at Geelong. So successful was Trowberry, a former minister, that people begged him to stay on (Farquhar, 1995, p. 61):

> Greenwood School fell in love with Trowberry. Here was a school head who was present on campus, who cared, who was optimistic and upbeat, who knew what to do next. He played his guitar for the kindergartners one minute and taught a class to high schoolers the next. The magnitude of the school's impoverishment under Morehouse's tenure – isolation from the larger educational community, lack of consistency and support from the top, the corrosive effects of an embittered proprietor – was amplified by the contrast with Trowberry.

Trowberry was offered, and accepted, a four-year contract. Like Hall at Boston, Trowberry had insisted originally that he would fill in for Morehouse and would not be a candidate for his replacement. Stakeholders, however, 'hounded him, the search committee, and Board members almost immediately to elevate him to permanent head' (Farquhar, 1995, p. 63).

As has been indicated so far, a leader's departure at any time to take up a new position during her or his career, but especially at the end of it, can be complicated for the individuals having to let go, as it was for Morehouse in this instance, and produces some odd behaviour. Sonnenfeld's (1986, p. 329) speculation is that this may be because 'by late career we are anxious to show that our accumulated wisdom is still deemed beneficial'. Whatever the reason, the net effect of a leader's departure can be for it to create a ghostly presence or cast a shadow over their successor.

Shadows

Gilmore and Ronchi (1995, p. 11) have defined a shadow as 'memories of a former leader [which] continue to shape the perceptions, emotions, and behaviour of people in the organization well beyond what would be expected from straightforward social-comparison processes'. The shadow phenomenon is an extension of the idea of the Rebecca myth. In respect of the post-departure behaviour of the predecessor, a shadow can be understood in a passive sense to mean nothing more than a nostalgia and hankering for the past by those who have had to establish new leadership allegiances. The affection felt for Gouldner's Old Doug is a good example: following his departure it was not necessary for Old Doug to do anything explicit to influence his former workmates, they simply had to call him to mind whenever Peele came into view. But there is a more active or interventionist understanding of the shadow idea that includes occasions in which departed leaders take steps to ensure that they are still remembered or that their presence is felt. The persistence of the shadow is a sure sign that the conversion or cognitive attribution switch identified by Heller has not occurred and that followers – perhaps because they 'have been jilted by previous leaders' (Gilmore and Ronchi, 1995, p. 21) or want to be assured that the new woman or man is not just passing through – are hedging their bets. Shadows or ghosts of the past may also mean that predecessors are actively doing their darnedest to ensure that an attributional switch to the successor never occurs.

Examples of these shadow effects are legion. At the benign end of the spectrum are to be found instances in which departing or retired leaders try to minimize the length of their shadow. Known (but undocumented) instances include a long-serving faculty dean who took a year-long sabbatical in a foreign country to ensure he was not seen as hovering – in the way that Mrs Thatcher was alleged to have been doing by looking over John Major's shoulder prior to the 1991 UK election – and a recently retired headmistress who not only stayed away from her former school but even changed her place of regular Sunday worship because of the parish's direct representation on the school's council. A slightly longer shadow is cast when an incumbent nominates her or his successor, an ill-advised practice, according to Levinson (1974), because to seek to do so is a sure sign that retiring incumbents are insecure within themselves and uncertain about exactly how the leadership legacy they have built up is going to fare in the future. Fortunately, however, most leaders are 'sufficiently secure in their own self-image as capable executives' to avoid such a temptation (Levinson, 1974, p. 61). On the other hand, the stronger the allegiance of a board of management or governing body to a predecessor, 'the more problematic it will be for a newcomer either to take actions that do not "parrot" those of the predecessor or to deliver organizational performance lower than the predecessor's' (Fredrickson *et al.*, 1988, p. 267).

Further along the spectrum a much longer shadow is cast when predecessors give voice to their concerns about their successors. In his memoirs, *Richly Rewarding*, Darling (1978, p. 117) expressed concern at his successor's preparedness to change arrangements which he had set firmly in place during the preceding 32 years:

> My successor [T.R. Garnett], for instance, thought it necessary to circulate *The Lanchester Tradition* by G.F. Bradby amongst the staff shortly after he took over. More tactful things have, I think, been done.

In this case the transition between Darling and Garnett turned out to be sticky (Bate, 1990, p. 223):

> In a community which had waited for the headmaster to give the nod, or had feared his frank rebuke, [Garnett's] new approach was perplexing. Staff felt uncertain about what Garnett wanted, when what he most wanted was for them to take initiatives. He also warned those parents who believed that the way to get things done was to go right to the top, that they would have to look more widely for assistance . . .

Because Darling himself was shocked by what he thought his successor was doing and because he made his concern known, his disappointment also hung like a black cloud over the scene: it was thought at the time that Garnett's proposals for change at Corio were known at the Melbourne Club long before they were general knowledge in the school.

According to Bate, feelings ran high when Garnett circulated Bradby's *The Lanchester Tradition* because the novel 'cut close to the bone in exploration of the power of precedent'. Further, it was difficult to tell whether Garnett's action was meant to be 'deliberately hurtful' or whether it was 'a brave attempt to make people face a serious situation – in line with Garnett's practice of enlivening members of staff constantly with ideas, articles and suggested reading'.

Way out on the end of the spectrum is the celebrated – or even notorious – instance of a predecessor's interference which occurred at Rugby School when the headmaster, Frederick Temple, was elevated to the See of Exeter and the trustees appointed the Revd Henry Hayman as his replacement in 1869. Some of the Rugby masters were soon in uproar against Hayman, mainly on grounds to do with what were thought to be inappropriate and inadequate testimonials. There was no eventual mutiny amongst the masters but even before his arrival Hayman had got wind of the ground-swell against him. He later sought the support of the trustees in dismissing the chief malcontent, E.A. Scott, but failed to secure it. Hayman's appointment had been widely discussed in the national press and, barely two months into his incumbency, some masters had tried to have the trustees' decision to appoint him queried in the House of Commons – the trigger for the new head's plea for the trustees' backing in his move against the opposition masters. Prior to his departure from Rugby Temple had invited Hayman and his wife to visit the school and, during a meeting with the assistant masters, Hayman 'gave an explanation of the character of his testimonials and begged them not to judge him without a trial' (Simpson, 1967, pp. 71–2). Back in Temple's study, Hayman, feeling that he had got absolutely nowhere with the masters, appealed to Temple to use his influence to secure their cooperation, whereupon Temple is said to have 'rounded on him' and to have told him 'that he considered the appointment a disastrous mistake, that Hayman ought to withdraw, and that it was his, Temple's, duty to write to the Trustees to give them his opinion'. And write he did (cited in Simpson, 1967, p. 72):

The plain truth is that he [Hayman] is quite incompetent to perform some of the most important duties of the place ... He has the ability implied in a clear perception of his own purposes, much power of expression, and extraordinary strength of will. But in true insight into character, which alone will enable a man to deal justly with the older boys, or to govern able and high-minded men, he is absolutely deficient. The result is certain: as far as mere strength goes towards good government he will govern the School. But his government of the VIth will assuredly fail, and he will never get men of high mark to work under him ... The staff will inevitably deteriorate ... the moral tone and the discipline will sink, and the confidence of the parents will be justly withdrawn. It would be natural that, on leaving, I should recommend my successor to the parents who consult me confidentially, but as an honest man I am unable to do so.

Temple chose to be silent, but 'silence in such cases is condemnation'.

A further attempt by Hayman to secure Scott's removal was rebuffed by the trustees. Amidst this unsavoury imbroglio, enrolments began to collapse. With his position steadily worsening, the composition of the governing body was changed in accordance with a new Act of Parliament in late 1871 and, to Hayman's horror, one of the new governors – elected by the University of London – was Temple. He protested, but in vain. Relations with the governors reached their nadir in 1872 when a confidential minute of rebuke was leaked to the press. At this point Temple was 'reported to have said that "he would like to see anyone who could stop his mouth" ' (Simpson, 1967, p. 83). In what must rate as one of the oddest twists in a succession battle ever recorded, Temple, Hayman's predecessor, then eventually became a leading party to his successor's removal for, in December 1873, the Rugby governors finally dismissed Hayman. The latter sought to appeal to the Court of Chancery but Temple (and another governor) thwarted him to the bitter end by raising a legal objection (a demurrer) to Chancery's right to decide the case. Sir R. Malins upheld Temple's objection but lambasted the governors, in particular Temple and a fellow governor for 'allowing themselves to be elected to the Governing Body and on their treatment of Hayman' (Simpson, 1967, p. 88).

The Rugby case, thankfully, was probably an extreme one, at least in education. Yet, along with all the other examples cited in this chapter it shows that, from all points of view, but especially from that of the aspirant leader and prospective incumbent, succession processes are fraught with all manner of unknowns, uncertainties and possibilities. If this is so, then one of the key questions which an aspirant leader needs to ask her or himself is: Are there some occasions and circumstances which are more desirable than others for taking charge? All that can be offered by way of reply is to observe that while no point in time is ever completely ideal for taking on leadership there are clearly some occasions in which it is ill-advised and some which are more propitious than others. Wily successors will no doubt have tried to the best of their ability before agreeing to become candidates for a vacancy to find out why a particular incumbent has departed and whether or not she or he has left under a cloud. Some applicants who succeed in making it to the selection table sense that they are about to be handed a poisoned chalice and withdraw there and then or refuse to accept an offer of appointment. But some, like Darling (1978, p. 117), profess themselves to be lucky: 'Probably I was more fortunate than [Garnett, his own successor] was, for my predecessor had left me one priceless tradition at least, namely, that the boss was always right, whoever the boss was.' Others, like Freeman (1981) – who took over a small, run-down regional boarding school for girls – much to their horror, find themselves ensnared in a nest of vipers. Still others, like the stern disciplinarian J.R. Sutcliffe (1977, pp. 110–11) – headmaster of Melbourne Grammar School from 1938 to 1949 and appointed after his predecessor's brief headmastership – make enemies right from the start and relish the challenge this presents.

Finally, no prospective leader can ever know in advance whether their incumbency is destined to be lengthy, like Darling's, or short-lived and acrimonious like that of the hapless Hayman. Nor can they be certain whether they will succeed or fail. Educational history is littered with brief incumbencies which often seem in retrospect to have been brief interludes between lengthy leadership eras in the historical life-cycles of schools, but during which the crucial groundwork is laid down on which subsequent appointees have been able to capitalize. In such cases forgotten leaders turn out to have been women and men before their time. Hopefully, then, it is with a full awareness of all of these succession vagaries and possibilities that a would-be leader allows her or his name to go forward as a candidate for selection as a replacement. And it is to the intricacies and dynamics of this vital phase of the overall succession process that the discussion now turns.

CHAPTER 8

Selecting leaders

Throughout this book I have been devoting a lot of attention in all sorts of ways to the idea of perception: the perceptual basis of attributions of leadership, the importance of appearances in legitimating leaders – as emphasized by Machiavelli – insight into one's sense of self, masks, mirrors, impression management, personas, images, reputations, shadows, the various messages signalled by a leader's actions and the prying, questioning eyes of one's colleagues and subordinates. It is true to say that every one of these aspects – indeed, the entire apparatus of perception – is brought to bear in some manner during the selection phase of the overall succession process. There are two occasions when the campaign to convince oneself and anyone else that one merits being treated as a leader can be won or lost. The second of the two comes when one is finally put to the test and inducted: when those responsible for having installed one as a leader get a long-awaited opportunity to see whether the proof of the pudding is indeed going to be in the eating. But for that new leader to have got to that point she or he has to have survived the demands imposed on them by the first and earlier prerequisite occasion: they will have had to perform convincingly before a selection panel. There, huddled amidst the collective micro-consciousness assembled around the selection table, shut off behind closed doors from prying outsiders, for what might seem to everyone involved to be an interminable period of time, a little drama will play itself out. It is there that the moment of truth for aspirant leaders and all that they prefer to believe about themselves has finally come. And it is also there that whatever hopes and aspirations those searching for a leader have had will either begin to bear fruit or will fade.

Yet selection clearly means a whole lot more than a simple agenda of questions and answers being uttered across an interview table, for its outcomes can make or break organizations. Selection is an important boundary-marking occasion in the life-cycle of organizations during which all the stakeholders involved – direct and indirect – put themselves and their credibility to the test. For successful leadership candidates their selection means that they have crossed an important validation line: they have sub-mitted themselves to public scrutiny and a new status has been conferred on them. For those whose job it has been to bestow that new official status and identity they have much to gain or lose as well, in particular responsibility for either prejudicing or safeguarding the interests of all the organization mem-bers concerned as well as those of its beneficiaries. And the wider community served by an organization, particularly if it happens to be a school, has its own interest in being assured that public resources have been soundly invested and deployed for the present and future well-being of the young.

Procedures governing the conduct of selection vary enormously between different educational contexts in the degree of formality required to be observed by selectors, so that the process is far from straightforward or cut-and-dried. For students interested in the dynamics of group behaviour and micro-political processes, then, selections merit detailed scrutiny. On all accounts selection rarely if ever follows a rational course and is really far better understood as like a game going on in the dark in which the aspirant leader has to keep guessing what the rules are by which the selectors are playing as she or he stumbles along, and as this recollection – despite its obvious embellishment – captures rather well (Darling, 1978, pp. 106–7):

> There we all were then, to be interviewed in turn. Surely some more humane procedure could be established for such an exercise as this. The candidates must all feel like parlourmaids, in the old days, waiting in the Registry Office, pretending to be insincerely friendly to each other. By the time that my turn came I was even more certain that I did not want to be selected but, having put my name down, I could not now refuse to go in to bat. There was a long table in the middle of which sat Monty Rendall [the retired head of Winchester College], whom I knew well. On his right was a smallish keen-looking man with grey hair and a small moustache, who was introduced to me as Mr Donald Mackinnon, Chairman of the [Geelong Grammar] School Council. On Monty's left was a large and red-faced clergyman who turned out to be Dr F.E. Brown's brother, Dr Brown being the retiring headmaster of Geelong. These three were flanked by two officials of the Board of Education ... I don't remember what we talked about but I am sure that I was quite indecently free from alarm and quite enjoying myself. Very soon it was clear that Brown's brother had been well briefed on the question of selection and that I was not his choice. Leaning over the table to me he asked, though it was clearly a question to which he knew the answer, 'Are you in Orders, Mr Darling?' 'No', I replied firmly. 'Are you contemplat-ing Orders?' 'No,' again. He sank back into his seat triumphant. Some minutes later he again took the floor. 'Are you married, Mr Darling?' – and he knew the answer to that well enough also. 'No,' I replied. 'Are you contemplating matrimony?' That fixed it. The simple answer would not have done, nor yet a lengthy disquisition on the advantages and disadvantages of married headmasters. The fatal words arrived in my mind and I replied, 'Well, not specifically.' As I said them I glanced at Mr Mackinnon and caught his eye. He was clearly amused and pleased. From that moment I think that his mind was made up and his mind was of course the mind that mattered ... After a few more minutes the interview was over. Nothing was said to enlighten me but I felt fairly sure of the result. Some days or weeks later I was informed that my name had been the first of two sent to Australia for decision by the Council. After that there was a long wait.

Darling turned out to be right about the interpersonal chemistry he felt between himself and Mackinnon, for he was offered, and accepted, the appointment as headmaster.

Despite the obvious hyperbole with which Darling has reconstructed this dialogue, it shows, *inter alia*, the personal connections which sometimes exist between selectors and incumbents (in this case filial), how apparently innocent questions are often designed to trap and embarrass the unwary but also how the cleverness of the questioner can backfire: in this case an entirely new set of assumptions were at work, for the council chairman signalled himself as perfectly content to entertain the prospect of a young, unmarried, lay headmaster in a church school. More importantly, what this little *mise-en-scène* shows is the invariably context-bound and coded nature of selection proceedings. Nowadays, in the current era of equal employment opportunity, questions about matrimony are *verboten* and deemed to be discriminatory – and seem touchingly quaint or archaic when read by modern eyes now that the contemporary concern is with managerial competencies – but in boys' boarding schools at that particular time (1929) wedlock and the ordained ministry still obviously counted when appointing headmasters.

In this chapter I begin by considering selection methods and whether the whole idea of a method makes any sense at all. I then examine the process of selection from the perspective of selectors and the kinds of assumptions they bring to bear in their preparation and questioning. Next I move around to the other side of the table to the candidates' chair and analyse how they prepare themselves, and the extent to which they strategize, as I foreshadowed earlier that they might. I then conclude with some observations about status conferral which was alluded to when introducing the chapter.

Methods of selection

It is surprising how much of our contemporary understanding of selection in education and beyond has been influenced by practices pioneered in the military, in particular by the Allied armies during World War II which were in turn influenced by the German *Wehrmacht*. The dominance of traditional ruling elites in the officer corps of the European powers persisted until well into the twentieth century before selection was instituted on a meritocratic and professional basis. Sporadic use was made of psychologists to assist with officer selection during the Great War, but it was the systematic employment of psychologists by Germany after the Treaty of Versailles which had a lasting effect on other Western countries (Jones, 1991, p. 64). The standard method of British Army officer selection had been to take young men with the School Certificate from schools with an Officer Training Corps. For about 20 minutes or so an interview board of three would question an officer candidate whose answers, along with 'such traits of character or deportment as he betrayed' (Morris, 1949, p. 220), provided the basis of an assessment of suitability. After the evacuation from Dunkirk in 1940 and the reorganization of the British Army, however, it was realized that there was a high failure rate in Officer Cadet Training Units amongst candidates recommended for commissions by their officers. One possible reason may have been that the officers were 'orientated to assessing men with "a public school" background, but were out of their depth when it came to assessing men with very different backgrounds to themselves' (King, 1989, p. 24). The collapse of the traditional system in 1940–1 produced deleterious outcomes for it was 'not scientifically based' (Morris, 1949, p. 221) and in the summer of 1942 a new system of War Office Selection Board (WOSB) officer selection was introduced.

Each WOSB comprised a president (usually an army colonel), a military testing officer – or MTO – (a major or captain), a psychiatrist (again a major or captain) and a psychologist (a subaltern). Testing of potential officers lasted for three days, during which time they completed a battery of written tests (questionnaires, intelligence tests, psychological tests to indicate personality characteristics, and a mathematics paper), a series of practical tests conducted by the MTO and three interviews (to do with officer quality, and psychiatric and technical aspects). The tests conducted by the MTO included simulated individual and command group situations and, interestingly, leaderless group situations – such as military-related group tasks or group discussions – in which (Garforth, 1945, pp. 102–3):

> the observer watches above all the interpersonal reactions of the group, and the significance of the contributions to direction or execution made by each member of the group. It is by no means always the candidate who talks the loudest or most, or apparently takes the lead, that gets the highest grading.

It was then open to the WOSB to have candidates appear before a final board conference, following which, after the observations of the various officers had been pooled and appropriate records (e.g. medical) consulted, a final grading decision would be made by the president. According to Garforth (1945, p. 107) the new WOSB approach was not 'wholly "scientific" ' but it at least attempted to compensate for the human prejudice and error of the previous haphazard, casual and intuitive methods it replaced. Its virtue was that it relied on trained, concentrated, multiple and organized observations (Garforth, 1945, p. 108). Satisfaction levels amongst commanding officers with WOSB nominees during subsequent military campaigns were found to be high (Morris, 1949, p. 225).

A number of interesting developments emerged from these pioneering military initiatives. The first was the growing popularity and refinement of approaches to personality assessment for selection and other purposes during the 1940s and 1950s (see Taft, 1959 for an early review of the technicalities involved). Intelligence testing was by no means confined to the armed forces and psychological expertise had already been utilized fairly widely in education for vocational guidance and student placement. Moreover, with the emergence of personnel departments as a result of the growing popularity of the human relations movement in industry there was considerable interest in testing for things like workers' job adjustment, loyalty and satisfaction levels. Indeed, by the early 1950s industrial psychology and testing were thought by concerned observers to be in the ascendancy, so much so that when one of them, W.H. Whyte – the editor of *Fortune*, a leading US business magazine – surveyed US corporations he discovered that a significant proportion of them were using personality tests, mostly for screening job applicants but also for checking on whether or not employees should be promoted. Whyte (1963, p. 163) viewed this growing fetish for testing with alarm and was irate at proponents' claims that testing was scientific.

Blinkhorn and Johnson (1990, p. 672) claim that 50 per cent of UK firms still use personality tests for selection or assessment. They surveyed three of the personality tests most widely used for selecting recruits and could find 'precious little evidence that [they] predict job performance and a good deal of evidence of poorly understood statistical methods being pressed into service to buttress shaky claims'. Testing amounted to pseudo-science at best. Whyte held a similar view and scandalized many of his critics at the time by recommending that whenever an individual was required by an organization to reveal these kinds of innermost, private thoughts and opinions in a test then 'he [*sic*] has a duty to himself to give answers that serve his self-interest rather than that of The Organization. In a word he should cheat' (Whyte, 1963, p. 163). This advice was outlined in the celebrated appendix to his widely read book, *The Organization Man*, which was entitled 'How to cheat on personality tests'. The moral of Whyte's rather impishly worded recommendation can be found in the opening two lines: were one, as a candidate, ever required to be assessed then Whyte's (1963, p. 373) advice was that 'you don't win a good score', on a personality test, instead 'you avoid a bad one'. In short, he was inviting those at the mercy of the tester to play safe by, in effect, feigning an identity and contriving a desired test score: 'you should try to answer as if you were like everybody else is supposed to be'. The real trick for the individual in successfully negotiating a testing regime, therefore, was to be able to engineer a test result 'without departing too far from your own true self' (Whyte, 1963, p. 374).

The second feature of wartime experience concerns the weakness of selection interviewing as the sole or most important predictor of subsequent leadership performance. I provide a more detailed analysis of interviewing shortly (when I also return to the matters of feigning and being true to self touched on by Whyte). For the moment the point is that, 50 or so years after these defects with interviewing first became widely known, it is still by far the most significant source of leader selection judgements in schooling and education – although that importance is slowly beginning to change. The weakness of interviews is that they promote candidate behaviour which really amounts to display or, as Cecil A. Gibb (1946, p. 65) – a wartime psychologist with the Australian Army Psychology Service and later a noted leadership commentator – observed:

> It is inevitable that the factors which create the greatest impression in the interview situation are those of maturity, poise, self-confidence, verbal fluency and the like, whereas other fundamentals of executive capacity, intelligence, tolerance of others and good 'contact' are practically inaccessible.

Yet Gibb's is far from the last word on interviewing, for Silverman and Jones's (1976) investigation of selection processes in a UK public sector organization shows that recruitment specialists who are conversant with both relatively firm and invariant definitions of candidate acceptability, and with typical candidate attributes, can be very adept and economical in screening applicants for the necessary prerequisites for appointment. Their book *Organizational Work* suggests that interview experience and expertise are important in drawing valid inferences from interview behaviour. Indeed, recruiters were observed to adhere to well-tried and well-rehearsed techniques of discrimination (Silverman and Jones, 1976, pp. 28–9):

> From the accounts that selectors have offered us on being played tapes of selection interviews, 'acceptability' is recognized in a 'performance' which implies that the candidate is prepared to stand up for himself [*sic*], 'sell himself', yet to defer to the accumulated wisdom of the Selection Board. One of the selectors on each Board is deliberately allocated an 'abrasive' role: his job is to attack the candidate, in order to see if he can stand up to pressure in an 'acceptable' way, i.e. to 'sell himself' deferentially.

Candidates were also deemed acceptable when they were seen to eschew unduly abstract ideas in favour of practical-mindedness. One successful candidate, for example, had his performance highly praised by an officer of the organization who heard the tape of the interview for the manner in which the candidate approached political and social issues from an administrative frame of reference – a perspective taken to reflect an ability to get to the technical heart of an issue and to see it in practical terms.

The third important development forged in the exigencies of war was the assessment centre. Once again this was an approach pioneered by the German Army. A variation of it was also used in wartime by the US Office of Strategic Services (OSS) – the forerunner of the Central Intelligence Agency – to train special agents, and the assessment centre method continues to be the principal means of officer selection in the armies of Western Europe and the Commonwealth (Jones, 1991, pp. 70–1). In Germany, over two days at a testing centre controlled by a board of two military officers, a physician and three psychologists, applicants for commissions would undergo an analysis of their life histories and personal features such as their facial expressions, handwriting and speech quality; they were given intelligence tests and a battery of performance assessments – including a choice reaction test, a command test and a series of individual performance tests – and they were given a personal interview (Eaton, 1950, p. 624). Bass (1990, p. 872) has described the uniqueness and peculiar advantage of assessment centres as being:

> [their] use of the pooled judgements of staff psychologists and managers who have

been assigned as observers. The judgements are based on their observations of the candidates in action and the inferences they draw from the test results to reach consensus decisions about the leadership decisions of each candidate. The observers also use consensus to predict each candidate's likely performance as a manager and other aspects of the candidate's future performance.

The assessment centre is becoming increasingly popular in education. Perhaps the earliest and best-known application of assessment centres for the selection of school administrators is the Principals Assessment Centre (PAC) established by the National Association of Secondary School Principals (NASSP) in the USA. The assessment of 12 participants by six trained assessors over two days comprises six exercises: two leaderless groups, two in-basket activities, a fact-finding activity and an interview. Each candidate is rated on 12 skill dimensions and ratings are then aggregated into a profile of a candidate's readiness for administration (McCleary and Ogawa, 1989, and see Draper and McMichael, 1998, pp. 164–5 on candidates' perceptions of their own readiness for leadership). A study of the PAC by Schmitt *et al.* (1984, p. 213) concluded that such centres 'are valid predictors of job performance, not merely indicators of an individual's ability to survive within an organization'. The University of East London currently offers a diagnosis of heads' strengths and weaknesses at the Headteachers Assessment and Development Centre (Lyons *et al.*, 1993), and the assessment centre approach has now been adopted in Australia to identify discrepancies between frontline managers' current abilities and generic national competencies as part of the earlier-mentioned FMI initiative. Finally, in the state of Victoria all Leading Teachers employed by the Department of Education are being accredited by an assessment process in order to confirm that they possess designated leadership and management competencies, and to secure their higher pay and performance bonuses (Nesbit, 1997).

As McCleary and Ogawa (1989, p. 112) point out, while NASSP assessment centre profiles provide a clear basis for selection on merit they may be used by school districts as just one source of information when making principal appointments. Another possible consideration for district boards might also be to ensure that appointees' profiles are consistent with community norms. This was an overriding factor observed by Peshkin (1978, p. 81) in Mansfield, USA, a 'rural dominated tradition-oriented' community in which the board members were concerned less with the 'capacity to lead' than with a prospective superintendent's 'fit with their orthodoxy'. This kind of parochialism is admirably captured in Winifred Holtby's novel *South Riding* when Sarah Burton is being interviewed for the post of headmistress by the governors of Kiplington Girls' High School in Yorkshire and reveals that she once came from 'these parts'. Miss Burton, it transpired, was the daughter of the blacksmith from nearby Lipton-Hunter:

> The chairman, fumbling with his tongue for a bit of gristle caught in a hollow tooth, thought, 'Let them get on with it. A blacksmith's daughter. Good enough for Kiplington.'

There may, on the other hand, be occasions when countervailing arguments will invalidate community norms such as those running along the lines of 'more of the same' – that was clearly so at Oscar Centre when Peele was appointed and also seemed to be the case at Corio when Darling went to Geelong Grammar School. If, for example, selectors think of the needs of their particular organization in life-cycle terms then they are more likely to be attuned to casting tradition aside and to weigh up carefully the relative merits of appointing not only an outsider but one who is likely to break the mould. These points bring us to the kinds of implicit assumptions which weigh on the minds of selectors.

The selectors

Selection panels in education and beyond vary greatly in size, composition, level of expertise and the amount of responsibility they exercise in the selection of leaders. Such variations make generalizing about all possible selection contingencies and permutations extremely difficult. Assuming, however, that some degree of site-based involvement in selection is permitted – Fauske and Ogawa (1987, p. 36) report that there was none when Mr Brown resigned at Valley Elementary and there was precious little until the early 1980s in Australian government schools (see Watkins, 1991) – then three main selection mechanisms can be distinguished. First, there are site-based governing bodies or councils which, broadly, are stand-alone employing authorities (as in the fee-paying school sector) that either select and appoint candidates themselves or constitute panels to make nominations on their behalf, on the basis of which they then make offers of appointment. Second, there are site-based governing bodies or councils which are part of a system of schools or colleges and to which authority has been delegated by a minister of the Crown, a parliament, a local authority or their equivalents to select or nominate candidates to an employing authority (as in government sector schooling). In both cases the membership is small (typically 10 or less) and comprises a balance of elected or appointed local interests (old scholars, parents, members of the community, co-optees, etc.) and, in the second instance, includes system or employer authority representatives (advisers, inspectors or departmental officers). Third, a site-based governing body (usually of the stand-alone type) contracts a professional search committee or agency in much the same way that a commercial employer does either to screen and reduce prospective candidates who meet predetermined specifications down to a short-listed few, or to screen and assess a recommended rank order on its behalf for immediate appointment.

For each of these three selection types – stand-alone, site-and-system and search – there will usually be a summary job description or statement of the position to be filled which appears in an advertisement in the national press or (if it is a system-level appointment) in an official or quasi-official publication. At Worthington, a voluntary control primary school in the UK, the advertisement in the *Times Education Supplement* for a new deputy head said simply (Gronn, 1986a, p. 3):

> Applicants should be outstanding teachers, willing and able to contribute to curricu-
> lum development and to be fully involved in school administration and
> organization. Interest in Music, Art and Craft or Boys' Games an advantage.

The last four words quoted in the advertisement were deliberately contrived by the governors to circumvent the equal opportunity provisions obtaining in the LEA and to try and meet the female head's preference for a male deputy. Among voluntary aided sector schools in the UK – in which it is legally permissible to include denominational criteria in advertisements for headship vacancies – Foster (1996, p. 108) found a curious unintended effect of this denominational provision occurring in localities like Barset-shire where there was a high concentration of aided schools (295 of 591 primary schools), but in most of which there were small enrolments. To the extent that school governors in the few larger Barsetshire county schools attached a high priority to previous headship experience as a selection criterion, then within-county applicants who were unable to meet the denominational requirements found themselves at a disadvantage com-pared with their voluntary aided colleagues. This is because they had fewer available options in which to secure the requisite headship experience.

Depending on the degree of delegated authority accorded school site personnel the documents and detailed selection criteria devised by the selectors will encapsulate the profile desired of the prospective appointee. This profile is the outcome of site-based micro-political processes. It gives expression to the consensus- or majority-based assumptions about the desired replacement prevailing amongst the contending site-based interests repre-sented on the governing body (and its selection panel) – sometimes referred to as the dominant coalition – and symbolizes the public face of the organiza-tion to prospective candidates. At Worthington, an example of a site-and-system selection mechanism – 'candidates are selected by a lay interview panel of local authority members and school governors which is advised "professionally" by an education officer' (Morgan, 1986, p. 152) – the head set out her expectations of the new appointee in a document entitled 'The Role of the Deputy Head'. This was written in conjunction with the retiring male deputy, an incumbent of many years standing, and each of the six candidates short-listed for interview received a copy. The document emphasized leadership rather than what she termed 'petty tasks'. Because the new position was primarily a teaching role, however, the head sought a good teacher and someone who displayed the potential to lead. She and the governors had to be able to 'see Head material in them'. She therefore sought evidence of initiative, the willingness to lead and the capacity to 'inspire others to follow'. What the field of 43 applicants did not know, however, was her wish for a male deputy – a preference known and supported by the governors and which was an attempt to rectify the numerical gender bias towards women among her staff, to provide the significant proportion of children enrolled from single-parent families with a constant male role model and to ensure that the discipline of boys was undertaken by a man.

Unbeknownst to potential candidates, then – unless they happen to be insiders who are 'in the know' – there is often a hidden face or sub-text to selection lurking in what an organization discloses publicly. Sometimes candidates sense this. Thus, all six UK women heads in her research study told Valerie Hall (1996, p. 59) that during their final selection interviews they were convinced that their job would go to a male candidate. Although they happened to be proven wrong in their cases preferences in some succession processes, as Friedman and Olk (1995, p. 142) point out, are often known well in advance of selection. One of the six, Diana, was told by the chair of the governors that she was not the favoured candidate for the headship, 'felt she had nothing to lose' and was astonished when she got the job (Hall, 1996, p. 59).

The combination of two criteria – the extent of departing incumbent influence on a dominant coalition and advance knowledge of a dominant coalition's preferences – generate four main types of selections, each with their own peculiar consequences for the incoming leader: crown heir, horse race, coup d'état and comprehensive search (Friedman and Olk, 1995, p. 149). A crown heir is a person publicly designated and probably even groomed to succeed an incumbent. Indeed, she or he may be the incumbent's preferred choice and their nomination signals the desire for a smooth transition. This possibility would be most likely to occur in stand-alone selections and in such circumstances a crown heir is almost certain to be an inside appointment. Coups occur when an insurgent set of interests opposes an incumbent's regime and, perhaps well in advance, makes its preferred alternative candidate known. In schooling the incidence of coups would again tend to be confined to stand-alone contexts because the strength of the external monitoring and authority lines in site-and-system cases would preclude any secrecy and scheming against an incumbent. On the other hand, site-and-system instances in which system-level personnel (in the guise of inspectors or regional officials) are appealed to by governing bodies or their equivalents to intervene in circumstances of incumbent ill-health or incompetence, for example, are far from unknown. Comprehensive searches – Friedman and Olk's equivalent to my third selection category – provide probably the clearest instance of occasions in which an organization is determined to make an outside appointment and to introduce new blood, whereas horse races, according to Friedman and Olk, comprise a field of fairly evenly matched internal applicants. In schooling, searches are common in stand-alone situations but horse races comprising solely site-based personnel are rare.

The contrast in preferences for internal and external successors amongst these four types – particularly in the case of crown heirs and searches – is stark. A number of considerations might make an internal replacement an attractive possibility. In some contexts tradition exercises a remarkably strong influence. The Midtown Service Organization, for example, a voluntary agency studied by Zald (1965, p. 55), had 'always chosen its executives from among its own personnel' and seemed none the worse for having done so. Pressure for an internal appointee is also likely to be strong if a cabal of influential organizational staff covet advancement for themselves, in which case its members are likely to bear in mind 'that an insider is less likely to replace them than an outsider' (Kets de Vries, 1988, p. 58). An internal replacement usually signals stability and confidence in the quality of an organization's own people. Moreover, selectors may view an insider as some-one already well acculturated in the ways of the organization and who, having served a long apprenticeship, is forearmed with considerable accumulated wisdom and knowledge. On the other hand, from the perspectives of former peers and associates a newly promoted internal incumbent may be adjudged as the beneficiary of favouritism and become the object of resentment, bitterness and sour grapes as a result. Given their local cultural knowledge, of course, insiders are well placed to capitalize on a departing leader's legacy. Yet an insider replacement who is expected to be a clone who exactly mirrors their predecessor's style and values will not necessarily do so, for they might feel shackled and hamstrung, and not their 'own woman' or 'own man'. Another dimension to internal replacements is the strong likelihood that a favoured insider, who has been groomed or perhaps has anticipated being appointed, may miss out. The experience of being passed over typically results in hurt, a sense of betrayal or even ridicule sufficient for those concerned to try and sabotage and collude against a successor. The best example is vice-principals who have acted as school principals during an interregnum and yet an outsider is appointed over them. They are then left in the position of having to try and gracefully retreat to lick their wounds.

A different set of pressures predisposes selectors to nominate an external candidate. Whenever an organization's performance is perceived to have degenerated or lapsed into a moribund state then the desire for innovation or a shake-up will be strong and perhaps even overwhelming. One of the reasons J.R. Sutcliffe (1977, p. 109) was appointed to the headmastership of Melbourne Grammar School in 1938 appears to have been that he was meant to pull the school around after six changes of headmaster or acting head-master in the previous four years. A problem faced by an outsider who is intent on achieving new efficiencies or economies is that she or he has to deal with the 'old lieutenants' amongst middle managers. Their die-hard loyalties and the strong sense of their own entitlement can make life bad enough for an internal appointee, but when an external successor 'fails to respect these old obligations and their informally privileged position, they begin to resist' (Gouldner, 1954, p. 74). Regardless of their point of origin, successors may well try to come down hard on such old allegiances and privileges – as Peele did – but they might also try the opposite approach of appeasement, or what

Gouldner refers to as a policy of pseudo-gemeinschaft. That is, the newly selected incumbent may endeavour to create a superficial community of interests, consensus and solidarity by being friendly, by appearing to stroke people and by cultivating the common touch. The likely occurrence of either of these alternatives is difficult to predict because, as Gouldner (1965, p. 649) asserted, any complex institution 'reflects a compromise between formal and informal organization, between rational and non-rational norms'.

From the point of view of selectors the most helpful research into the relative merits of internal and external candidates was conducted by Carlson (1961–2), who proposed a number of interesting hypotheses based on a study of US school superintendents. Insiders – those whom Carlson (1961–2, p. 211) said wait for their chances to arise – tended to be place-holders or place-bound individuals who were more compliant and ready to fall into line with school district board policies. Outsiders, on the other hand – those who, like 'the man [sic] who does not wait' (Carlson, 1961–2, p. 211), were mobile and created their own opportunities for professional advancement – were career-bound. Insiders tended to be more pliable from a board's point of view whereas outsiders tended to make policy on their own terms and to feel less constrained to support their predecessor's way of doing things. The rule of thumb which Carlson (1961–2, p. 214) found to be operating in the selection of school superintendents was that 'in no case where the [previous] administration was considered unsatisfactory was an insider appointed'. Consistent with Gouldner's earlier hypothesis about the consequences of succession, Carlson also found that there was a stronger tendency for outsiders to bureaucratize school district administration in the early stages of their incumbencies by increasing staff numbers and by bringing in new staff. This was mainly because they were endeavouring to redirect their immediate subordinates' loyalties.

Because her or his commitment is to place rather than to career, therefore, an insider's length of incumbency will tend to be greater than that of an outsider because the latter is committed to career mobility. Significant organizational consequences follow for selectors from the pattern of consecutive succession appointments (Carlson, 1961–2, p. 223):

> The various comparisons between insiders and outsiders suggest the hypothesis that an organization would not be able to adapt itself and operate successfully under the impact of two successive insiders. A reputation would develop that the system was not developing an adequate program and able personnel could not be attracted. The community would complain about outmoded procedures and practices. Institutional integrity would be damaged, for the commitments of the insider suggest that [she or] he is more willing to make compromises than the outsider. In time, this could reflect on the professional standing of all administrators in the system and on the school board.

Of four likely succession patterns in school districts – insider succeeded by insider (I–I), insider by outsider (I–O), outsider by outsider (O–O) and outsider by insider (O–I) – Carlson (1961–2, pp. 224–5) found that in 103 successions over a 32-year period in 48 Californian school districts, I–I successions occurred on only seven occasions. Insider successors are predominantly domesticated individuals or system-maintainers who derive status from their new incumbencies, whereas outsiders are people who bring status to their new offices.

Armed with the foreknowledge of dominant coalition preferences, and the merits and demerits of internal and external candidates, the selectors finally prepare themselves to interview a few short-listed applicants. In keeping with the spirit of the observation by Gibb (1946) cited earlier, Fletcher (1990, p. 740) has argued that the highest priority in selections is invariably accorded candidates' interview behaviour which is 'taken as indicative of enduring [personality] dispositions'. From a candidate's point of view, on the other hand, she or he, naturally enough, 'is seen as wishing to be viewed in a positive light by others and as behaving in such a way as to maximize the chances of this'. If, however, as Fletcher argues, interviews should not be thought of as tests of personality, then an important question is: What valid inferences about leadership may be drawn from candidates' presentation strategies? Silverman and Jones (1976, p. 29, original emphases) found that experienced personnel recruiters in the public sector deemed interviews to be:

> a crude replication of the conditions that the candidate might experience if employed by the Organization ... the interview is important *not* as a means of gathering information about a candidate's *past* performance but about his *present* performance 'under fire' – 'getting by' in the interview is itself the test.

At Worthington the school governors took a more leisurely view of things and concentrated on trying to interpret the messages conveyed by the candidates' behaviour. These were first- and second-hand impressions based on perceptions of utterances, body positionings, moods, airs and graces, interpersonal feelings, and reputably sourced opinions (Gronn, 1986a, p. 11). What drove the head's judgement of whether or not she had read all of the candidates' signals correctly was, in the end, 'instinct on the day of the interview', 'an instinctive feeling this person is right because of personal qualities' (Gronn, 1986a, p. 1). Instinct and intuition, of course, work both ways. On the day of her headship interview Susan's intuition told her that Covington Primary School in the UK 'was right for her and she for the job' (Hall, 1996, p. 82). Her approach was to say what she thought had to be said. It worked.

The candidates

The steps in the selection process at Worthington following the receipt of applications included the completion of a short-list, the conduct of six interviews and then a post-interview reflection meeting of the selection panel. Initially, possible candidates for the post who stood out on the basis of their references and her own reading of their applications were invited by the head to visit the school. This provided an opportunity to 'assess them on a personal basis' and for their prospective colleagues to meet them, which was important because 'what is written on paper doesn't always live up to expectations' (Gronn, 1986a, p. 6). The short-listing was then completed by the head and an LEA adviser, both of whom sorted through the written applications and searched them for indicators of the candidates' attributes (particularly self and style) in everything they chose to say about themselves or elected not to mention. It is at this point in the selection process that all kinds of idiosyncrasies in the minds of selectors become evident. At Worthington the head was a reasonably tall woman. Immediately, the height and size of the new appointee became an issue for her, for it was no good appointing a small deputy, particularly 'if I'm towering over them', she said. Moreover, a man's smallness, in her view, would inhibit his capacity to 'say authoritatively [to staff] there's another way to do this' (Gronn, 1986a, p. 6). In this connection one of Hall's (1996, p. 59) six women heads was even informed after an unsuccessful interview for a deputy headship that 'she was considered too [physically?] attractive for the job'. In such circumstances candidates have no way of knowing about or even dealing with such expectations.

   Considerable attention was paid to the details of letters of application and accompanying curricula vitae at Worthington, including their content and form. This was because the head deemed these documents and their presentation to be measures of administrative capacity. 'You've really got to imagine that you're in the job, in a sense, haven't you?', she said. Moreover, both selectors and candidates knew exactly what was expected of them: the adviser commented during the short-listing that 'they've got to sell themselves', and one of the unsuccessful candidates (A) reflected after his interview that 'I didn't flog myself, you know, it's like you've got to be a bit like a salesman . . . punch it home.' But there was a fine balance to be struck in selling oneself. Some applicants were thought to have gone over the top in what they said about themselves – 'I personally wouldn't put down all those i.s.e. courses' – and in the manner in which they presented all their career details – 'my God' (a comment on the use of elaborate black scrolls and italic print). Others were thought to have under-sold themselves in what they claimed were their attributes – 'he hasn't put his heart into that, has he?' – and again in the way they presented the skimpy details – 'a bit drab too'. The particularly damning errors were misspellings (including the head's surname!) and, in the absence of a standard pro-forma application, ill-chosen paper. Again, these kinds of responses were taken as signalling something about the personality of the applicant. One confirmatory instance was given of a candidate's letter written on lined paper:

> it's small, the presentation is small, he was a small person, he was awe-inspired when he walked in here, so obviously he needs not only lines to write on but lines to guide him in life.

Misspellings and careless syntax were particularly damning signs that 'it's not an important enough application from their point of view to make a particular effort'. In all of these ways, then, a written application was considered to be a worthy test of administrative capacity for 'if they can't put a proper application together then they're not suitable to take on a responsible post' (Gronn, 1986a, pp. 6–7, 14).

This imperative to sell oneself is one immediate pressing determinant of the jockeying and preening which form part of aspirants' accession strategies. Prudent candidates are careful to make themselves known by visiting schools, by attending official functions, by coming under the watchful eye of advisers and officials and by being seen to accrue what are known euphemistically as brownie points: going out of one's way, perhaps, to acquire formal qualifications and to participate in professional development programmes. Candidates also rehearse to try and ensure their eventual successful appointment by regularly applying for promotion vacancies. Two problems arise. The first concerns the extent to which in selling oneself one necessarily compromises what I quoted Whyte (1963, p. 374) describing earlier as one's 'own true self'. Is it possible to convey a sense of who one really is while at the same time trying to promote oneself as a kind of desirable self? The second problem, which follows as a consequence of the first, concerns the extent to which selectors have evidence before them of a false, rather than a true, self and whether there is any means of discriminating between the two. These problems no doubt explain why the head and the adviser at Worthington were so insistent that there should be no standard application form, because in the absence of one it was easier for applicants to betray unintended details about themselves. These problems also account for the selectors' intuition that whenever they came across a feral application detail they thought they could smell a rat. But for all kinds of legitimate reasons – pressures of time and existing commitments, personal inadequacies, the desire to maximize their likelihood of success – leadership aspirants in the 1990s may be promoting misleading details about themselves because they are increasingly tempted to submit applications which are ghost-written on their behalf by commercial resumé-writing firms. When an applicant is an insider discrepancies between what is known through first-hand experience and what is included and exaggerated in a commercially prepared application are easier to detect, but this is less easy when an applicant is an outsider.

These problems touch on the other matter mentioned by Whyte which was to do with feigning and deceit. The imposter – Winnicott's (1965) false self – was the subject-matter of an early article by Greenacre (1958, p. 359, original emphasis) and was described as 'not only a liar, but a very special type of liar who *imposes* on others fabrications of his [*sic*] attainments, position, or worldly possessions':

> This he may do through misrepresentations of his official (statistical) identity, by presenting himself with a fictitious name, history, and other items of personal

identity, either borrowed from some other actual person or fabricated according to some imaginative conception of himself.

But there two sides to imposture. As Kets de Vries (1990, p. 674) notes, an imposter has 'an uncanny talent for putting others under [her or his] spell', but also requires an audience to validate or endorse the illusion that she or he is trying to sustain. A benign way in which this observation applies to selection interviews is to recognize that candidates will invariably try to gild the lily where their attributes are concerned and that panels are often reluctant to make unduly harsh, critical judgements. Citing Greenacre on this very point, Kets de Vries (1990, p. 671) notes 'the necessity of the confirming reaction of the audience to help the imposter to establish a realistic sense of self'. Pathological examples of imposture at the highest levels of the public and corporate sectors came to light with alarming frequency in financial scandals in a number of countries during the entre-preneurial 1980s. The abundance of everyday words like charlatan, con, scam and sting indicate the extent and prevalence of deception. From time to time superficially convincing leadership applicants who survive the initial screening process overreach themselves and their true selves stand revealed. Candidate E for the Worthington deputy headship is a good example. After being welcomed at his interview E sat down knees crossed sideways across his chair, reclined on his arm and quipped: 'Bit like Mastermind isn't it really?' The governors subsequently paid out on him unmercifully, dismissing him with such words as nonchalance, facile, fly-by-night, beyond the pale, woolly, patronizing, cocky and half-baked (Gronn, 1986a, pp. 9, 12).

Perhaps forewarned is forearmed, particularly given the distorted self-perception and lack of a balanced sense of reality to which the narcissistic personalities mentioned in Chapter 4 are invariably hostage. Rangell (1976) – a childhood contemporary of Richard Nixon – argued shortly after the president's resignation following the Watergate scandal that in his case being forwarned ought to have meant being forearmed. Sufficient informa-tion was available on the public record, Rangell claimed, to indicate a long career built on political opportunism, distortion, fabrication and cover-up. Yet Americans only changed their perceptions of Nixon and 'moved from apathy and denial to a belated and begrudging acknowledgment of [the] evidence when this could no longer be denied' (Rangell, 1976, p. 39). In this case forewarned proved not to be forearmed. Other, humbler, examples, such as the Worthington one in which the selectors sensed that candidate E was trying to 'put one over them', might be cited in opposition to any argument that selection is a purely technical matter or something best left to expert committees. On the other hand, there might be a good case for sensitizing selectors to the typical kinds of impression-management strate-gies resorted to by candidates, and their effects, 'so that [selectors] can identify them more readily and take account of them in their decision-making process' (Fletcher, 1990, p. 747).

Despite all of the qualms expressed by commentators about flaws inherent in interviewing, it needs to be remembered that the initiative lies with the interviewer rather than the interviewee. This sense of power imbalance comes through very strongly in the first part of Kress and Fowler's (1979, pp. 63-4, emphasis added) discussion of English commercial employment agency interviews:

> [The interviewer] is in control of the mechanics of the interview: he [*sic*]starts it, he has the right to ask questions, and he has the privilege of terminating it. Through his choice of questions he selects the topics which may be introduced and . . . he even has the prerogative to ask questions so designed structurally that *no* new information can be introduced . . . In the hands of an experienced practitioner, the devices for control granted to the interviewer by the format and situation of the interview itself constitute a formidable armoury.

The official record of what was known as a milk-round interview with Chadwick, a 21-year-old economics graduate, compiled by Milburn, the interviewer, and cited by Silverman and Jones (1976, pp. 31–2), provides a vivid illustration of the results of merciless questioning about acceptability:

> **Name:** Chadwick
> 1. **Appearance** Tall, slim, spotty-faced, black hair. Dirty grey suit.
> 2. **Acceptability** Non-existent. Rather uncouth.
> 3. **Confidence** Awful. Not at all sure of himself.
> 4. **Effort** High.
> 5. **Organization** Poor.
> 6. **Motivation** None really that counts.
> **Any other comments** Reject.

Chadwick had nothing like the kind of carefully prepared presentation strategy foreshadowed above by Fletcher and certainly did not impress Milburn (Silverman and Jones, 1976, p. 32, original emphasis):

> *I found that he was . . . um . . . not particularly confident. He seemed to me to be rather diffident altogether . . . um the sort of chap who was . . . the sort of chap who really, coming from the background he did . . . er . . . was about what you would have expected. That is to say without, I mean it sounds terribly snobbish, but um, he was the sort of bloke who had got there by hard work and, and it seemed to me had got very little out of being at university, except perhaps a degree – which I suppose is all important!*

Fortescue, a 21-year-old English undergraduate, on the other hand, sent all the correct signals to Milburn (Silverman and Jones, 1976, p. 36, original emphasis), because he struck him as '*being a reasonable sort of bloke – British and proud of it, you know, stiff upper lip and all that . . . one had to admit that one could see him fitting in extremely well in this sort of atmosphere*'.

Many of the questions asked of candidates at Worthington also illustrate Kress and Fowler's observation about power for they were very direct and presumed a fairly precise and full knowledge of contemporary UK educational developments. Examples included (Gronn, 1986a, p. 8):

- What do you believe to be the purpose of primary education?
- Does spelling matter?
- How would you draw on [a recently published report] to implement a Mathematics programme?
- Would you like to tease out those aspects [of another recent report] particularly in terms of creative language which are important to language development?
- As a deputy head how would you try to influence a colleague whose teaching methods are pedestrian? And if you found that none of this had any effect?
- If you could isolate one quality which a deputy head ought to possess which quality would it be?

In fact it was her one-word answer to this last question which brought a young woman applicant's interview completely undone: 'tactfulness'. When the governors met later to consider the six candidates both the clergyman and the parent observer burst in simultaneously with 'Not for this school' as soon as the chairman called for comments on D:

Advisor (2):	Except for 'tactfulness' ... I'm still unhappy.
Head:	[Interrupting] Oh it was a bit thin wasn't it thin?
Advisor (2):	About that.
Head:	For someone who has been in a school where she will have seen a very good deputy at work it rather surprised me she hadn't picked up from that what sort of things were involved in the total responsibility.
Advisor (1):	Slick ideas yes hm.

Even though D was thought to have an excellent grasp of the curriculum and was an impressive class teacher these attributes were not enough. Moreover, her motives for applying were queried because her interview performance was seen by everyone to belie the idea of tactfulness she espoused and would have had to embody had she been selected for the role. As one governor reflected later:

> If she had no more patience and resources at her disposal than she demonstrated in the interview in answer to that question then the tactfulness might not have been there.

After the selection was over D reflected that even though she lived within walking distance of Worthington she had not bothered to pay the school a preliminary visit because she was not aware that it was essential to do so. Unlike Heather, who felt confident and relaxed at her interview (Hall, 1996, p. 60), D lamented the fact that she and the head had seemed incapable of getting on the same wavelength: 'I couldn't understand what she was wanting from me'; 'I didn't mention the role of sort of taking on responsibility for the school because I assumed every Deputy Head does that when the Head's out anyway' (Gronn, 1986a, pp. 10, 13).

Selection as a status passage

Earlier on I cited Gibb's (1946, p. 60) incisive observation about verbal fluency, self-confidence and poise – in other words precisely the kinds of desired personal qualities which I suggested in Chapter 4 were the ones leaders would wish to project – as being typically manifested in interviews. The reason for categorizing these attributes as typical of display, is that they are analogous to the kinds of features to which judges are attuned in events as seemingly disparate as livestock sales, mannequin parades, mardi gras and festive processions. In each of these examples various types of pedigree animals and human beings are on show or are seen to be showing off and parading the magnificence of bloodlines, produce, garments, artistic creativity and so on. Applicants for leadership vacancies are in a similar position of being on show and displaying their prospective wares in a selection interview and it is frequently on the basis of such impressions that predictive judgements about leadership capacity are made. As a member of the Worthington panel remarked later: 'appearance matters tremendously doesn't it? All of the body language stuff'; and as the head said: 'A lot of it's in the eyes and the face' (Gronn, 1986a, p. 15).

That was one thing which struck me about selection at Worthington. The other thing about Worthington was that the status of the successful candidate (C) as a deputy head and prospective leader was legitimated but the remaining five, while unsuccessful but not failures, had to be cooled out. One of them (F) said immediately after his interview that he felt 'really grotty now', and then later on remarked that he and the others had been given only 'a very brief chat' by one of the advisers and he still wanted to know why he was not chosen. Another unsuccessful applicant (B) – who had already been short-listed for interview on nine occasions without luck – said later that 'the truth isn't you're a failure, you're one of the six that were collected out of forty-three' (Gronn, 1986a, pp. 12, 13). This same young woman had striven hard to remain true to self in her interview and later observed of an interviewee's answers to questions '*they've got to be yours . . . to be honest to the job and yourself*' (Gronn, 1986a, p. 15, original emphasis). To secure an appointment, therefore, meant that a candidate's career leadership aspirations and status were being either confirmed or disconfirmed. From an appointee's point of view the conferral of her or his new status can be viewed as analogous to a rite of passage, an event or ceremony marking the transition or crossing-over from one identity to another: in baptism, this means admission to the faith; in traditional versions of marriage, the movement from celibacy to a lifelong partnership and fidelity; in funerals, the paying of last respects, the celebration of and thanksgiving for a life.

For newly promoted individuals a shift in their official identity also means that they are likely to begin perceiving themselves differently as people. Sometimes, as in Betty Freeman's (1981, p. 20) case, this prospect takes a while to sink in:

When the Chairman, on driving me back to my motel [after the formal interview for the headship and a lavish supper], asked me if I were interested in taking the position, I was somewhat surprised at the suddenness of the proposal, and not wanting to commit myself without further thought, but not wanting to discourage an offer, I played for time. I said honestly that I needed time to think – that there was much that I liked, but uprooting my family was a serious move. However, I left him with the general feeling that if such a proposal eventuated, it would be favourably considered.

Other new appointees, like C at Worthington – for whom to get to an interview was 'the extent of my serious ambition' (Gronn, 1986a, p. 14) – are pleasantly surprised at the prospect. The final new element of promotion for successful candidates, if she or he happens to have been an outside applicant, is that, having been invited by the panel to outline their particular philosophy or vision for education, and to provide some indication of their style, is that they now have to put these things to work in an entirely unfamiliar context. Not only have they been promoted to a new role but membership of a new organization has been conferred on them as well. When these two aspects – occupational status change and a new organizational allegiance – are combined, they mean in leadership career terms that aspirants have successfully negotiated accession and are about to begin what, from their point of view, will hopefully be the first of a number of satisfying and worthwhile incumbencies. Having seen what it means for them to have got on in their careers, it remains to see how they work their way through the process of getting into and accepted in their new environment, which is the subject of the next chapter.

CHAPTER 9

Inducting leaders

Well into the narrative of *Rebecca*, long after Maxim and the second Mrs de Winter had driven through the entrance gates to Manderley, the sombre, brooding and embittered housekeeper, Mrs Danvers, devoted forever to Rebecca, the longed-for first Mrs de Winter, steadfastly refuses to be reconciled to the presence and authority of her new mistress:

> 'Why don't you go?' she said. 'We none of us want you. He doesn't want you, he never did. He can't forget her. He wants to be alone in the house again, with her. It's you that ought to be lying there in the church crypt, not her. It's you who ought to be dead, not Mrs de Winter.'

Should any successor ever be the object of this kind of deep-seated personal animosity at any stage of their new incumbency, let alone well down the track and into it, then she or he would be quite justified in wondering whether they had done the right thing by accepting an offer of appointment. Yet this level of enmity does not have to be directed solely at the new leader, for it can also be deeply embedded in the culture of the organization they have just joined. The first staff meeting Betty Freeman (1981, p. 38) chaired in her new role as headmistress, for instance, was one she would 'never forget', for it quickly became apparent that she had taken over a bitterly divided school staff and 'the abuse and plain malice were appalling'.

Experiences such as these would truly constitute any incoming leader's worst induction nightmares. Ms Marshall, the principal of Fairview Elementary School in the USA, and Catherine, who was the principal of Waverley High School in the rural south-west region of the state of Western Australia, fared ever so much better when they took up their appointments. LeGore and Parker (1997, p. 381) report that Marshall received 'virtually unanimous endorsement from the staff early in her succession and was accorded the informal power or authority to control the school', and a colleague of Catherine's is quoted as saying that when she first arrived 'the ethos changed dramatically. We now had an innovative principal who loved her job' (Wildy and Wallace, 1997, p. 140). These two contrasting sets of examples are far from idiosyncratic and, as will be seen throughout the course of this chapter, could be duplicated many times over. For that reason alone they suggest a number of understandable areas of concern to the parties directly involved in the induction of the new leader. The first is to identify the range of factors which shape a new leader's and an organization's experience of induction. Already the examples cited disclose a mix of elements: the newcomer, post-arrival effects of the newcomer, a departed predecessor, the predecessor's legacy, the predecessor's ghost, discontented or contented staff, aggrieved third parties and a series of implied situational unknowns. The second is to establish how and why it is that these (and any other) personal and con-textual ingredients combine to produce such wildly divergent sets of outcomes. And the third, given the enormous material and emotional investment by organizations and prospective newcomers in minimizing disruptive leadership transitions, is whether the various ways in which these factors are likely to play themselves out can be known in advance.

My focus in this chapter is on the personal and organizational manage-ment of role entry. I take an emergent perspective on induction by giving some indication, first of all, of what is involved in winning acceptance and recognition as a leader, and I particularly emphasize the importance of antecedent factors in role assumption. I then say something about the ways in which newcomers come to terms with their roles and begin constructing new identities for themselves. I next consider what it means for an inductee to claim role mastery and when it is timely to do so. Here I consider some of the typical anxieties associated with induction and how these are managed by the various parties. The important point to be borne in mind throughout is that for first-time leaders (such as beginning principals) the socialization they undergo is twofold, professional as well as organizational: not only do they have to learn to become a principal, for example, but they have to learn to become a principal *here* or *there*.

Coming on board

I am less inclined than Gabarro (1988) to typify the arrival phase of succession as the process of taking charge because this notion conveys an unnecessarily instrumental view of what a successor is immediately able to do. The problem with such a description is not only that it carries with it the imputation that a new leader's first encounter with an organization is all one way – her or his effect on it – but that it awards the leader's agency far too much licence. In fact organizational induction provides a perfect laboratory within which to inspect the interplay between agency and structure. The reason is that on the occasion of an induction the volition and choice of the individual leader come hard up against the task-structuring properties of the organization, four of them in particular: its long-term life-cycle position; its external alignments and dependencies; its culture; and the particular role demands with which it confronts the newcomer. In this emergent induction process there will always be scope for intentionality on the part of the leader,

yet these four factors will also impose significant constraints on the realization of one's purposes. The precise ambit of discretion will vary from context
to context, but will invariably comprise choices from amongst a range of
structured options. Sometimes the degrees of freedom available will be
sufficient to call forth proactive leadership – such as in an expanding
organization 'where opportunities are plentiful and the competition for
scarce resources is consequently less intense' (Izraeli, 1975, p. 69) – while at
others the leader will find her or himself confined to merely reacting. And
the result of the mutual adjustment which transpires over time between the
successor and the host organization ensures that some degree of continuity
with the past will be retained but that changes will also occur. As part of the
realist theoretical standpoint adopted in this book, then, structure always
pre-dates the actions which transform it and structural elaboration necessarily post-dates the (individual and collective) actions which have brought
about its transformation (Archer, 1995, p. 157).

Leaving aside culture, for the moment I want to say something about the
other three structuring properties. Implicit in my earlier discussion about
the relative merits of appointing insider or outsider successors was a connection between the long-term position of an organization in the minds of
selectors and the person whom they were about to appoint. Sometimes there
turns out to be a perfect match – the appointee and the cyclically determined
location of the organization find themselves to be in synchronization or
harmony – while at others the two are out of kilter. On occasions like the
latter the appointees are referred to as people 'out of their time' or, more
charitably perhaps, as people 'ahead of their time'. Baliga and Hunt (1988, p.
131) have posited an organizational life-cycle model which incorporates the
sequential phases of birth, growth and maturity through to arrival at a Y-fork,
at which time the possibilities of either revitalization or organizational
mortality await. Sensibly, Baliga and Hunt do not restrict each developmental
cycle to precisely defined time periods but, as organizations enter each phase,
the particular demands, constraints and choices (Stewart, 1989, p. 7) –
or, in my terms, the structural determinants and the scope for the leader's
agency – will, needless to say, vary. Not only that, but key individuals'
personal resources – cognitive abilities and emotional make-up – will also
account in some measure for variations in collective responses at each life-
cycle point (Baliga and Hunt, 1988, p. 133). To take just a couple of
illustrative examples, proactive and visionary leadership thinking would
clearly be called for during the birth or start-up phase of a cycle and – as the
Timbertop example suggested, when survival and growth of the school were
matters of pressing concern – also at the Y-fork. The need to oversee
consolidation, and the streamlining of assets and resources, on the other
hand, is more likely to be called for by leaders during the phase of organizational maturation.

Baliga and Hunt are careful to suggest that at any point of the cycle the
particular choices, constraints and demands will vary according to the level

of organizational leadership in question – be it at the strategic apex, at middle management or amongst supervisors or frontline managers. With the strategic apex or upper-echelon level primarily in mind some of the difficulties in sychronizing incumbencies with cyclic switches can be illustrated by examples of school heads whose inductions proved to be uncomfortably rocky. The selection of the Revd Charles Tasman Parkinson, for example – a man whose vision was said to be '30 to 40 years ahead of his time' (Waddy, 1981, p. 155) – as headmaster of the King's School, Parramatta, Sydney, in 1933 was one such case. His appointment was botched from the outset. In a remarkable contrast to what had happened just five years earlier at Geelong Grammar with the appointment of Darling, the King's School council limited itself solely to a choice of Church of England clergymen and, incredible as it now seems, left the nomination entirely in the hands of an English committee. The result was that the selection committee (Waddy, 1981, p. 156):

> made an eminently qualified choice of a good headmaster for an English Public School in England. The trouble was that Parkinson was to succeed Louis XIV [the Revd E.M. Baker: 'Work hard, play hard, pray hard' – p. 139] at Parramatta. It was a hard act to follow.

Parkinson was the committee's unanimous choice. Yet it soon became obvious to everyone that there was hardly one point of similarity between Parkinson and his predecessor. Moreover, Parkinson 'had one fatal flaw . . . an inability to comprehend that others might think and feel differently, when he was so absolutely, subjectively and objectively, correct'. Symbolic of the change from the previously stiff regime to the new and looser one, and publicly available for the entire King's community to draw the visual comparison, is an early photograph in the school magazine from the time: 'It showed the headmaster flanked by dignitaries [and his family], strolling along, smoking a cigarette' (Waddy, 1981, p. 158).

The smoothness of inductions is often facilitated by a mandate (Hambrick and Fukutomi, 1991, pp. 727–8) given new leaders by the bodies responsible for appointing them. One of the differences between Darling and Parkinson was that Darling had a mandate from the school council (Gronn, 1992, p. 74) whereas Parkinson did not. Even so, Darling stuck closely to two personal rules of thumb. The first was 'when you come into a new place you must first try to discover what are its firm traditions and you must build on those' (Darling, 1978, p. 118) and the second was to stay in touch with his predecessor, Dr Brown (who had returned to England), and to seek his advice from time to time on the practicality of various possible schemes. So well did their relationship prosper that on Darling's advice the new school boarding house built at Corio in 1937 was named Francis Brown House. In his efforts to liberalize boy management and to introduce cultural and aesthetic pursuits at King's, however, Parkinson ran foul of a small coterie of self-appointed guardians of school tradition amongst the masters. As with Hayman at Rugby these senior men challenged Parkinson's authority. An

old boy master was deputed to approach the school council, which responded by hastily convening an inquiry. In 1935 Parkinson offered to resign but
this was rejected by council. He eventually staggered on until early 1938
when, with enrolments tumbling – in fee-paying schools, perhaps the most
heinous and unforgivable of succession outcomes – he resigned. His successor, H.D. Hake, a housemaster at Haileybury, England, later told Parkinson
he would never have come to King's but for what Parkinson had achieved in
his short stay. 'Like a prophet in the wilderness, eating locusts and wild
honey, and eventually losing his head', notes the school historian (Waddy,
1981, p. 168), 'he had prepared the way for one who came after him'.

And that, in life-cycle terms, is precisely the point. Brief incumbencies like
Parkinson's, in which the newcomer's values and style do not quite fit in are,
nonetheless, important transitional interludes between organizational
cycles. It is as if the cultural unfreezing or thawing out as a pre-condition of
the change about which Schein (1992, pp. 298–301) writes so ably has to be
a drawn-out and attenuated process before cracks begin to appear in the old
order. A similar kind of fate befell Peter Thwaites in his first headmastership
at Guildford Grammar School in Western Australia in 1950. In this instance
the second of the three structuring factors suggested above – external
organizational alignments and dependencies – compounded Thwaites's
problem because for much of its history Guildford, with few endowments,
had struggled on mostly in a state of severe financial penury. Thwaites later
went on to become the headmaster of two church schools until he retired in
1975. He was a reformer, and had been a pupil at Geelong Grammar in the
first decade of Darling's headmastership. His predecessor, Canon R.E.
Freeth, was a rather austere Anglo-Irish clergyman who for 21 years had
'imposed his cold and forbidding personality on the school though sheer
Olympian presence, command of administrative detail, the respect of all
concerned and the exercise of unquestioned authority' (White, 1993, p.
2).

Thwaites began as Darling was to later advise and spent most of 1950
carefully analysing the school's needs. At the start he also had the solid
backing of the council. The situation began to unravel for him, however,
when he proposed an expansionary programme including a doubling of
enrolments to 650 boys. Like Parkinson, Thwaites had also tried hard to
broaden the curriculum and to introduce a redemptive, rather than a
brutally physical, regime of pupil discipline, and he regularly consulted staff
opinions on policy and various operational matters. These measures were
quite unanticipated. Complaints about cheekiness and slack student behaviour increased, and events reached their nadir one evening when the
headmaster 'was pelted with bread rolls at one old boys' dinner to which the
then captain of the school had been invited' (White, 1993, p. 10). Thwaites
resigned in 1956. The next year the school council commended his replacement as headmaster for having improved the Leaving Certificate results
attained in that year. Ironically, it took the only remaining master from

Freeth's era to put these achievements into their proper perspective for he is reported to have explained 'that the improved results had their roots in reforms instituted by Thwaites' (White, 1993, p. 10). Credit, it seemed, where credit was due. Again, as Parkinson had apparently done for Hake, Thwaites's reforming efforts had 'made the way much easier for his successor to break free of the pre-war cultural straightjacket' (White, 1993, p. 12).

The same year that Thwaites arrived at Guildford saw Michael Searle follow H.L. Tonkin's 17 years of 'gentleness and warmth' (Hansen, 1986, p. 198) at Camberwell Grammar School, a Church of England day school in Melbourne. Searle had been a master at Maidstone Grammar School in Kent, where he had taught languages, and was an accomplished musician. He was well connected: one of his referees was his headmaster at Marlborough College, the distinguished G.C. Turner, and his best friend at school had been Harry Fisher, son of the Archbishop of Canterbury. (Both Turner and the Archbishop, on visits to Australia in 1954, met Searle at Camberwell.) When he heard of Searle's appointment, Darling – still more than a year off the launch of his Timbertop scheme – wrote to the school council congratulating them on their excellent choice (Hansen, 1986, p. 201). Everything augured well, apart from one small detail: like Parkinson before him, the council had taken Searle sight unseen, for he had been interviewed on their behalf by a firm of solicitors in London. 'But young, handsome, public school and Oxford, distinguished war service: what more could a school want in a headmaster? Here was the kudos Camberwell needed' (Hansen, 1986, p. 202). When council decided not to renew Searle's appointment from the end of 1954, he resigned. The causes of the steady but irreversible erosion of his relationship with the council, and in particular its honorary secretary, the tough, gritty J.G. Robinson – 'not only right-wing in politics but reactionary', and 'over-bearing and dictatorial' (Hansen, 1986, p. 262) – were complex and multi-stranded. They involved the collapse of Searle's vision splendid for the school's expansion into the adjacent expanding suburbs of Melbourne, concerns about eroding scholastic standards and discipline, the headmaster's slightly eccentric manner, loss of staff and the feeling that Searle 'was striding forward too fast'. Again, it seemed to be a case in which the 'soil for change had been turned over and watered [with] the increase to come later' (Hansen, 1986, pp. 232, 221).

Headmistresses of girls' schools are by no means immune from these kinds of induction ructions. In 1937, Miss Winifred Allen, a shy but slightly unorthodox English headmistress from Grahamstown in South Africa, was appointed headmistress of Toorak College, near Melbourne. Miss Allen was 'cautious in making changes' (Robinson, 1987, p. 170) but after six years she had had enough and resigned in 1942. Dogged by small enrolments, shortages of staff and the privations of wartime, for nearly six years Miss Allen had put up with the added incubus of her two predecessors, the Misses Isobel and Robina Hamilton, the much-loved joint headmistresses since 1908 (and, until 1928, co-proprietors), who filled two vacancies on the council and thereby instantly became her employers. Compared with the previous authority of the Hamiltons, the directors had severely limited Miss Allen's powers. Not only had she succeeded them but Miss Allen 'was to work in their long shadow as well' for 'the sisters were frequent visitors to the school' (Robinson, 1987, p. 169). The presence of the Misses Hamilton on council is said to have made her 'diffident', and Toorak's was a council which 'displayed a general disposition to regard change as threatening' (Robinson, 1987, p. 184).

Apart from brief incumbencies like these, which prepare the ground for a subsequent successor to lead the organization relatively smoothly through the next cyclic phase, there are equally brief incumbencies, in which the inductions are trouble-free, but which mostly perpetuate the existing cyclic phase. It is to be expected that successors in these circumstances would be older and trusted insiders. Harold Stewart's appointment at 56 for a five-year term as headmaster of Wesley College, Melbourne, from the beginning of 1933 is a case in point. Stewart replaced the legendary L.A. ('Dicky') Adamson, the head of Wesley for 30 years until his death in December 1932. For most of those three decades Stewart had been Adamson's loyal deputy and the two had worked in tandem. Stewart had already been acting headmaster on four occasions over this period and, to many people, had been unofficial headmaster since the Great War. Never in the school's history 'has a master looked more like a headmaster' (Blainey *et al.*, 1967, p. 160). What is more, Adamson – a Rugbeian and the quintessence of the muscular Christian headmaster – had expressed publicly his confidence that while Stewart was at Wesley he would 'carry on the traditions which I have established'. Indeed, when it extended Stewart's tenure by two years in 1937 the council said as much itself for it referred to Stewart as having carried on 'the Adamson tradition' which had been such a successful formula for nearly 40 years (Blainey *et al.*, 1967, pp. 161, 163). And, if further confirmation was needed that the Wesley community was well aware of the school's then cyclic position, one eminent old boy said in reference to Stewart's appointment that 'to have imported new blood at the present juncture would have been a great mistake' (Blainey *et al.*, 1967, p. 162). Clearly, then, Stewart, a loyal and faithful servant, was given a mantle but not a mandate. Yet, ironically, while providing Wesley with considerable continuity of ethos, it was Stewart who was to oversee the beginning of the end of the Adamson era, in particular the demolition of the old man's much-loved, but inadequate, school buildings and their reconstruction following the receipt of a huge financial gift to the school (Blainey *et al.*, 1967, p. 163).

Of these examples it is worth mentioning in passing that Stewart's case, particularly, shows the force and endurance of the fourth of the factors listed above, organizational culture. With the possible exception of Miss Allen, each of the examples highlights the significance of strategic-level thinking, in life-cycle terms, as an element in the other factor not yet considered, the particular role demands facing a newcomer. The intricate historical details which would indicate why these five inductions transpired as they did are, of course, no longer available (and in a sense no longer matter), but it is a fairly safe bet that then, as now, a plausible explanation would be found in the idea of role enactment. With the swing towards symbolism in leadership and managerial studies in the 1980s documented at the beginning of this book, 'enactment' has been a process receiving very powerful endorsement amongst leading commentators. But enactment is a bit like the idea of taking charge: we have to be careful that the newcomer's agency is not exaggerated and assume that it is she or he who does all of the enacting and has unlimited discretion at their disposal. If it is a formal position of leadership which we have in mind, such as a school or college principalship, then the role as such will be defined, presumably, in a job description or position statement – as we saw earlier at Worthington – but there will also be a host of accompanying intangibles: unspoken assumptions, conventions persisting from time immemorial but never inscribed and, most importantly, expectations. As Fondas and Stewart (1994) quite rightly argue, it is expectations which form the main contextual component of the antecedents of any process of role assumption. Moreover, it is during their enactment that a leader's particular attributes will be either confirmed as in accordance with, or disconfirmed and flying in the face of, those expectations.

Expectations take root in a whole host of ways. They may be formally spelt out, in the hope that they will not be violated, as in the case of the aforementioned mantle and a mandate. They may also be left implicit, in which case speculation about them can still be fuelled in a number of ways. Sometimes a fleeting glimpse of newcomers prior to their arrival is sufficient to feed the organizational rumour-mill or grapevine. At other times such sightings take on the character of an informal inspection. When working their way through lists of possible appointees, for example, lay members of Anglican incumbency committees are known to make a point of worshipping in a clergyman or woman's current parish to get a feel for their priestly presence in the Eucharist which they can then report back to their colleagues. At other times sightings of newcomers are entirely inadvertent. At Worthington, for example, after the selection interviews had been completed, two of the female governors were overtaken in the street by F, who said to them reassuringly 'I'm not following you.' Their response to him was that (Gronn, 1986a, p. 12):

> He looked like an overgrown schoolboy. I couldn't believe it was the same person. He just looked like a gangly sixth former. It was so funny.

And when A had initially visited Worthington, the head later informed the governors, 'he was darting about; his gaze was not fixed, it was darting around and I found that disconcerting' (Gronn, 1986a, p. 12). But newcomers do not even have to make themselves visible because their reputations, known or even presumed, can precede them and are sufficient to influence both legitimate and unwarranted expectations. Searle's distinguished record certainly preceded his arrival at Camberwell and Dr Hamilton, Brown's replacement at Valley Elementary in the USA, was reputed to be a 'teacher's principal' which, the faculty told Ogawa (1991, p. 42), was deserved – at least initially in his induction. Moreover, prospective follower expectations can range from the most ethereal to the most trivial. When Hart (1987, p. 5) arrived as the new principal at a junior US high school – an outsider in a school suspicious of appointments from beyond the district, but head-hunted by the district board, aged 35, enrolled in a doctoral programme and female – some staff saw her appointment as a sure sign of an impending purge. On the other hand, Hart discovered to her chagrin that she was even expected to perform such trivial pursuits as selecting colleagues 'to say grace at faculty parties, [something which] made her squirm' (Hart, 1987, p. 9). Her induction was cushioned by the fact that the assistant principal – male, in his 40s, informed by Hart's predecessor that he would almost certainly replace him and disgruntled that he had not done so – quickly swallowed his pride and swung in solidly behind her. In fact such one-on-one socialization of newcomers by insiders has been claimed to enhance commitment to the organization's values and norms (Sutton and Louis, 1987, p. 356). If that is so, then this assistant principal's response invites a closer analysis of what is entailed in according leadership legitimacy to an inductee.

The construction of a new identity

Just as with the overall process of succession a whole host of euphemisms capture the induction experience of which it is a part in the popular mind, including: easing oneself in, settling in, learning the ropes, getting on top of things, finding one's feet, coming up to speed and plain sailing. Some systems and organizations farewell their departing predecessors with 'parties, speeches, gift-giving and picture-taking to mark the ending of a leadership phase' (Austin and Gilmore, 1993, p. 56) – at Valley Elementary, for example, there was a retirement dinner with songs and poetry for Mr Brown (Fauske and Ogawa, 1987, p. 38). Organizations also try and smooth the transition to the new incumbency with a formal or informal ceremony – perhaps an initiation rite, an investiture or, in the case of monarchies, by coronations. Thus, masonic lodges establish installation nights for new masters, ships' crews pipe their new commodores aboard, parishes formally induct new priests and university departments hold special morning teas to welcome new staff. Such ceremonies fulfil a variety of purposes, but one is a boundary-marking function designed to delineate the old order from the new. As with other aspects of succession researchers until fairly recently have been flying blind in regard to induction for, as a recent review (Parkay *et al.*, 1992, p. 44) of research into the professional socialization of educational administrators notes, 'little is known about [it]'. Indeed, there is a 'dearth of studies on the socialization experiences of those who assume a new principal-ship'. And on the wider front beyond education, Gabarro (1988, p. 237) observes that 'very little [research] has focused on the activities and prob-lems faced by the new manager after he or she actually takes charge'.

As part of this recent quest for a better appreciation of induction has come an understandable urge by commentators to try to specify the seasonality of a first-time leader's tenure. Thus far, agreement has proven elusive. Gabarro (1988, pp. 244–5) claimed there were five phases spread over three-years – taking hold, immersion, reshaping, consolidation and refinement – and, for new school principals, Parkay *et al.* (1992, p. 56) suggested a slightly different five: survival, control, stability, educational leadership and pro-fessional actualization. Based on his observations of Dr Hamilton, however, Ogawa (1991) detected only three phases: three months of enchantment until the novelty of Hamilton wore off, followed by a switch in attributions to disillusionment and disenchantment – in which there was something of a communication vacuum because neither Hamilton nor his staff let their expectations be known to one another – and then an accommodation or the reaching of a *modus vivendi*. Interestingly, however, in her year-long field-work study of 19 first-year sales and marketing managers in two US security firms and computer companies Hill (1992, p. 322, original emphases) found no sustained evidence of periodicity in the transition to management, even though she confessed she expected to. Instead, her sample of new managers was 'learning *what* they needed to learn only *when* they needed to learn it. Time was not the organizing principle that would explain my data; problems and surprises would do so.' And, finally, on the basis of her own successor experience, Hart (1988, p. 335) detected only 'a gradual replacement of preconceived perceptions, expectations, and speculations about intentions with a social network of interaction and support (and pockets of resistance) in the school'.

What these interpretations share, with the possible exception of Hill, is a recognition of shifts in the relative position of the newcomer as part of role enactment. Sometimes the terms convey binary differences in kind (as in attributional responses like enchantment–disenchantment) while at others they provide differences in the degree of a newcomer's control (as in taking hold and refinement). But while it might be pointless pursuing matters of timing, what can be done is to clarify the factors which give the mechanics of role enactment this apparent kind of push-and-pull and give-and-take quality that occurs during the posited stages. At the everyday interpersonal level, role enactment boils down to the development of what Gabarro (1978, 1987) has termed satisfactory working relationships. He investigated the process of role definition and expansion in four US companies as newly appointed presidents developed their working relations with key immediate subordi-nates. The managers' evolving relations with these subordinates began with 'a period of initial impression-making and culminate[d] in a stage in which both parties had worked out a relatively stable set of mutual expectations'

(Gabarro, 1978, p. 292). Initially, exploratory feelers were put out about each other's expectations, then followed a deeper and more sustained exploration of them, and then the mutual negotiation of differences in expectations. These interpersonal moves occurred formally and informally in meetings and in routine task-based interactions, and were crucial for the development of trust. And it was that trust which provided the basis for the expression of mutual influence between managers and their immediate subordinates.

Mutual influence entails mutual dependence and reciprocity. Provided there is interpersonal trust then dependence becomes a matter of choice, with the result that 'to the extent that either party [leader and immediate subordinates] allows himself [*sic*] to become more influenced by the other, he also allows himself to become more dependent on the other' (Gabarro, 1978, p. 300). Clearly there was trust at the basis of Adamson and Stewart's working duopoly. Furthermore, as the following extract from an interview with Cadman, the clinical director of the MPI, confirms, a previous history of working together can be indispensable to the development of trust and mutual dependence between people at the highest echelons (Hodgson *et al.*, 1965, p. 271, original emphasis):

> Cadman [clinical director, and unsuccessful candidate for director]: I've known Frank [Suprinn, the new director] for 20 years, and he knew what sort of person I was ... I decided that Frank and I had common interests, a mutuality of purpose, that could allow me to work with him, and not always be trying to work against him, show him up, and trying to take over his job rather than *helping* him with it. I decided there was a personal compatibility between Frank and me as persons that was strong enough to let us work together. I think that the most important thing between two people in this type of situation is a personal compatibility. Otherwise they wouldn't be able to work together.

In contrast to this example, newcomers, especially first-timers, tend to be dependent initially on colleagues and subordinates out of sheer necessity. There are four main ways in which this dependency on others expresses itself: first, newcomers lack local cultural knowledge; second, they may have incurred sponsorship debts in securing their appointments and these have to be repaid; third, they are deficient in power; and, fourth, they lack information.

As regards cultural knowledge, the best analogy for the newcomer's experience is that she or he is like a stranger – a tourist in a foreign country unable to speak the language – who encounters an experiential barrage of contrasts, differences, surprises and uncertainty (Louis, 1980). Immigrants often find themselves totally alone and utterly reliant on their own resources. They are tense and ever-alert, but also disoriented and unsure of themselves. Analogies aside, as Beeson and Matthews (1992, p. 325) suggest, the reality is probably that most newcomer leaders commence 'with varying mixes of confidence and apprehension', as did their sample of beginning principals. Tony Bishop's first day on the job is illustrative. Bishop (1993), a new principal chosen under local selection guidelines at Bayside Primary School, in Melbourne, kept a journal of his experiences in his first year in the job which began in the middle of the school year. Bishop's feet hit the ground running. He arrived in his new school on a bleak wintry Monday morning in July choked up with influenza. Apart from a teacher ally who had been a member of the selection panel, and who was on-side, he knew no-one. His previous principal telephoned to wish him luck and was at the ready with advice: 'Half seriously, I told him to stand by!' (Bishop, 1993, p. 17). Bishop got through his first day with no bones broken and, looking back later on his very first decisions – which included quickly sorting out an administrative cock-up when two relieving teachers arrived unannounced to replace a staff member on long service leave, and then doing his stint of rostered yard duty – he saw them as indicators to the staff of how he would eventually fare. First impressions for them, he believed, were to be lasting ones.

Like it or not, such impressions, especially if they are unfavourable, will stimulate the kind of invidious Rebecca-like comparisons which commence this chapter. But the making of comparisons, suggest Gilmore and Ronchi (1995, p. 11), is inevitable and the kinds of differences between predecessors and successors are often noted 'with uncanny insight' by subordinates. US President Lyndon Johnson is reported to have been 'tormented by his own reckoning of the lingering presence of JFK in the Johnson White House' (Gilmore and Ronchi, 1995, p. 12). Rarely, it seems, will a successor be able to, or want to, exactly fill the shoes of her or his predecessor, not even the devoted Stewart at Wesley. On the other hand, some shadows and ghosts can be experienced as benign. Harry, a rookie US secondary school principal, for example, took over from a man who was thought to be a legend at his school, whereas his fellow principal Herb succeeded a rather *laissez-faire* predecessor who was summed up as having virtually 'retired on the job' (Parkay *et al.*, 1992, p. 60) – an instance sounding suspiciously like a case in which 'job mastery gives way to boredom; exhilaration to fatigue; strategizing to habituation' (Hambrick and Fukutomi, 1991, p. 731). Examples like the latter one can be turned to a newcomer's advantage. Prinn, the high school principal mentioned earlier, was a woman for whom staff felt a deep affection. Her predecessor had never consulted them about anything and, as one of them said, 'there was civil war'. 'He gradually got rid of everybody who opposed him.' Described as 'semi-competent' this man was caricatured as an autocrat who had his own inner cabal: 'He would veto so many things, refuse to discuss, refuse to vote on them, and so on.' One teacher recalled the feelings he engendered:

> When [he] stood up in the staff meeting last year my stomach would instantly churn: 'What's coming? Oh God, what's coming?'

Further, '[he] would do appalling things like carpet a staff member without naming them in the [staff] meeting and everyone knew who it was . . . and the poor woman's sitting here'. He 'had this big cloak of secrecy around him; the less that people know, the less they can whinge about or try to disrupt'. Life was exceedingly unpleasant: 'Anyone that disagreed with him got yelled at, basically.' Prinn's style was the antithesis of all this and, starved of professional recognition, the staff felt nourished by her and fed her in return (Gronn, 1986c, p. 32).

Provided newcomers can quickly sense prevailing cultural norms, as Prinn did then, as Louis (1990, p. 107) points out, it is always open to them to test the limits of new-found tolerance by deviating appreciably from what is expected and acceptable. They can also take soundings, and watch, listen and soak up information. Thrust into her new role, Hart (1987, p. 4) made it her business to get onto the learning curve quickly and to find out as much as possible about her new school's history. Moreover, contrary to Darling's wait-and-see approach, and against her predecessor's advice, Hart (1988, p. 349) moved fairly swiftly with changes: 'Had I followed this advice [to hasten slowly], the negative atmosphere might have become entrenched.' One can always position oneself so that one observes whatever is happening from different angles – by sitting in on various meetings in which one may not be the central player, perhaps, and by positioning oneself unobtrusively at gatherings at which one is able to be out of the limelight. But always, according to Louis (1990, p. 110), in the manner of the traditional ethnographic researcher and participant observer, one is endeavouring to get a perspective on what is happening through the eyes of the veterans and old-guard organization members. The result is that the learning of most newcomers proceeds incrementally – as a study of 20 newly appointed assistant principals found (Marshall and Mitchell, 1991, pp. 410–11):

> They learn from small mistakes; they learn what resources they can call on; they watch the politics in their districts (and beyond); they gossip and listen to the grapevine; they build networks of friends (other APs or principals) on whom they can rely for advice; and they respond by adjusting to what works.

These experiences have to be set against those of Ms Marshall, of course – an inside principal appointee from the school district who behaved like an outsider by making changes based on her vision right from the start, and who, unlike Hart, deliberately chose not to consult her predecessor. Her induction defied Ogawa's (1991) three-stage pattern for, at the end of the school year 'the teachers were very supportive of Ms. Marshall's leadership' (LeGore and Parker, 1997, p. 379).

In regard to succession debts, any incoming leader 'is under political and social pressure to display the exact orientation for which he or she was selected' (Hambrick and Fukutomi, 1991, p. 722). There are two significant costs to be endured in debt repayment. First, backers and supporters anticipate that their preferred candidate will deliver on any promises and undertakings upon assuming office. Second, if there has been a ground-swell of pressure to secure the appointment of X, or if the choice of X was seen as a foregone conclusion – so that selectors are perceived to have barely gone through the motions when interviewing the other candidates – then X's appointment is likely to be viewed as tarnished by selection irregularities. Friedman and Olk (1995, p. 157) describe this eventuality as the breach of a propriety norm: 'propriety is enhanced to the extent that candidates are seen as having been truly tested during the selection process (i.e., they can be said to have got the job fairly and squarely) and so have earned the appointment'. As has been seen, irregularities with his selection testimonials formed a large part of Hayman's legitimacy problems at Rugby. But Friedman and Olk (1995, p. 157) also distinguish an endorsement norm, in which 'informal power ... may be used to convince organization members of a successor's rightful claims to top leadership, such as through politicking and informal lobbying efforts by powerful actors who are supporters of different candidates'. Should such activities overreach themselves or be performed in too heavy-handed a way then the legitimacy of a successor may also be prejudiced. Moreover, when it comes to actually returning favours and debts once on board then there is bound to be speculation about the likely beneficiaries of such spoils, and about any colleagues seen to be positioning themselves and creating new allegiances in anticipation of forthcoming favours and privileges (Austin and Gilmore, 1993, p. 55).

As for augmenting a newcomer's power and influence, key insiders will definitely need to be on-side when expanding what Izraeli (1977) terms one's power base. Power expansion occurs when the newcomer 'attempts to advance his [sic] own interests rather than merely react to the pressures [peers and subordinates] exert on him' (Izraeli, 1977, p. 137). A good example of the difficulties this can sometimes entail was to be seen in the early episodes of the recent English television drama series *The Governor*, in which the incoming prison governor was not merely new to the particular prison, but a new, young woman starting out in an incredibly entrenched male world. Successful power expansion dictates that key people will have to be kept on-side: the chairwoman or chairman of a school council, perhaps, and other high-profile councillors; immediate subordinates, such as a principal's deputy (who proved such a key ally for Hart), and other significantly positioned and aligned personnel. These potential lieutenants form a part of what Fondas and Stewart (1994, p. 85) refer to as an incumbent's role set and they 'help label and thus shape how members experience the work setting' (Louis, 1990, p. 93). When the Archbishop of Canterbury visited him at Camberwell in 1954, for reasons best known to himself Searle kept the visit informal and so low-key that the school council was not present when Fisher inspected the school. This proved to be a grievous miscalculation by the new headmaster for, in the margin beside the relevant passage in the headmaster's report, Robinson noted, waspishly, 'Council ignored' (Hansen, 1986, p. 225).

The last of the four ways in which newcomers are vulnerable and dependent on others is in relation to the procurement of information. This information-dependency takes one of two forms, the first sinister, the second benign. The first type comprises sins of commission in which, as Macmillan

(1996, pp. 141–2) notes, 'staff may purposely withhold or downplay the importance of crucial bits of information required to make the right decision'. These actions may occur for all manner of reasons but usually betoken some form of reprisal or are a calculated attempt to embarrass a new arrival. The second type is more a sin of omission, so that in the absence of existing files, data and documentation, for example, newcomers are left to start from scratch. Her own frustrating experiences in this regard prompted Gai McMurtrie (1997), a primary principal in the state of New South Wales, to focus her recent research on what she calls the pre-entry needs of beginning principals – that period between the announcement of their appointment and their appearance on-site. In 1996 McMurtrie (1997, p. 89) surveyed 57 beginning principals and found that well over 80 per cent of them rated a formal hand-over, a meeting with new school personnel, access to a 'survival for the first-time principal' handbook and access to site-based documents before their arrival as being moderately or extremely important. Journalists are fond of saying that for such newly elected political figures as presidents and prime ministers there is generally a honeymoon – that 'period of time following the arrival of a successor in which subordinates are willing to: 1) overlook the new leader's mistakes, and 2) allow the successor to press the limits of his/her discretion' (Johnson and Licata, 1995, p. 406). But to be told by a teacher on one's first day, as a principal in McMurtrie's (1997, p. 90) sample was, that because he (the principal) had not unlocked the gates (when he wasn't aware he had to) 'there are people out there angry because they can't get into the school', suggests that for appointee leaders in schooling such honeymoon periods might be rare. In Tony Bishop's case there was certainly no honeymoon, and instead it was a case of learn-as-you-go for him, just as it had been for other incomers like Hart.

Role mastery

Provided the majority of the indications and signs during one's early weeks and months provide positive feedback, at some future point in their incumbencies newly appointed leaders will begin to feel that they getting on top of things. Six months down the track Tony Bishop (1993, p. 25, original emphasis) noted in his diary: 'one week to Xmas holidays and everything *major* has just about been completed – Monday main task is to finalize staff with Region'. On reflection he thought this entry indicated that he had 'attained greater control over the job and possessed a much more positive approach to events'. Yet there were still glitches – such as his deputy's inability to properly organize his role and about which staff complained (Bishop, 1993, p. 20) – but he felt well on the way towards being successful. Promotion to such a formal leadership role as the principalship marks an important personal developmental shift from being the young woman or man of promise to the person exercising formal responsibility. If the thrust of the argument being advanced in this book is correct then this change will

likely have entailed a prolonged internal self-appraisal of existing commitments, talents, values and priorities. But not all of these matters will ever be
satisfactorily worked through once and for all. They will continue to be
wrestled with as, at a moment of crisis in *Rebecca*, the young, nervous Mrs de
Winter caught herself doing:

> My old fears, my diffidence, my shyness, my hopeless sense of inferiority, must be
> conquered now and thrust aside. If I failed now I should fail forever. There would
> never be another chance. I prayed for courage in a blind despairing way, and dug my
> nails into my hands.

Sizing up newcomers in respect of style and personality does not stop with
people's initial prying gazes. Rather, it is just at its most intense immediately
after a new incumbent's arrival (Johnson and Licata, 1995, pp. 407–8). A
survey of over 3,000 US teachers found that what better disposed them
towards newly incumbent principals was the latter's willingness to allow
teachers to retain predictability and control over their classroom work – an
expectation harking back, perhaps, to earlier points about indulgency
patterns. Thus, any successor 'whose leadership style and policies function to
challenge this predictability and control is viewed less favourably by teachers
than one whose style and policies maintain and enhance these features'
(Johnson and Licata, 1995, p. 413).

The one study which has thoroughly investigated role mastery is Linda
Hill's (1992) *Becoming a Manager.* One of the reasons Hill was consulted by
the previously mentioned Australian Industry Taskforce on Leadership and
Management Skills was because of her detailed research on a cohort of first-
time female and male managers. Her sample was aged in their early 30s and
they each managed between 5 and 80 subordinates. Hill investigated the
transition from being part of the production process to what it meant to
become a manager. The contrast the sample experienced between their
recently acquired role and that which they had discarded she described as
comprising more than the acquisition of competencies and the building of
relationships but instead as a profound transformation in which 'individuals
learn to think, feel and value as managers' (Hill, 1992, p.5). The four
personal transformation tasks were: to learn what it means to be a manager;
to develop interpersonal judgement; to acquire self-knowledge and to cope
with stress and emotion. Nonetheless, Hill's sample found themselves
trapped in conflicting sets of expectations about their roles. On the one
hand as new incumbents they saw themselves as invested with formal authority and geared their minds to the accomplishment of tasks. Yet their
subordinates, on the other hand, were far more interested in their capacity
to deal with people. Moreover, the newcomers soon discovered that the fine
details of their subordinates' expectations of them were contradictory: not
only did subordinates want the autonomy to get on with their own jobs – in
the same way that Johnson and Licata's (1995) teachers expected of their
principals – but also they expected their bosses to intervene and solve their
problems (Hill, 1992, p. 60). This personal transformation for the new

managers was often experienced as profoundly emotionally unsettling –
principally because they 'had to *act* as managers before they understood
what the role was ... the meaning and importance [of which] they could not
grasp ahead of time' (Hill, 1992, p. 47, original emphasis). Their biggest
surprise, reminiscent of Khleif's (1976) observations about rookie school
superintendents, was that they all had to unlearn their previous roles: 'Only
as they gave up that identity could they begin to accept their identity as a
manager' (Hill, 1992, p. 52). These first-timers also had to come to terms
very quickly with heavy workloads, a fast-paced work-flow and, not surprising,
the fact of their (unanticipated) dependence on others in order to complete
their work. In this respect these first-time managers had to learn to persuade
other people rather than to direct them (Hill, 1992, p. 106). *Becoming a
Manager*, therefore, describes a group of new managers who learn by the end
of their first year that managing is less a matter of technical competence
(although this recognition died hard with the sample – Hill, 1992, p. 170)
than one of handling people.

   Hill found that the greatest impact of the changed role was on each
manager's sense of identity and her or his understanding of themselves as
persons. This identity shift required them to come to grips with their own
limitations, to try to discover and build on their personal strengths, to carve
out for themselves a preferred style of management and to work on the
development of their personal qualities (Hill, 1992, pp. 171–82). Discarding
a former understanding of their work role and their old identities – as
Mealyea (1988) found as well – was experienced as stressful, and was
compounded by factors inherent in their new managerial work such as
fluidity, overload, ambiguity and conflict (Hill, 1992, pp. 189, 191). Nevertheless, the sample had begun to learn to live with factors like negativity,
imperfection, bearing the burden of responsibility and the diffuse boundaries existing between their personal and working lives (Hill, 1992, pp.
202–3). The first year for the incomers, then, had been one of considerable
hardship and self-doubt. But if the accumulated evidence from psycho-
dynamic studies leadership is any indication, then these short bursts of
emotional flickering would be far from the end of it, for most leaders
undergoing career moves beyond their initial appointments have been
found to be susceptible to nagging inner doubts and fears.

   One of the most common experiences with which upwardly mobile
leaders are required to come to terms is a growing sense of isolation or
aloneness. With career movement there come changes in one's immediate
reference group, so that relationships with former close associates amongst
peers and colleagues have to be recast. One is no longer at liberty to swap
quite the same intimacies as before and, indeed, one's circle of intimates
shrinks. Increasingly one finds more in common with people of equivalent
status in other organizations rather than in one's own. With appointment to
ever more senior leadership roles comes even greater responsibility and
accountability, more confidential information, increased visibility, a greater

likelihood that one will be the object of scorn and criticism, and yet all the time the feeling of being constrained to pretend that all is well and to try to keep up appearances. Jackson (1977), a senior educational administrator, claimed that in his case there were two aspects to leadership isolation. The first was the sheer existential experience of literally being the only person at the very top, and the second was his capacity to live with that fact without succumbing to feelings of abandonment. Some leaders find themselves much better equipped to deal with these changes than others. In her worst moments, for example, Mary – a new principal in Parkay *et al*.'s (1992, p. 63) beginning principals study – confessed to being plagued by doubts about herself as a principal and wanted her old job back:

> I have not slept. I can document that. I work during sleep. It seems to be almost ongoing, and I don't know that I want to pay the price of being so tired that I can't relate to my family in a productive, positive manner. I am so spent that all I want to do is crawl upstairs and lie in bed in a fetal position and say, 'That's it! That's it! That's it!'

Likewise, Klerman and Levinson's (1969, p. 422) Dr P – the Director-designate in a US psychiatric hospital – found his new job to be a mixed blessing. Desirous of promotion he became anxious about the change in his life goals and career direction. 'He looked forward to the new and broader professional responsibilities, yet suffered from corrosive doubts about his ability to manage them. "Did I truly merit this rapid advancement, or has excessive ambition led me to perpetrate a fraud?"'

The first sign to a subordinate or colleague that all may not be well with a leader, according to Zaleznik (1966, p. 36), is their inability to take a stand on a problem. If, therefore, they appear inclined to talk out of both sides of their mouth at once, then 'the chances are reasonably good that you have come across a [woman or] man in the throes of status anxiety'. There are a number of typical ways in which leaders tend to try and resolve any doubts they harbour about their new-found status. The first is to try to cultivate a nice-guy image. This takes a number of forms: the insistence, for example, that a leader's door is always open, of making a point of always being on first-name terms with colleagues and by trying to be one-of-the-girls or one-of-the-boys. These initiatives tend to create familiarity, and familiarity, as the adage says, breeds contempt. The flipside of projecting oneself as a kind of nice-guy is that former colleagues of the new leader still expect to be able to treat her or him in much the same old way despite their changed status. Jim, a secondary principal interviewed by Macmillan (1996, p. 141), reported on an acquaintance's experiences as follows:

> I also saw from him that he was someone returning to the school where he had been a teacher. And I also saw from him the loneliness of office, the fact that you can't be one of the boys the way it was expected that he could be. He was welcomed back by his 'cronies' thinking 'Terrific!' and he wasn't what had left the school. He had changed and I think they hadn't. And they were a bit rough on him because he wasn't the person he had been when he left.

Another adjustment tactic, particularly by outside appointees who find acceptance by subordinates difficult, is to distance themselves by not over-identifying with their new surroundings. This they do by seeking to remain interpersonally aloof or by retreating – as is captured by the expression about locking oneself in one's bunker – or by maintaining psychological distance and trying to keep out of the heat. They may also seek to differentiate themselves – as Dr Hamilton did at Valley Elementary with his constant references to objects and aspects of his lifestyle (such as his boat and his regular tennis engagements) which made him look superior – or they may over-idealize their old organization and its ways. On this latter point, few statements are better calculated to wear new colleagues' patience thin, and to point up their inadequacies, than constant references to how something always used to be done differently elsewhere – the implication being, of course, that different means better. This is a case of using the Rebecca myth in reverse.

These personal considerations to do with identity and status on which I have been concentrating are a sure indication to the newcomer that the rigours of incumbency are beginning to be felt. Their appearance also marks the end of their accession: all the rehearsing is over and at long last this first experience is a taste of the real thing. It is unlikely, however, having just come on board, that they will yet feel themselves to be entirely the mistress or the master of their own house. On the other hand, given time, they will certainly become less and less like a stranger in their own land. Years after his retirement, for example, Darling (1978) was able to look back on the early part of his headmastership and label it the halcyon years, despite its corre-spondence with much of the period known as the Great Depression. Coming a long way forward in time it goes without saying of the current generation that, as new leaders for the new millennium – be they incumbents with formal executive status or informal leaders lacking the authority bestowed by position and rank – new arrivals will confront previously undreamed-of organizational problems. Perhaps the one wider element in their favour which sets them apart from the generations of their predecessors is the breadth of the current interest in, and experimentation with, different learning modes and technologies. Truly, learning-is-in-the-air: rarely does one nowadays hear a description like the learn*ed* professions; instead the preferred term is fast becoming professional learning, which takes its place alongside other popular trends such as the learning organization and the learning society, as part of the shift to customization. Provided newly inducted leaders are comfortable and can work with the possibilities opened up by this new environmental climate in which they will have to operate – which will mean constantly signalling their own preparedness to learn – then exciting possibilities will lie ahead of them. Hopefully, when they look back later to the period of their first induction they, too, will derive satisfaction from knowing that they measured up in their own eyes and those of others to the challenges with which they were confronted.

Concluding comments

This book has been written with the needs of prospective educational leaders in mind. I divided the discussion into three parts. In Part I my purpose was to provide three ways for the aspiring leader to begin thinking about leadership: first, as follower-centred meaning framing in a particular here-and-now situational context; second, and developmentally, as a career with its own unique time frames, phases, transition points, seasonality and rhythms; and third as a role which in the 1990s is open to potentially anyone and for which the requisite preparation has been progressively de-mystified historically to a point where it has become specifically role-related. In Part II I focused on what I maintained were the three key aspects of an individual leader's make-up which would likely be of concern to their prospective followers: identity, values and style. I relied on the historical example of the formation of young English men for leadership roles in Chapter 2 to indicate how the various socialization agencies productive of various identities, values and styles between them shaped the character of leaders. In Part III quite deliberately I shifted the focus of the analysis to a level falling somewhere between the macro and micro concerns of the previous two parts in order to consider the reception accorded aspiring leaders and the strategies for securing recognition. Chapter 7 discussed the potential barriers to a successful transition created by a predecessor's departure. Chapter 8 looked at what happened when the candidates were on show and selectors were convinced by their performances. Finally, I gave some indication of the factors which would make for a satisfactory or unsatisfactory reception for the new arrival.

'Leadership. Everyone talks about it, everyone wants it. But who are the people who will lead us into the new millennium?' So begins a special report on 'Our leaders of the 21st century', a lift-out supplement in the Melbourne *Herald Sun Weekend* for 4 July 1998. If this 11-page form guide of 16 young up-and-comers, complete with their brief vision summaries for the millennium, is any indication, then the issues dealt with in this book will continue to engage the general public. In one way this kind of appetite to identify rising stars and faces-to-watch, and the cataloguing of their notable accomplishments, tells us something about people's craving for celebrities, but in another way it is also saying something about public awareness of the necessity to replace one generation of leaders with another. Even beyond that, I suppose, this urge to try and spot talent is further confirmation of Meindl's thesis about the romance of leadership and just how deeply entrenched our attachment to leaders can become.

But the popular fascination with leadership goes even further. One month earlier, the Melbourne *Age* carried two reports, one in the main part of the paper and the other in its colour supplement, on two prominent and high-ranking public figures. Both reports were short biographical pieces, the first on Australia's current federal Treasurer and the other on the new head of Victoria's Department of Premier and Cabinet and former head of the federal Industry Commission. The interest in these two articles for students of leadership is that when read side by side they catalogue stories of two individuals coming from completely different family and social backgrounds – the one working-class, the other lower middle-class – but who publicly espouse remarkably similar commitments to the need for micro-economic reform, and a reliance on market principles to deliver public sector reform and efficiencies. Looking back at the their different biographies in the articles to the time when they were children who could possibly have predicted this outcome, let alone the likelihood that their future public careers would ever have intersected? A similar question could be asked of the youngsters who were the original members of the *Seven Up* programme and who are now moving as a cohort through middle age.

The two sets of newspaper reports address key dilemmas to do with leader formation. On the one hand, the *Age* articles look back and enquire, in effect, how it was that two men began life when and where they did, and yet ended up where they are now and what were the factors which shaped them. The *Herald Sun*, on the other hand, looks forward and conjectures at possible future careers that might or might not come to fruition for a pool of young talent. Both instances, however, point to the difficulties in trying to predict and control the means by which leadership is replenished. Notwithstanding the ascriptive examples considered in Chapter 3, society-wide systems of leader formation and replacement, by and large, retain a happenstance or hit-or-miss character. This is understandable because, unlike an organiza-tion, people do not join a social system: rather, they are born into one. Societies, therefore, have to take what they get and make the best of the talent they have on offer. And over time, fortunately, leadership has become less and less an accident of birth, family, social class and the like, although it still remains substantially an accident of gender.

Organizations, on the other hand are in the fortunate position of being able to pick and choose their memberships according to desired profiles. And that is why succession processes are so potentially divisive and engage so many people's energies and emotions. Successions, in a very real way, are the occasions during which nearly all the core themes in the relations between leaders and followers – perceptions, attributions, expectations, impressions, discretion and so on – become the focus of virtually everyone's attention and are put to the test. Hall (1989, p. 12, original emphasis) compared succession planning in two US companies, Healthco and PowerInc, and found that in each case '*the design of the executive continuity system mirrors the larger organization design*', which is another way of saying that organizations remake themselves in their own image. Some of the reasons for that were set out in Chapters 5 and 6 when we saw why dominant values and styles took root across organizations. Healthco managed to identify individual talent and sought to nurture it through a range of measures including profiles of desired leadership performance, and developmental initiatives such as management training and assessment centres. At PowerInc, however, it was a case of sink-or-swim, find-your-own-feet and get-ahead-in-your-own-way. The problem for the incumbent generation of leaders in any organization as regards its future, then, remains one of 'how and why to grow talent in a systematic way' (Hall, 1989, p. 23).

The overall argument of this book has been that the status of educational leader cannot be taken for granted. The idea that without followers there can be no leaders is often dismissed as a statement of the obvious, which of course it is. Yet that cliché also expresses a truer statement of the position than is evident when simply dismissed at face value. The bottom line of leadership, as was pointed out in Chapter 1, is that this status is ascribed or conferred by followers who perceive their expectations being fulfilled in conformity with the particular prototypes or implicit theories of leadership to which they adhere. From that starting-point the analysis in this book has been built around two different sets of perspectives. On the one hand I have sought to bring to light what has to happen if individuals are to project themselves as leaders and then to say something about the kinds of organizational processes which those individuals have to endure if they are to realize their ambitions. On the other hand, I have also endeavoured to make clear what it is that organizations do when they legitimate people with the status of leader and some of the traps involved in bestowing leadership status on people who have to be taken on trust as unknown quantities. In both of these ways my purpose was to try and rectify a gap in our understanding of how and why it is that leaders get to be leaders. My hope is that this purpose has been achieved.

References

Anderson, R.H. (1982) *In Limbo: Organisational and Career Commitment among Relieving School Principals*, M.Ed Studies Project, Monash University.

Andrews, K.C. and Moyle, C.R. (1986) Administrative training in Australia: A new model, *Theory into Practice*, 25(3): 191–6.

Annan, N. (1988) Gentlemen and players, *New York Review of Books*, 29 September.

Archer, M.S. (1995) *Realist Social Theory: The Morphogenetic Approach* (Cambridge: Cambridge University Press).

Argyris, C. (1979) How normal science methodology makes leadership research less additive and less applicable, in J.G. Hunt and L.L. Larson (eds), *Crosscurrents in Leadership* (Carbondale, IL: Southern Illinois University Press), pp. 47–63.

Armstrong, J.A. (1973) *The European Administrative Elite* (Princeton, NJ, Princeton University Press).

Arthur, M.B. and Rousseau, D.M. (1996) Introduction: The boundaryless career as a new employment principle, in M.B. Arthur and D.M. Rousseau (eds), *The Boundaryless Career: A New Employment Principle for a New Organizational Era* (New York: Oxford University Press), pp. 3–20.

Austin, M.J. and Gilmore, T.N. (1993) Executive exit: Multiple perspectives on managing the leadership transition, *Administration in Social Work*, 17(1): 47–60.

Australian Competency Research Centre (1997) *Final Report of the National Trial of the Frontline Management Initiative*, Typescript, Australian Competency Research Centre.

Avolio, B. and Bass, B.M. (1988) Transformational leadership, charisma and beyond, in J.G. Hunt, B.R. Baliga, H.P. Dachler and C.A. Schriesheim (eds), *Emerging Leadership Vistas* (Lexington, MA: D.C. Heath), pp. 29–49.

Baliga, B.R. and Hunt, J.G. (1988) An organizational life cycle approach to leadership, in J.G. Hunt, B.R. Baliga, H.P. Dachler and C.A. Schriesheim (eds), *Emerging Leadership Vistas* (Lexington, MA: D.C. Heath), pp. 129–49.

Barber, J.D. (1974) Strategies for understanding politicians, *American Journal of Political Science*, 18(3): 443–67.

Barber, J.D. (1977) *The Presidential Character: Predicting Performance in the White House*, 2nd edition (Englewood-Cliffs, NJ: Prentice-Hall).

Barnard, C.I. (1956) *Organization and Management* (Cambridge, MA: Harvard University Press).

Barnard, C.I. (1982 [1938]) *The Functions of the Executive* (Cambridge, MA: Harvard University Press).

Barnett, C. (1972) *The Collapse of British Power* (Gloucester: Alan Sutton).

Bass, B.M. (1985) *Leadership and Performance Beyond Expectations* (New York: Free Press).

Bass, B.M. (1990) *Bass and Stogdill's Handbook of Leadership: Theory, Research and Managerial Applications*, 3rd edition (New York: Free Press).

Bate, W. (1990) *Light Blue Down Under: The History of Geelong Grammar School* (Melbourne: Oxford University Press).

Baum, H.S. (1992) Mentoring: Narcissistic fantasies and oedipal realities, *Human Relations*, 45(3): 223–45.

Beeson, G.W. and Matthews R.J. (1992) Beginning principals in Australia, in F.W. Parkay and G.E. Hall (eds), *Becoming a Principal: The Challenges of Beginning Leadership* (Boston: Allyn and Bacon), pp. 308–28.

Bendix, R. (1956) *Work and Authority in Industry: Ideologies of Management in the Course of Industrialisation* (New York: Harper & Row).

Benjamin, W. (1977) The work of art in the age of mechanical reproduction, in J. Curran, M. Gurevitch and J. Woollacott (eds), *Mass Communication and Society* (London: Edward Arnold), pp. 384–408.

Bensimon, E.M. (1990) Viewing the presidency: Perceptual congruence between presidents and leaders on their campuses, *Leadership Quarterly*, 1(2): 71–90.

Bensimon, E.M. (1991) The social processes through which faculty shape the image of a new president, *Journal of Higher Education*, 62(6): 637–60.

Berg, J. (1996) Context and perception: Implications for leadership, *Journal of School Leadership*, 6(1): 75–98.

Biggart, N.W. (1981) Management style as strategic interaction: The case of Governor Ronald Reagan, *Journal of Applied Behavioral Science*, 17(3): 291–308.

Biggart, N.W. and Hamilton, G.G. (1987) An institutional theory of leadership, *Journal of Applied Behavioral Science*, 23(4): 429–41.

Bishop, A.A. (1993) *A Perspective on Executive Succession from the Point of View of a New Incumbent*, M. Ed Studies Project, Monash University.

Blainey, G., Morrissey, J. and Hulme, S.E.K. (1967) *Wesley College: The First Hundred Years* (Melbourne: Robertson and Mullins).

Blinkhorn, S. and Johnson, C. (1990) The insignificance of personality testing, *Nature*, 348(6303): 671–2.

Bond, A.H. (1986) Virginia Woolf and Leslie Stephen: A father's contribution to psychosis and genius, *Journal of the American Academy of Psychoanalysis*, 14(4): 507–24.

Brown, S.L. and Eisenhardt, K.M. (1997) The art of continuous change: Linking complexity theory and time-paced evolution in relentlessly shifting organizations, *Administrative Science Quarterly*, 42(1): 1–34.

Bryman, A. (1987) The generalizability of implicit leadership theory, *Journal of Social Psychology*, 127: 129–41.

Bryman, A. (1992) *Charisma and Leadership in Organizations* (London: Sage).

Burnham, J. (1962) *The Managerial Revolution* (Harmondsworth: Penguin).

Burns, A.J. (1991) *Non-Renewal of Contracts: A Study of the Effects of Non-Renewal of Contracts on Catholic Secondary School Principals*, M. Ed Studies Project, Monash University.

Burns, J.M. (1978) *Leadership* (New York: Harper & Row).

Byrt, W. (1989) Management education in Australia, in W. Byrt (ed.), *Management Education: An International Survey* (London: Routledge), pp. 78–103.

Calder, B.J. (1977) An attribution theory of leadership, in B.M. Staw and G.R. Salancik (eds), *New Directions in Organizational Behavior* (Chicago: St Clair), pp. 179–204.

Carlson, R.O. (1961–2) Succession and performance among school superintendents, *Administrative Science Quarterly*, 6: 210–27.

Chandler, A.D. (1977) *The Visible Hand: The Managerial Revolution in American Business* (Cambridge, MA: Belknap Press).

Chandler, A.D. (1984) The emergence of managerial capitalism, *Business History Review*, 58(4): 473–503.

Coleman, M. (1996) The management style of female headteachers, *Educational Administration and Management*, 24(2): 163–74.

Connell, W.F. (1983) Innovative headmistress – D.J. Ross, in C. Turney (ed.), *Pioneers of Australian Education: Studies of the Development of Education in Australia, 1900–50*, vol. III (Sydney: Sydney University Press), pp. 200–30.

Connell, W.F. (1993) The school as a democratic community: The educational ideas of D.J. Ross, in R. McCarthy and M.R. Theobald (eds), *Melbourne Girls Grammar School Centenary Essays, 1893–1993* (Melbourne: Hyland House), pp. 88–109.

Crow, G. (1989) The use of the concept of 'strategy' in recent sociological literature, *Sociology*, 23(1): 1–24.

Cunningham, K.S. and Radford, W.C. (1963) *Training the Administrator: A Study with Special Reference to Education* (Melbourne: Australian Council for Educational Research).

Darling, Sir James (1978) *Richly Rewarding* (Melbourne: Hill of Content).

Davies, A.F. (1972) The concept of administrative style, in A.F. Davies (ed.), *Essays in Political Sociology* (Melbourne: Cheshire), pp. 118–33.

Davies, A.F. (1980) *Skills, Outlooks and Passions: A Psychoanalytic Contribution to the Study of Politics* (Cambridge: Cambridge University Press).

Day, C. and Bakioglu, A. (1996) Development and disenchantment in the professional lives of headteachers, in I.F. Goodson and A. Hargreaves (eds), *Teachers' Professional Lives* (London: Falmer), pp. 205–27.

De Roche, C.P. (1994) On the edge of regionalization: Management style and the construction of conflict in organizational change, *Human Organization*, 53(3): 209–19.

Dixon, N.F. (1983) *On the Psychology of Military Incompetence* (London: Jonathan Cape).

Draper, J. and McMichael, P. (1998) Preparing a profile: Likely applicants for primary headship, *Educational Management and Administration*, 26(2): 161–72.

Drucker, P. (1993) *Post-Capitalist Society* (New York: HarperCollins).

Eaton, J.W. (1950) Is scientific leadership selection possible?, in A.W. Gouldner (ed.), *Studies in Leadership* (New York: Russell and Russell), pp. 615–43.

Epstein, J. (1981) *A Golden String: The Story of Dorothy J. Ross* (Melbourne: Greenhouse).

Evetts, J. (1987) Becoming career ambitious: The career strategies of married women who became primary headteachers in the 1960s and 1970s, *Educational Review*, 39(1): 15–29.

Evetts, J. (1992) Dimensions of career: Avoiding reification in the analysis of change, *Sociology*, 26(1): 1–21.

Evetts, J. (1993) Careers and partnerships: The strategies of secondary headteachers, *Sociological Review*, 41(2): 302–27.

Fairhurst, G.T. (1993) The leader–member exchange patterns of women leaders in industry: A discourse analysis, *Communications Monographs*, 60(4): 321–51.

Farquhar, K. (1991) Leadership in limbo: Organization dynamics during interim administrations, *Public Administration Review*, 51(3): 202–10.

Farquhar, K. (1995) Not just understudies: The dynamics of short-term leadership, *Human Resource Management*, 34(1): 51–70.

Fauske, J.R. and Ogawa, R.T. (1987) Detachment, fear, and expectation: A faculty's response to the impending selection of its principal, *Educational Administration Quarterly*, 23(2): 23–44.

Fidler, B. (1992) Strategic management: Where is the school going? A guide to strategic thinking, in B. Fidler and G. Bowles (eds), *Effective School Management: A Strategic Approach* (London: Longman), pp. 19–35.

Fidler, B. (1997) School leadership: Some key ideas, *School Leadership and Management*, 17(1): 23–37.

Firestone, W.A. (1990) Succession and bureaucracy: Gouldner revisited, *Educational Administration Quarterly*, 26(4): 345–75.

Fletcher, C. (1990) The relationship between candidate personality, self-presentation strategies, and interviewer assessments in selection interviews: An empirical study, *Human Relations*, 43(8): 739–49.

Fondas, N. (1996) Feminization at work: Career implications, in M.B. Arthur and D.M. Rousseau (eds), *The Boundaryless Career: A New Employment Principle for a New Organizational Era* (New York: Oxford University Press), pp. 282–93.

Fondas, N. and Stewart, R. (1994) Enactment in managerial jobs: A role analysis, *Journal of Management Studies*, 31(1): 83–103.

Foster, R. (1996) Selecting primary school headteachers: Potential bias in Barsetshire, *School Organisation*, 16(1): 101–09.

Fredrickson, J.W., Hambrick, D.C. and Baumrin, S. (1988) A model of CEO dismissal, *Academy of Management Review*, 13(2): 255–70.

Freeman, M.E. (1981) *Being an Administrator: Reflections on Two Years Spent as a Headmistress*, M. Ed Minor Thesis, Monash University.

Friedman, S.D. and Olk, P. (1995) Four ways to choose a CEO: Crown heir, horse race, coup d'état and comprehensive search, *Human Resource Management*, 34(1): 141–64.

Gabarro, J.J. (1978) The development of trust, influence, and expectations, in A.G. Athos and J.J. Gabarro (eds), *Interpersonal Behavior: Communication and Understanding in Relationships* (Englewood Cliffs, NJ: Prentice Hall), pp. 290–303.

Gabarro, J.J. (1987) The development of working relationships, in J. Galeghar, R.E. Kraut and C. Egido (eds), *Intellectual Teamwork: Social and Technological Foundations of Co-operative Work* (Hillsdale, NJ: Lawrence Erlbaum), pp. 79–110.

Gabarro, J.J. (1988) Executive leadership and succession: The process of taking charge, in D.C. Hambrick (ed.), *The Executive Effect: Concepts and Methods for Studying Top Managers* (Greenwich, CT: JAI Press), pp. 237–68.

Gardiner, L. (1993) Back into line, in R. McCarthy and M.R. Theobald (eds), *Melbourne Girls Grammar School Centenary Essays, 1893–1993* (Melbourne: Hyland House), pp. 128–46.

Gardner, H. (1995) *Leading Minds: An Anatomy of Leadership* (New York: Basic Books).

Garforth, F.I. de la P. (1945) War Office selection boards (OCTU), *Occupational Psychology*, 19(2): 97–108.

Gathorne-Hardy, J. (1979) *The Public School Phenomenon, 597–1977* (Harmondsworth: Penguin).

Gathorne-Hardy J. (1985) *The Rise and Fall of the British Nanny* (London: Weidenfeld and Nicolson).

Gemmill, G. and Oakley, J. (1992) Leadership: An alienating social myth, *Human Relations*, 45(2): 113–29.

Gephart, R.H. (1978) Status degradation and organizational succession: An ethnomethodological approach, *Administrative Science Quarterly*, 23(4): 553–81.

Gerth, H.H. and Mills, C.W. (1964) *Character and Social Structure: The Psychology of Social Institutions* (New York: Harcourt, Brace & World).

Gibb, C.A. (1946) The selection of leaders, *Australian Quarterly*, 18(4): 52–66.

Gibb, C.A. (1968) Leadership, in G. Lindzey and E. Aronson (eds), *The Handbook of Social Psychology*, vol. IV, 2nd edn (Reading, MA: Addison-Wesley), pp. 205–83.

Gifford, H. (1982) Raison d'être, in P. Grimshaw and L. Strahan (eds), *The Half-Open Door: Sixteen Modern Australian Women look at Professional Life and Achievement* (Sydney: Hale & Iremonger), pp. 172–93.

Gilmore, T.N. and Ronchi, D. (1995) Managing predecessors' shadows in executive transitions, *Human Resource Management*, 34(1): 11–26.

Goffman, E. (1975) *Frame Analysis: An Essay on the Organization of Experience* (Harmondsworth: Penguin).

Goffman, E. (1976a) *Asylums: Essays on the Social Situation of Mental Patients and Other Inmates* (Harmondsworth: Penguin).

Goffman, E. (1976b) *The Presentation of Self in Everyday Life* (Harmondsworth: Penguin).

Gouldner, A.W. (1950) Introduction, in A.W. Gouldner (ed.), *Studies in Leadership* (New York: Russell & Russell), pp. 3–49.

Gouldner, A.W. (1954) *Patterns of Industrial Bureaucracy* (New York: Free Press).

Gouldner, A.W. (1965) The problem of succession in bureaucracy, in A.W. Gouldner (ed.), *Studies in Leadership* (New York, Russell & Russell), pp. 644–62.

Graham, J.W. (1991) Servant-leadership in organizations: Inspirational and moral, *Leadership Quarterly*, 2(2): 105–19.

Greenacre, P. (1958) The imposter, *Psychoanalytic Quarterly*, 27: 356–82.

Greenfield, T.B. and Ribbins, P. (eds) (1993) *Greenfield on Educational Administration: Towards a Humane Science* (London: Routledge).

Greening, W.A. (1964) The Mannix thesis in Catholic secondary education in Victoria, in E.L. French (ed.), *Melbourne Studies in Education 1961–2* (Melbourne: Melbourne University Press), pp. 285–302.

Greenstein, F.I. (1983) Reagan and the lore of the modern presidency: What have we learned?, in F.I. Greenstein (ed.), *The Reagan Presidency* (Baltimore: Johns Hopkins University Press), pp. 159–87.

Gregory, A. (1987) *Lord Somers: Something of the Life and Letters of Arthur, 6th Baron Somers* (St Kilda, Vic.: Lord Somers' Camp and Power House).

Griffin, R.W., Skivington, K.D. and Moorhead, G. (1987) Symbolic and interactional perspectives on leadership: An integrative framework, *Human Relations*, 40(4): 199–218.

Gronn, P. (1979) *The Politics of School Management: A Comparative Study of Three School Councils.* Ph.D Thesis, Monash University.

Gronn, P. (1986a) Choosing a deputy head: The rhetoric and reality of administrative selection, *Australian Journal of Education*, 30(1): 1–22.

194   References

Gronn, P. (1986b) The boyhood, schooling and early career of J.R. Darling, *Journal of Australian Studies*, 18: 30–42.

Gronn, P. (1986c) *The Psycho-Social Dynamics of Leading and Following* (Waurn Ponds, Vic.: Deakin University Press).

Gronn, P. (1989) J.R. Darling and the Public School Empire Tour to New Zealand, *History of Education Review*, 18(1): 43–59.

Gronn, P. (1990) An experiment in political education: 'V.G.', 'Slimy' and the Repton Sixth, 1916–1918, *History of Education*, 19(1): 1–21.

Gronn, P. (1991) 'A drag on the war effort'?: Geelong Grammar School, 1940–1945, *Journal of the Royal Australian Historical Society*, 77(2): 53–76.

Gronn, P. (1992) Schooling for ruling: The social composition of admissions to Geelong Grammar School, 1930–1939, *Australian Historical Studies*, 25(98): 72–89.

Gronn, P. (1993a) Bewitching the lcd: Hodgkinson on leadership, *Journal of Educational Administration and Foundations*, 8(1): 29–44.

Gronn, P. (1993b) Psychobiography on the couch: Character, biography and the comparative study of leaders, *Journal of Applied Behavioral Science*, 29(3): 343–58.

Gronn, P. (1994) Educational administration's Weber, *Educational Management and Administration*, 22(4): 224–31.

Gronn, P. (1995) Greatness re-visited: The current obsession with transformational leadership, *Leading and Managing*, 1(1): 14–27.

Gronn, P. (1996) From transactions to transformations: A new world order in the study of leadership?, *Educational Management and Administration*, 24(1): 7–30.

Gronn, P. (1997) Leading for learning: Organizational transformation and the formation of leaders, *Journal of Management Development*, 16(4): 274–83.

Gronn, P. (1999) Substituting for leadership: The neglected role of the leadership couple, *Leadership Quarterly*, 9(1) (forthcoming).

Gronn, P. and Ribbins, P. (1996) Leaders in context: Postpositivist approaches to understanding educational leadership, *Educational Administration Quarterly*, 32(3): 452–73.

Guest, R.H. (1962) Managerial succession in complex organizations, *American Journal of Sociology*, 68(1): 47–54.

Gunz, H. (1989) The dual meaning of managerial careers: Organizational and individual levels of analysis, *Journal of Management Studies*, 26(3): 225–50.

Halberstam, D. (1987) *The Reckoning* (London: Bloomsbury).

Hall, D.T. (1989) How top management and the organization itself can block effective executive succession, *Human Resource Management*, 28(1): 5–24.

Hall, D.T. (1995) Unplanned executive transitions and the dance of the subidentities, *Human Resource Management*, 34(1): 71–92.

Hall, D.T. (1996) Protean careers of the 21st century, *Academy of Management Executive*, 10(4): 8–16.

Hall, D.T. and Mirvis, P.H. (1996) The new protean career: Psychological success and the path with a heart, in D.T. Hall (ed.), *The Career is Dead – Long Live the Career: A Relational Approach to Careers* (San Francisco: Jossey-Bass), pp. 15–45.

Hall, V. (1996) *Dancing on the Ceiling: A Study of Women Managers in Education* (London: Paul Chapman Publishing).

Hambrick, D.C. and Brandon, G.L. (1988) Executive values, in D.C. Hambrick (ed.), *The Executive Effect: Concepts and Methods for Studying Top Managers* (Greenwich, CT: JAI Press), pp. 3–34.

Hambrick, D.C. and Finkelstein, S. (1987) Managerial discretion: A bridge between polar views of organizational outcomes, in L.L. Cummings and B.M. Staw (eds), *Research in Organizational Behavior*, vol. IX (Greenwich, CT: JAI Press), pp. 369–406.

Hambrick, D.C. and Fukutomi, G.D.S. (1991) The seasons of a CEO's tenure, *Academy of Management Review*, 16(6): 719–42.

Hambrick, D.C. and Mason, P.A. (1984) Upper echelons: The organization as a reflection of its top managers, *Academy of Management Review*, 9(2): 193–206.

Hansen, I.V. (1986) *By Their Deeds: A Centenary History of Camberwell Grammar School, 1886–1986* (Melbourne: Camberwell Grammar School).

Hart, A.W. (1987) Leadership succession: Reflections of a new principal, *Journal of Research and Development in Education*, 20(4): 1–11.

Hart, A.W. (1988) Attribution as effect: An outsider principal's succession, *Journal of Educational Administration*, 26(3): 331–52.

Hart, A.W. (1991) Leader succession and socialization: A synthesis, *Review of Educational Research*, 61(4): 451–74.

Heifetz, R.A. (1994) *Leadership Without Easy Answers* (Cambridge, MA: Harvard University Press).

Heller, T. (1989) Conversion process in leadership succession: A case study, *Journal of Applied Behavioral Science*, 25(1): 65–77.

Hill, L. (1992) *Becoming a Manager: Mastery of a New Identity* (Boston: Harvard Business School Press).

Hodgkinson, C. (1978) *Towards a Philosophy of Administration* (Oxford: Blackwell).

Hodgkinson, C. (1983) *The Philosophy of Leadership* (Oxford: Blackwell).

Hodgkinson, C. (1991) *Educational Leadership: The Moral Art* (New York: SUNY Press).

Hodgkinson, C. (1996) *Administrative Philosophy: Values and Motivations in Administrative Life* (Oxford: Pergamon).

Hodgson, R.C., Levinson, D.J. and Zaleznik, A. (1965) *The Executive Role Constellation* (Boston: Graduate School of Business Administration, Harvard University).

Hofstede, G. (1994) *Cultures and Organizations: Software of the Mind – Inter-*

cultural Cooperation and its Importance for Survival (New York: HarperCollins).

Hogan, R., Curphy, G.J. and Hogan, J. (1994) What we know about leadership: Effectiveness and personality, *American Psychologist*, 49(6): 493–504.

Honey, J.R.deS. (1977) *Tom Brown's Universe* (London: Millington Books).

Horney, K. (1950) *Neurosis and Human Growth* (New York: W.W. Norton).

Hosking, D.M. (1988) Organizing, leadership and skilful process, *Journal of Management Studies*, 25(2): 147–66.

House, R.J. (1977) A 1976 theory of leadership, in J.G. Hunt and L.L. Larson (eds), *Leadership: The Cutting Edge* (Carbondale, IL: Southern Illinois University Press), pp. 189–207.

Hunt, J.G. (1991) *Leadership: A New Synthesis* (Newbury Park, CA: Sage).

Industry Task Force on Leadership and Management Skills (1995) *Enterprising Nation: Renewing Australia's Managers to Meet the Challenges of the Asia-Pacific Century* (Canberra: AGPS).

Izraeli, D.N. (1975) The middle manager and the tactics of power expansion: A case study, *Sloan Management Review*, 16(2): 57–70.

Izraeli, D.N. (1977) Settling-in: An interactionist perspective on the entry of the new manager, *Pacific Sociological Review*, 20(1): 135–60.

Jackson, P.W. (1977) Lonely at the top: Observations on the genesis of administrative isolation, *School Review*, 85(3): 425–32.

James, W. (1901) *The Principles of Psychology*, vol. I (London: Macmillan).

Janda, K.F. (1966) Towards the explication of the concept of leadership in terms of the concept of power, *Human Relations*, 13(4): 345–63.

Jaques, E. (1970) On being a manager, in E. Jaques, *Work, Creativity and Social Justice* (London: Heinemann), pp. 130–45.

Jaques, E. and Clement, S.D. (1995) *Executive Leadership: A Practical Guide to Managing Complexity* (Oxford: Blackwell).

Johnson, B.L. and Licata, J.W. (1995) School principal succession and teachers on successor effectiveness, *Journal of School Leadership*, 5(5): 394–417.

Jones, A. (1991) The contribution of psychologists to military officer selection, in R. Gal and A.D. Mangelsdorff (eds), *Handbook of Military Psychology* (London: Wiley and Sons), pp. 63–80.

Kaplan, R.E. (1990a) Introduction: Why character and leadership?, *Journal of Applied Behavioral Science*, 26(4): 417–22.

Kaplan, R.E. (1990b) The expansive executive: How the drive to mastery helps and hinders organizations, *Human Resource Management*, 29(3): 307–26.

Katz, E. and Dayan, D. (1986) Contests, conquests, coronations: On media events and their heroes, in C.F. Graumann and S. Moscovici (eds), *Changing Conceptions of Leadership* (New York: Springer-Verlag), pp. 135–44.

Kearl, M.C. and Hoag, L.J. (1984) The social construction of the midlife crisis: A case study in the temporalities of identity, *Sociological Inquiry*, 54(3): 279–300.

Kernberg, O. (1978) Leadership and organizational functioning: Organizational regression, *International Journal of Group Psychotherapy*, 28(1): 3–25.

Kernberg, O. (1984) The couch at sea: Psychoanalytic studies of group and organizational leadership, *International Journal of Group Psychotherapy*, 34(1): 5–23.

Kets de Vries, M.F.R. (1988) The dark side of CEO succession, *Harvard Business Review*, 66(1): 56–60.

Kets de Vries, M.F.R (1989a) Leaders who self-destruct: The causes and the cures, *Organization Dynamics*, 17(4): 5–17.

Kets de Vries, M.F.R (1989b) The leader as mirror: Clinical reflections, *Human Relations*, 42(7): 607–23.

Kets de Vries, M.F.R. (1989c) Alexithymia in organizational life: The organization man revisited, *Human Relations*, 42(12): 1079–93.

Kets de Vries, M.F.R. (1990) The imposter syndrome: Developmental and societal issues, *Human Relations*, 43(7): 667–86.

Kets de Vries, M.F.R. (1991a) On becoming a CEO: Transference and the addictiveness of power, in M.F.R. Kets de Vries (ed.), *Organizations on the Couch: Clinical Perspectives on Organizational Behavior and Change* (San Francisco: Jossey-Bass), pp. 120–39.

Kets de Vries, M.F.R. (1991b) Whatever happened to the philosopher-king?: The leader's addiction to power, *Journal of Management Studies*, 28(4): 339–51.

Kets de Vries, M.F.R. (1993) *Leaders, Fools and Imposters: Essays on the Psychology of Leadership* (San Francisco: Jossey-Bass).

Kets de Vries, M.F.R. and Miller, D. (1984) *The Neurotic Organization* (San Francisco: Jossey-Bass).

Khleif, B.B. (1975) Professionalization of school superintendents: A socio-cultural study of an elite program, *Human Organization*, 34(3): 301–8.

Khleif, B.B. (1980) Modes of professionalization, *Sociologica Internationalis*, 18: 207–16.

King, P. (1989) Activities of British psychoanalysts during the second world war and the influence of their inter-disciplinary collaboration on the development of psychoanalysis in Great Britain, *International Journal of Psycho-Analysis*, 16(1): 15–33.

Klapp, O. (1964) *Symbolic Leaders* (Chicago: Aldine).

Klerman, G.L. and Levinson, D.J. (1969) Becoming the director: Promotion as a phase in person-professional development, *Psychiatry*, 32(4): 411–27.

Kohut, H. (1978) Thoughts on narcissism and narcissistic rage, in P.H. Ornstein (ed.), *The Search for Self* (New York: International Universities Press), pp. 615–58.

Kotin, J. and Sharaf, M.R. (1967) Management succession and administrative style, *Psychiatry*, 30(3): 237–48.

Kotter J. (1982) *The General Managers* (New York: Free Press).

Kotter, J. (1990) What leaders really do, *Harvard Business Review*, 90(3): 103–11.

Kram, K.E. (1985) *Mentoring at Work* (Glenview, IL: Scott Foresman and Co.).

Krantz, J. (1989) The managerial couple: Superior–subordinate relationships as a unit of analysis, *Human Resource Management*, 28(2): 161–75.

Krantz, J. and Gilmore, T.N. (1990) The splitting of leadership and management as a social defense, *Human Relations*, 43(2): 183–204.

Kress, G. and Fowler, R. (1979) Interviews, in R. Fowler, B. Hodge, G. Kress and T. Trew (eds), *Language and Control* (London: Routledge and Kegan Paul), pp. 63–80.

Laing, R.D. (1966) *The Divided Self: An Existential Study in Sanity and Madness* (Harmondsworth: Penguin).

Langer, W.C. (1973) *The Mind of Adolf Hitler* (London: Secker and Warburg).

Lantis, M. (1987) Two important roles in organizations and communities, *Human Organization*, 46(3): 189–99.

Laski, H. (1940) The danger of being a gentleman: Reflections on the ruling class in England, in H. Laski, *The Danger of Being a Gentleman and Other Essays* (London: Allen and Unwin), pp. 13–31.

LeGore, J.A. and Parker, L. (1997) First year principal succession: A study of leadership, role, and change, *Journal of School Leadership*, 7: 369–85.

Leinster-Mackay (1984) *The Rise of the English Prep School* (Lewes: Falmer).

Lerner, M. (1985) Of presidents and their splendours and miseries, *Encounter*, 65(1): 33–9.

Levinson, D.J., Darrow, C.N., Klein, E.B., Levinson, M.H. and McKee, B. (1978) *The Seasons of a Man's Life* (New York: Ballantine Books).

Levinson, H. (1974) Don't choose your own successor, *Harvard Business Review*, 52(6): 53–62.

Lifton, R.J. (1993) *The Protean Self: Human Resilience in an Age of Fragmentation* (New York: Basic Books).

Lipman-Blumen, J. (1996) *The Connective Edge: Leading in an Interdependent World* (San Francisco: Jossey-Bass).

Locke, R.R. (1984) *The End of Practical Man: Entrepreneurship and Higher Education in Germany, France and Great Britain, 1880–1940* (Greenwich, CT: JAI Press).

Locke, R.R. (1985) Business education in Germany: Past systems and current practice, *Business History Review*, 59(2): 231–53.

Lord, R.G. and Maher, K.J. (1993) *Leadership and Information Processing: Linking Perceptions and Performance* (London and New York: Routledge).

Louis, M.R. (1980) Surprise and sense making: What newcomers experience in entering unfamiliar organizational settings, *Administrative Science Quarterly*, 25(2): 226–50.

Louis, M.R. (1990), Acculturation in the workplace: Newcomers as lay ethnographers, in B. Schneider (ed.), *Organizational Climate and Culture* (San Francisco: Jossey-Bass), pp. 85–129.

Lyman, S.M. and Scott, M.B. (1968) Coolness in everyday life, in M. Truzzi (ed.), *Sociology and Everyday Life* (Englewood Cliffs, NJ: Prentice Hall), pp. 92–101.

Lyons, G., Jirasinghe, D., Ewers, C. and Edwards, S. (1993) The development of a headteachers' assessment centre, *Educational Management and Administration*, 21(4): 245–8.

Machiavelli, N. (1967 [first published in English 1640]) *The Prince*, trans. G. Bull (Harmondsworth: Penguin).

Macmillan, R.B. (1996) New principals' experiences with leadership: Crossing the cultural boundary, in S.L. Jacobson, E.S. Hickcox and R.B. Stevenson (eds), *School Administration: Persistent Dilemmas in Preparation and Practice* (Westport, CT: Praeger), pp. 137–45.

Marshall, C. (1985) Professional shock: The enculturation of the assistant principal, *Education and Urban Society*, 18(1): 25–58.

Marshall, C. and Mitchell, B.A. (1991) The assumptive worlds of fledgling administrators, *Education and Urban Society*, 23(4): 396–415.

Martin, N.H. and Strauss, A.L. (1956) Patterns of mobility within industrial organizations, *Journal of Business*, 29(2): 101–10.

Martinko, W.L. and Gardner, M.J. (1988) Impression management: An observational study linking audience characteristics with verbal self-presentations, *Academy of Management Review*, 31(1): 42–65.

McCall, M.W. (1993) Developing leadership, in J.R. Galbraith and E.E. Lawler (eds), *Organizing for the Future: The New Logic for Managing Complex Organizations* (San Francisco: Jossey-Bass), pp. 256–84.

McCarthy, R. (1993) MCEGGS in a time of change: The era of Edith Mountain, 1957–74, in R. McCarthy and M.R. Theobald (eds), *Melbourne Girls Grammar School Centenary Essays, 1893–1993* (Melbourne: Hyland House), pp. 147–69.

McCleary, L.E. and Ogawa, R. (1989) The assessment centre process for selecting school leaders, *School Organisation*, 9(1): 103–13.

McMurtrie, G. (1997) Combating the traumas of taking charge: Pre-entry support for NSW beginning principals, *Leading and Managing*, 3(2): 81–96.

Mead, G.H. (1974 [1934]) *Mind, Self and Society: From the Standpoint of a Social Behaviorist*, ed. C.W. Morris (Chicago: University of Chicago Press).

Mealyea, R. (1988) *Confirmed Tradies: A Study of a Mature-Age Technical Teacher Education Programme*, Ph.D Thesis, Monash University.

Meindl, J.R. (1990) On leadership: An alternative to the conventional wisdom, in B.M. Staw and L.L. Cummings (eds), *Research in Organizational Behavior*, vol. XII (Greenwich, CT: JAI Press), pp. 159–203.

Meindl, J.R. (1993) Reinventing leadership: A radical, social psychological approach, in J.K. Murnighan (ed.), *Social Psychology in Organizations:*

Advances in Theory and Research (Englewood Cliffs, NJ: Prentice Hall), pp. 89–118.

Meindl, J.R. (1995) The romance of leadership as a follower-centric theory: A social constructionist approach, *Leadership Quarterly*, 6(3): 329–41.

Meindl, J.R., Ehrlich, S.B. and Dukerich, J.M. (1985) The romance of leadership, *Administrative Science Quarterly*, 30(1): 78–102.

Mintzberg, H. (1973) *The Nature of Managerial Work* (New York: Harper & Row).

Miskel, C. and Cosgrove, D. (1985) Leader succession in school settings, *Review of Educational Research*, 55: 87–105.

Morgan, C. (1986) The selection and appointment of heads, in E. Hoyle and A. McMahon (eds), *The Management of Schools* (London: Kogan Page), pp. 152–63.

Morgan, D.H. (1989) Strategies and sociologists: A comment on Crow, *Sociology*, 23(1): 25–9.

Morris, B.S. (1949) Officer selection in the British Army, 1942–1945, *Occupational Psychology*, 23(4): 219–34.

Muslin, M. and Desai, P. (1985) The transformations in the self of Mahatma Gandhi, in C.B. Strozier and D. Offer (eds), *The Leader* (New York: Plenum Press), pp. 111–32.

Nesbit, K. (1997) *Accrediting Leading Teachers in Schools of the Future*, Seminar presentation for staff and postgraduate students, Monash University.

Neumann, A. (1995) Context, cognition and culture: A case analysis of collegiate leadership and cultural change, *American Educational Research Journal*, 32(2): 251–79.

Neustadt, R.E. (1961) *Presidential Power: The Politics of Leadership* (New York: Wiley and Sons).

Neustadt, R.E. (1964) Kennedy in the White House: A premature appraisal, *Political Science Quarterly*, 79(3): 321–34.

Newsome, D. (1961) *Godliness and Good Learning: Four Studies on a Victorian Ideal* (London: Cassell).

Nicolson, H. (1984) Pity the pedagogue, in G. Greene (ed.) *The Old School: Essays by Divers Hands* (Oxford: Oxford University Press), pp. 83–100.

Norwood, C. (1929) *The English Tradition of Education* (London: John Murray).

Ogawa, R.T. (1991) Enchantment, disenchantment, and accommodation: How a faculty made sense of the succession of its principal, *Educational Administration Quarterly*, 27(1): 30–60.

Ogawa, R.T and Bossert, S. (1995) Leadership as an organizational quality, *Educational Administration Quarterly*, 31(2): 224–43.

Park, S.H. (1996) An evaluation of T.B. Greenfield's subjectivism in educational administration, *Leading and Managing*, 2(4): 284–303.

Parkay, F.W., Currie, G.D. and Rhodes, J.W. (1992) Professional socialization: A longitudinal study of first-time high school principals, *Educational Administration Quarterly*, 28(1): 43–75.

Parker, P. (1987) *The Old Lie: The Great War and the Public School Ethos* (London: Constable).

Pascale, C. and Ribbins, P. (1998) *Understanding Primary Heads and Headship* (London: Cassell).

Percival, A. (1969) *The Origins of the Headmasters' Conference* (London: John Murray).

Perkin, H. (1996) *The Third Revolution: Professional Elites and the Modern World* (London: Routledge).

Perrow, C. (1996) The bounded career and the demise of civil society, in M.B. Arthur and D.M. Rousseau (eds), *The Boundaryless Career: A New Employment Principle for a New Organizational Era* (New York: Oxford University Press), pp. 297–313.

Peshkin, A. (1978) *Growing Up American* (Chicago: Chicago University Press).

Pettigrew, A. (1992) On studying managerial elites, *Strategic Management Journal*, 13(Special): 163–82.

Pollard, S. (1965) The genesis of the managerial profession: The experience of the industrial revolution in Britain, *Studies in Romanticism*, 4(2): 57–80.

Ragins, B.R. (1989) Barriers to mentoring: The female manager's dilemma, *Human Relations*, 42(1): 1–22.

Ragins, B.R. (1995) Diversity, power, and mentorship in organizations: A cultural, structural, and behavioral perspective, in M.M. Chemers, S. Oskamp and M.A. Costanzo (eds), *Diversity in Organizations: New Perspectives for a Changing Workplace* (Thousand Oaks, CA: Sage), pp. 91–132.

Ralston, K. (1990) Getting new things done: The work performance of an academic entrepreneur, *International Journal of Qualitative Studies in Education*, 3(4): 321–34.

Ramamurti, R. (1987) Leadership styles in state-owned enterprises, *Journal of General Management*, 13(2): 44–55.

Rangell, L. (1976) Lessons from Watergate: A derivative for psychoanalysis, *Psychoanalytic Quarterly*, 45(1): 37–61.

Renshon, S.A. (1994) A preliminary assessment of the Clinton presidency: Character, leadership and performance, *Political Psychology*, 15(2): 375–94.

Ribbins, P. and Rayner, S. (1998) *What's So Special About Headship in Special Education?* (London: Cassell).

Riesman, D., Glazer, N. and Denney, R. (1961) *The Lonely Crowd: A Study of the Changing American Character*, abridged edn (New Haven: Yale University Press).

Ritchie, R.B. (1980) *The School Council*, paper presented at the annual conference of the National Council of Independent Schools (Sydney).

Roberts, N.C. (1985) Transforming leadership: A process of collective action, *Human Relations*, 38(11): 1023–46.

Roberts, N.C. and Bradley, R.T. (1988) Limits of charisma, in J.A. Conger and R.N. Kanungo (eds), *Charismatic Leadership: The Elusive Factor in Organizational Effectiveness* (San Francisco: Jossey-Bass), pp. 253–75.

Robinson, J. (1987) *The Echoes Fade Not: A History of Toorak College* (Hawthorn, Vic.: Hudson Publishing).

Rosener, J.B. (1990) Ways women lead, *Harvard Business Review*, 68(6): 119–25.

Rowles, K. (1990) *Learning the Job on the Job: Experiences of an Acting Primary School Principal*, M. Ed Studies Project, Monash University.

Rubinstein, W.D. (1983) Entrepreneurial effort and entrepreneurial success: Peak wealth-holding in three societies, 1850–1939, *Business History Review*, 25(1): 11–29.

Rubinstein, W.D. (1994) *Capitalism, Culture, and Decline in Britain, 1750–1990* (London: Routledge).

Rustow, D.A. (1970) The study of leadership, in D.A. Rustow (ed.), *Philosophers and Kings* (New York: Russell & Russell), pp. 1–32.

Sanderson, M. (1988) The English civic universities and the 'industrial spirit', 1870–1914, *Historical Research*, 61(144): 90–104.

Schein, E.H. (1991) The individual, the organization, and the career, a conceptual scheme, in D.A. Kolb, I.M. Rubin and J.S. Osland (eds), *The Organizational Behavior Reader*, 5th edn (Englewood Cliffs, NJ: Prentice Hall), pp. 128–45.

Schein, E.H. (1992) *Organizational Culture and Leadership*, 2nd edn (San Francisco: Jossey-Bass).

Schmitt, N., Noe, R.A., Meritt, R. and Fitzgerald, M.P. (1984) Validity of assessment center ratings for the prediction of performance ratings and school climate of school administrators, *Journal of Applied Psychology*, 69(2): 207–13.

Schwartz, F.N. (1989) Management women and the new facts of life, *Harvard Business Review*, 67(1): 65–76.

Selznick, P. (1957) *Leadership in Administration: A Sociological Interpretation* (Evanston, IL: Row, Peterson & Company).

Senge, P. (1993) *The Fifth Discipline: The Art and Practice of the Learning Organization* (Sydney: Random House).

Sergiovanni, T. (1996) *Leadership for the Schoolhouse: How is it Different? How is it Important?* (San Francisco: Jossey-Bass).

Serle, G. (1982) *John Monash: A Biography* (Melbourne: Melbourne University Press).

Shapiro, E.C., Haseltine, F.P. and Rowe, M.P. (1978) Moving up: Role models, mentors and the 'patron system', *Sloan Management Review*, 19(3): 51–8.

Silverman, D. and Jones, S. (1976) *Organizational Work: The Language of Grading and the Grading of Language* (London: Collier MacMillan).

Simpson, J.B.H. (1967) *Rugby Since Arnold: A History of Rugby School From 1842* (London: Macmillan).

Skidelsky, R. (1978) Keynes and his parents, *Daedalus*, 107(4): 71–9.

Smircich, L. and Morgan, G. (1982) Leadership: The management of meaning, *Journal of Applied Behavioral Science*, 18(2): 257–73.

Smith, F.B. (1982) *Florence Nightingale: Reputation and Power* (London: Croom Helm).

Sonnenfeld, J. (1986) Heroes in collision: Chief executive retirement and the parade of future leaders, *Human Resource Management*, 25(2): 305–33.

Sonnenfeld, J. (1988) Chief executive exit: The hero's reluctant retirement, in D.C. Hambrick (ed.), *The Executive Effect: Concepts and Methods for Studying Top Managers* (Greenwich, CT: JAI Press), pp. 269–99.

Spaulding, A. (1997) Life in schools – a qualitative study of teacher perspectives on the politics of principals: Ineffective leadership behaviors and their consequences upon teacher thinking and behavior, *School Leadership and Management*, 17(1): 39–55.

Spierings, J. (1990) *Magic and Science: Aspects of Australian Business Management, Advertising and Retailing, 1918–1940*, Ph.D Thesis, University of Melbourne.

Stebbins, R. (1970) Career: The subjective approach, *Sociological Quarterly*, 11(1): 32–49.

Sternberg, R.J. and Horvath, J.A. (1995) A prototype view of expert teaching, *Educational Researcher*, 24(6): 9–17.

Stewart, R. (1989) Studies of managerial jobs and behaviour: The ways forward, *Journal of Management Studies*, 26(1): 1–10.

Strauss, A.L. (1977) *Mirrors and Masks* (London: Martin Robertson).

Sutcliffe, J.R. (1977) *Why be a Headmaster?* (Melbourne: Melbourne University Press).

Sutton, R.I. and Louis, M.R. (1987) How selecting and socializing newcomers influences insiders, *Human Resource Management*, 26(3): 347–61.

Taft, R. (1959) Multiple methods of personality assessment, *Psychological Bulletin*, 56(5): 333–52.

Trow, D.B. (1961–2) Executive succession in small companies, *Administrative Science Quarterly*, 6: 228–39.

Turner, L. (1998) Turning around a struggling school: A case study, in L. Stoll and K.Myers (eds), *No Quick Fixes: Perspectives on Schools in Difficulty* (London: Falmer), pp. 96–106.

Urban, G. (1981) Was Stalin (the terrible) really a 'great man', *Encounter*, 57(5): 20–38.

Vanderslice, V.J. (1988) Separating leaders from followers: An assessment of the effect of leader and follower roles in organisations, *Human Relations*, 42(9): 677–96.

Volkan, V.D. (1980) Narcissistic personality organisation and 'reparative' leadership, *International Journal of Group Psychotherapy*, 30(2): 131–52.

Waddy, L. (1981) *The King's School, 1831–1981: An Account* (Sydney: The King's School).

Watkins, P. (1991) Devolving educational administration in Victoria: Tensions in the role and selections of principals, *Journal of Educational Administration*, 29(1): 22–38.

Weber, M. (1978 [1922]) *Economy and Society: An Outline of an Interpretive Sociology*, vol. I, eds G. Roth and C. Wittich (Berkeley: University of California Press).

Weick, K.E. (1976) Educational organizations as loosely coupled systems, *Administrative Science Quarterly*, 21(1): 1–19.

White, D.M. (1972) The problems of power, *British Journal of Political Science*, 2: 479–90.

White, M. (1993) *'Between a Rock and a Hard Place': Peter Thwaites at Guildford Grammar School, 1950–1956*, paper presented at the joint conference of the Australian and New Zealand History of Education Society and the Association Canadienne D'Histoire de L'Education (Melbourne).

Whitely, W.T. and Coetsier, P. (1993) The relationship of career mentoring to early career outcomes, *Organization Studies*, 14(3): 419–41.

Whitley, R., Thomas, A. and Marceau, J. (1981) *Masters of Business?: Business Schools and Business Graduates in Britain and France* (London: Tavistock Publications).

Whyte, W.F. (1965) *Street Corner Society: The Social Structure of an Italian Slum* (Chicago: University of Chicago Press).

Whyte, W.H. (1963) *The Organization Man* (Harmondsworth: Penguin).

Wiener, M.J. (1982) *English Culture and the Decline of the Industrial Spirit* (Cambridge: Cambridge University Press).

Wildy, H. and Wallace, J. (1997) Devolving power in schools: Resolving the dilemma of strong and shared leadership, *Leading and Managing*, 3(2): 132–46.

Wilkinson, R. (1964) *The Prefects: British Leadership and the Public School Tradition* (London: Oxford University Press).

Winnicott, D.W. (1965) Ego distortion in terms of true and false self, in D.W. Winnicott, *The Maturational Processes and the Facilitating Environment: Studies in the Theory of Emotional Development* (London: Hogarth Press), pp. 140–52.

Woods, P. (1979) *The Divided School* (London: Routledge).

Woolf, V. (1938) *Three Guineas* (New York: Harcourt Brace Jovanovich).

Yukl, G. (1989) Managerial leadership: A review of theory and research, *Journal of Management*, 15(2): 251–89.

Zald, M.N. (1965) Who shall rule?: A political analysis of succession in a large welfare organization, *Pacific Sociological Review*, 8(1): 52–60.

Zaleznik, A (1964) Managerial behavior and interpersonal competence, *Behavioral Science*, 9(2): 155–66.

Zaleznik, A. (1966) *Human Dilemmas of Leadership* (New York: Harper & Row).

Zaleznik, A. (1967) Management of disappointment, *Harvard Business Review*, 45(6): 59–70.

Zaleznik, A. (1977) Managers and leaders: Are they different?, *Harvard Business Review*, 55(3): 67–78.

Zaleznik, A. (1990) *The Managerial Mystique: Restoring Leadership in Business* (New York: Harper & Row).

Index

Mills, C.W. *see* Gerth, H.H.
Mintzberg, H.   23
Minutiae Corporation   118
mirroring relationships   67–8, 80, 82
Miskel, C. and Cosgrove, D.   132
mission and mission statements   92, 94
Monash, Sir John   53, 59, 73–4
Monash University   xi, 93
Montgomery, E.H.   98, 109
moral leadership   2, 26, 87–8, 90, 94, 96
moral order in schools   101, 103–4
Morehouse, Ed   133, 140
Morgan, D.H.   41, 43
Morgan, G. *see* Smircich, L.
Morgenstern, Christian   72
Mt Eliza Administrative Staff College   60–1
Mountain, Edith   85–6, 101, 106, 117, 124
Mulgrave Castle School   50
Muslin, M. and Desai, P.   75
'myself', sense of   70

nannies   48–9
narcissism   79–83, 117, 136, 160
National Association of Secondary School
    Principals (NASSP), US   151
natural leaders   xii, xiv; *see also* born leaders
Neumann, Anna   18
neurosis   71–2, 80, 113, 116
Neustadt, R.E.   108–9
Nicolson, Harold   50–1
Nightingale, Florence   76
Nixon, Richard, President   75, 160
norms   29, 46, 151–2, 177
Norwood, Cyril   48, 50–2, 55–6

occupational careers and ideologies   25, 29
Ogawa, R.T.   174, 177; *see also* Fauske, J.R.;
    McCleary, L.E.
Olk, P. *see* Friedman, S.D.
Oscar Centre   128, 152
outlooks   90

paranoid leadership   117–18
Parkay, F.W. *et al.*   173–4, 182
Parker, L. *see* LeGore, J.A.
Parkinson, Charles Tasman   168–70
Parsons, Diane   111, 124
Peele, Vincent   128, 131, 134, 140, 152, 155
perceptions   8, 13, 70–1, 114, 145
Percival, A.   47
Perkin, H.   xiii
Perrow, C.   30
personal qualities and characteristics of
    leaders   10–11, 15, 34, 81, 121, 124, 181
personality assessment   148–9
Peshkin, A.   151
Phillips, A.A.   86
poise   77–8, 163
Pollard, S.   58
prearrival factors   126–7, 131
preferred style   34, 36, 105–6, 112, 114, 181
preparatory schools   49–50
presence   76–8

presidents
    of the USA   75, 78, 79, 105, 107–9, 113
    of universities   78–9
proactive leadership   167
professionalization of management   58–61
protean careers   30–1, 83, 137
prototyping   12–14, 187
public figures   70–1
public personas   66, 78
public schools   45–53, 55–7, 96, 148·

Ragins, B.R.   54
Ralston, K.   116
Ramamurti, R.   115–16
Rangell, L.   160
Rayner, S. *see* Ribbins, Peter
Reagan, Ronald, President   109
Rebecca and the Rebecca myth   127–8, 134, 140,
    165, 176, 180
Rendall, Monty   146
renewal of leadership   17
Repton School   51–2, 56, 101
repudiation of departing leaders   134
Ribbins, Peter   ix, x, 40–1
    and Rayner, S.   43
Richardson, David   118
Ricketson, Staniforth   60
Riesman, D. *et al.*   83
Ritchie, R.B.   139–40
Roberts, Nancy   120–1
    and Bradley, R.T.   121
Robinson, J.G.   170, 178
Roddick, Anita   31
role models   53, 154
roles
    enactment of   106–7, 172, 174, 179–81, 185
    nature and definition of   36, 75, 107, 114
romance of leadership (RL)   13, 16, 186
Ronchi, D. *see* Gilmore, T.N.
Roosevelt, Franklin D., President   17, 108
Rosener, J.B.   122–3
Ross, Dorothy   86, 94, 97–101, 103–4, 106, 124
Roundthorn County Primary School   139
Rousseau, D.M. *see* Arthur, M.B.
Rowles, K.   138–9
Rubinstein, W.D.   56–7
Rugby School   142–3, 168

Salem School   95
Schein, E.H.   27, 91, 119, 169
schizoid organizations   117
Schmitt, N. *et al.*   151
school principals   38–9, 76, 79, 129, 138
    'relieving' and 'acting'   138
    unfilled vacancies for   xiii, 126
Schwartz, Felice   122
scientific management   60
Scott, E.A.   142–3
Scott, M.B. *see* Lyman, S.M.
Searle, Michael   170, 172, 178
selection of leaders   xiv, 45, 145–64
    hidden criteria for   154, 158
    in the army   147–50
    internal and external candidates   155–7, 167